CORPORATE POWER, AMERICAN DEMOCRACY, AND THE AUTOMOBILE INDUSTRY

This book offers a critical history of government policy toward the U.S. automobile industry in order to assess the impact of the large corporation on American democracy. It offers the first book-length treatment of the power of the nation's largest industry. Drawing together the main policy issues affecting the automobile industry over the past forty years – occupant safety, emissions, fuel economy, and trade – the work examines how the industry established its hegemony over the public perception of vehicle safety to inhibit federal regulation and the battle for federal regulation, which succeeded in toppling this hegemony in 1966; the subsequent efforts to include pollution emissions and fuel economy under federal mandates in the 1970s; the industry's resurgence of influence in the 1980s; and the mixed pattern of influence in the 1990s. The analysis seeks to uncover those factors that enhance corporate political influence and those that constrain corporate power, allowing for public interest forces to be successful.

Stan Luger is Associate Professor in the Department of Political Science, University of Northern Colorado. He received his Ph.D. from the Graduate Center of the City University of New York. Professor Luger has published articles in the *Journal of Policy History, Presidential Studies Quarterly, Environmental History Review, PS: Political Science and Politics,* and *In These Times,* as well as contributed a book chapter to the collection of essays *Trade Unions and Public Policy.*

Corporate Power, American Democracy, and the Automobile Industry

STAN LUGER
University of Northern Colorado

CAMBRIDGE
UNIVERSITY PRESS

PUBLISHED BY THE PRESS SYNDICATE OF THE UNIVERSITY OF CAMBRIDGE
The Pitt Building, Trumpington Street, Cambridge, United Kingdom

CAMBRIDGE UNIVERSITY PRESS
The Edinburgh Building, Cambridge CB2 2RU, UK   http://www.cup.cam.ac.uk
40 West 20th Street, New York, NY 10011-4211, USA   http://www.cup.org
10 Stamford Road, Oakleigh, Melbourne 3166, Australia
Ruiz de Alarcón 13, 28014 Madrid, Spain

First published 2000

Printed in the United States of America

Typeface Times Roman 10/12 pt.   *System* MagnaType ™[AG]

A catalog record for this book is available from the British Library.

Library of Congress Cataloging-in-Publication Data
Luger, Stan, 1956–
Corporate power, American democracy, and the automobile industry /
Stan Luger.
p.   cm.
Includes index.
ISBN 0-521-63173-4
1. Automobile industry and trade – Government policy – United
States. I. Title.
HD9710.U52L84   1999
338.4′76292′0973 – dc21   909-21388
                                                 CIP

ISBN 0 521 63173 4 hardback

Contents

Acknowledgments   *page* vii

Introduction   1

1. Studying Power in America   16

2. The Structure of the Auto Industry   34

3. Corporate Political Hegemony and Its Decline:
   1916–1966   54

4. The Politics of Compromise: 1967–1978   76

5. The Resurgence of Corporate Power: 1979–1981   97

6. The Triumph of Corporate Power: Regulatory Policy,
   1981–1988   113

7. The Triumph of Corporate Power: Trade Policy,
   1981–1985   135

8. Interregnum: 1989–1996   154

Conclusion: Corporate Power and American Democracy   182

Index   197

Acknowledgments

An initial version of this work was completed as a dissertation at the City University of New York Graduate Center. CUNY has long been a special institution in American higher education, providing access for the working class and an intellectual vitality that is sorely in short supply today. I am proud to have studied there. Sadly, it is being ravaged by those who seek to constrict the public sphere and undermine a critical social pillar of democracy in the United States.

I had the good fortune to have a dissertation committee of extraordinary individuals who each in his or her own way was a model of political engagement and scholarly excellence: Robert Engler, Martin Fleisher, the late Robert Lekachman, the late Ralph Miliband, and Frances Fox Piven. Since my days at CUNY, Frances Piven has continued to demonstrate a unique measure of support and concern.

Undergraduate courses in American politics and political theory taught by Bill Scheuerman sparked my interest in political economy, and through his example I was attracted to the academic life. His influence, while never intended, has been profound.

Over the years, I have benefited from an ongoing conversation with Brian Waddell on the theoretical issues involved in the study of power. As this work neared completion, he graciously commented on the entire manuscript. Sid Plotkin also provided insightful feedback on a number of issues central to this study. Sarah Raskin helped me to understand the science of traumatic brain injury.

A considerable debt is owed to Bill Sites, who at a pivotal stage of this work carefully read the entire manuscript and made extensive suggestions throughout, improving significantly both the prose and the narrative flow of the material.

Madeline Milian came into my life toward the end of this project and made finishing it all the more enjoyable.

Other debts are owed, of course, but remain harder to identify. Suffice it to say that no scholarly endeavor is simply the work of an individual author but builds on the work of an intellectual community. I hope this work contributes to the tradition of critical scholarship from which I have benefited.

Introduction

The proverbial man from Mars, looking at us afresh, would doubtless come to the conclusion that the automobile was the dominant fact in our producing, consuming, and perhaps our fantasy lives; he could plausibly conclude that the four-wheeled creatures run the society and that the two-legged creatures are its servants.

Douglas Dowd[1]

The automobile industry offers a compelling example of the dominance of corporate power in American society. Fundamental questions about democratic governance and institutional responsibility are raised by examining the power of the nation's largest industry, and one that arguably has been the dominant industry of the twentieth century. This study focuses on the U.S. auto industry's political influence to show its inordinate impact on public policy. It is written for those who are interested in understanding the exercise of corporate power in America and its effect on democratic possibilities. This work is not intended for two audiences: car buffs, who want to read a celebration of the automobile, and those scholars who insist that the sole legitimate approach for social inquiry is statistical testing of hypotheses.

The corporation has long been acknowledged as one of the central institutions of modern society, rivaling, if not surpassing, the state in its impact on contemporary life. Accordingly, long-time business analyst Peter Drucker wrote decades ago:

---

[1] Statement of Douglas Dowd in U.S. Congress, Senate, Select Committee on Small Business, *The Role of Giant Corporations in the American and World Economies. Part 1, The Automobile Industry. Hearings before the Subcommittee on Monopoly,* 91st Cong., 1st sess. (July 1969), p. 527.

1

What we look for in analyzing American society today is therefore the institution which sets the standard for the way of life and mode of living of our citizens; which leads, molds and directs; which determines our perspective on our own society; around which crystallize our social problems and to which we look for their solution. . . . And this, in our society today, is the large corporation.[2]

Fifty years after Drucker penned these words, the large corporation occupies an even greater role in American society. While in 1950 the top 100 corporations in the United States controlled 39.8 percent of all industrial assets, in 1992 they controlled 74.6 percent.[3] The percentage rate continued to climb throughout the 1990s, with massive mergers across a number of industries.

Previous generations of scholars and journalists gave far greater attention to the issues related to corporate power than do scholars and journalists today. Indeed, what was of central concern to the populists of the late nineteenth century and to Progressive Era reformers of the early twentieth century, as well as a critical issue for debate during the New Deal, has largely disappeared from public discussion and scholarly study. Today, as big business becomes increasingly dominant, exercising ever more power over social life, public officials remain eerily silent or, worse, are involved in efforts to strengthen corporate concentration. With corporate control over the media firmly in place, journalists have joined in the celebration of the corporate world. Gone are the days of the muckraker.

For many scholars, corporate power seems to lie outside standard disciplinary boundaries. Lack of attention by political scientists is so prevalent that one recently wrote, "corporate power persists as one of the great enigmas of political science."[4] Most economists, similarly, are simply indifferent to corporate power. Thus, two prominent economists could write that their discipline's conception of power "has remained remarkably unchanged, unidimensional, and, in all, anemic and innocuous."[5] While the broad issues related to living in a corporate society receive insufficient attention, less effort is given to analyzing the exercise of power by particular corporate giants. The quiescence of most political leaders, journalists, and scholars has left the citizenry without a major institutional voice to articulate or challenge the institutional parameters or ideological position of the large corporation in American society today.

---

[2] Peter Drucker, *The Concept of the Corporation* (New York: John Day Company, 1946), pp. 6–7.

[3] Thomas Dye, *Who's Running America?: The Clinton Years,* 6th ed. (Englewood Cliffs: Prentice Hall, 1995), p. 15.

[4] Scott Bowman, *The Modern Corporation and American Political Thought* (University Park: Pennsylvania State University Press, 1996), p. 1.

[5] Walter Adams and James Brock, "Bigness and Social Efficiency: A Case Study of the U.S. Auto Industry," in Warren Samuels and Arthur Miller, eds., *Corporations and Society: Power and Responsibility* (New York: Greenwood Press, 1987), p. 219.

Since the issue of corporate power has been neglected, it is necessary to pose again a basic question: What exactly *is* meant by corporate power? It is the power over what is produced, how these products are distributed, how work is organized, which skills workers need to develop, which advertising images are used to shape consumer consciousness, what kind of technology is developed, and what kinds of pollutants are created. Corporate power shapes the distribution of income, the conditions and location of employment, and thus the future of communities and nations.

An emphasis on corporate power stands in contrast to the standard focus of mainstream economists on markets, viewed as neutral clearing mechanisms between abstract producers and consumers. Those scholars who have been concerned about corporate power see nothing abstract about the power exercised by the modern corporation.[6] In light of the scope of corporate power, many have concluded that the corporation is itself a private government. And the resources available to the large corporation give it leverage over the public government that is often unmatched. Accordingly, a political science that avoids examining these issues is one that cannot fulfill an ancient promise: understanding the nature of the good community.

As the preceding summary of the scope of corporate power suggests, corporate power is far more extensive than those actions directed to influencing government policy. However, this study focuses primarily on corporate influence over government policy and not, for example, the internal structure of the corporation and its decision-making processes or the impact of the auto industry on American society. Several reasons guide this decision. To begin with, there already exists a large literature on various aspects of the impact of the car and the internal dynamics of the automobile industry, yet little has been written documenting the influence of the industry over public policy. In addition, by choosing this focus, this study seeks to meet the challenge set out for critics of corporate power by those political scientists who have insisted that studying key government decisions is necessary before any conclusions concerning power can be asserted. Thus, this study attempts to challenge conventional social science explanations of power on their own terrain to show that, in fact, the large corporation has a pervasive influence over public policy. To do this, the contours of political power of an entire industry over an extended period of time are examined. In this way, momentary variations in influence are located

---

[6] See, for example, Vernon Mogensen, *Office Politics: Computers, Labor, and the Fight for Safety and Health* (New Brunswick: Rutgers University Press, 1996); Sidney Plotkin and William Scheuerman, *Private Interest, Public Spending: Balanced-Budget Conservatism and the Fiscal Crisis* (Boston: South End Press, 1994); Walter Adams and James Brock, *The Bigness Complex: Industry, Labor, and Government in the American Economy* (New York: Pantheon Books, 1986).

within a perspective that yields a more thorough and rooted account than can be developed by treating a single issue, organization, or period.

To accomplish this goal, policy developments are grouped together according to historical periods so that material on a particular issue (e.g., fuel economy) appears in more than one chapter if policy battles in this area continued over time, and seemingly unrelated policy issues are addressed together when history brought them together. This form of presentation is essential to reveal the common patterns among different policy areas that, in turn, illustrate larger patterns of corporate influence and historical change. The approach used in this study focuses on the instrumental resources available to large corporations, the structural forces that enhance these resources, and the historical conditions that shape the circumstances within which contests occur. A framework for studying power that comprises these three elements is provided in the next chapter. It offers an approach to uncover those circumstances under which policy makers have been subject to the full force of economic power, as well as the conditions under which this same economic power has been constrained.

This study examines the central components of public policy explicitly directed to the auto industry: occupant safety, fuel economy, pollution emissions, and trade policy. Antitrust issues are also examined. The primary focus will be on those policies that affect passenger cars, as opposed to all motor vehicles. Except for a brief discussion that follows in this introduction, transportation policy and the development of the Interstate Highway System, clearly relevant to a comprehensive treatment of the politics of the automobile industry, are excluded because they have been thoroughly examined by others. An exploration of every policy decision or battle related to the automobile industry is well beyond the limits of any one book; only the central issues of each historical period will be addressed.[7]

Government policy toward the auto industry involves a large number of decision-making points, made by a vast array of government entities, including Congress, the president and the United States trade representative (USTR), the Justice Department's Antitrust Division, the Federal Trade Commission (FTC), the International Trade Commission (ITC), the Department of Transportation and the National Highway Traffic Safety Administration (NHTSA), and the Environmental Protection Agency (EPA). The federal courts are fre-

---

[7] The industry's political involvement extends far beyond the core issues examined and in recent years has included North American Free Trade Agreement (NAFTA) and fast track legislation, President Bill Clinton's health care reform proposals, U.S. sanctions against Iran and Cuba, electricity deregulation, immigration law enforcement, patent legislation, frequency spectrum auction, Mexico's financial stability, product liability, Commerce Department reorganization, Medicare and Medicaid, no-fault insurance, defense spending, the striker replacement ban, bankruptcy law revisions, copyright protection, "Made in USA" label criteria, and mortgage insurance. See *Automotive News,* December 29, 1997, p. 30.

quently involved in adjudicating issues considered (or avoided) by these governmental bodies. In light of this broad institutional network and the centrality of the automobile industry to American society, the patterns that emerge from studying auto-related policy are more instructive than those derived from a narrower policy network.

Much has been written about the auto industry. Books have lampooned,[8] celebrated,[9] and criticized[10] the car's impact on the social environment. There are comprehensive works on the evolution of highway traffic regulations[11] and the development of U.S. transportation policy.[12] There are books on automakers and the labor process,[13] the United Auto Workers,[14] General Motors's

[8] See, for example, John Keats, *The Insolent Chariots* (Philadelphia: J. B. Lippincott, 1958).

[9] See, for example, John Rae, *The Road and Car in American Life* (Cambridge: MIT Press, 1971), and John Rae, *The American Automobile Industry* (Boston: Twayne Publishers, 1984).

[10] The best critical work on autos is Peter Freund and George Martin, *The Ecology of the Automobile* (Montreal: Black Rose Books, 1993). A more popular account can be found in Jane Holtz Kay, *Asphalt Nation: How the Automobile Took Over America,* and *How We Can Take It Back* (New York: Crown Publishers, 1997); See also Steve Nadis and James Mackenzie, *Car Trouble* (Boston: Beacon Press, 1993).

A flurry of works were written in the 1970s on the consequences of the automobile. See, for example, Kenneth Schneider, *Autokind v. Mankind* (New York: Schocken Books,1971); Ronald Buell, *Dead End* (Englewood Cliffs: Prentice-Hall, 1972); John Jerome, *The Death of the Automobile* (New York: Norton, 1972); W. H. O'Connell, *Ride Free, Drive Free* (New York: John Day, 1973); Terrence Bendixson, *Without Wheels* (Bloomington: Indiana University Press, 1975); James Flink, *The Car Culture* (Cambridge: MIT Press, 1975); For a response to these "antiauto" works, see B. Bruce-Briggs, *The War Against the Automobile* (New York: E. P. Dutton, 1975).

[11] See, for example, Edward Fisher and Robert Reeder, *Vehicle Traffic Laws* (Evanston: Traffic Institute, Northwestern University,1974).

[12] See, for example, David St. Clair, *The Motorization of American Cities* (New York: Praeger Publishers, 1986); Glenn Yago, *The Decline of Transit* (New York: Cambridge University Press, 1984); Gary Schwartz, "Urban Freeways and the Interstate System," *California Law Review* vol. 49 (1976), pp. 406–513; Helen Leavitt, *Superhighway-Superhoax* (New York: Ballantine Books, 1970).

[13] See, for example, William Green and Ernest Yanarella, eds., *North American Auto Unions in Crisis: Lean Production as Contested Terrain* (Albany: SUNY Press, 1996); Nelson Lichtenstein and Stephen Meyer III, *On the Line: Essays in the History of Auto Work* (Urbana: University of Illinois Press, 1989); David Gartman, *Auto Slavery: The Labor Process in the American Automobile Industry, 1897–1950* (New Brunswick: Rutgers University Press, 1986); Stephen Meyer III, *The Five Dollar Day: Labor Management and Social Control in the Ford Motor Company, 1908–1921* (Albany: SUNY Press, 1981). For an irreverent firsthand account of life on the assembly line, see Ben Hamper, *Rivethead: Tales from the Assembly Line* (New York: Warren Books, 1991).

[14] See, for example, Nelson Lichtenstein, *The Most Dangerous Man in Detroit: Walter Reuther and the Fate of American Labor* (New York: Basic Books, 1995); Martin

(GM's) contribution to modern corporate structure,[15] and a number of works about the personalities who have been involved with the Ford Motor Company.[16] There are works that examine the internal corporate decision-making process[17] and those that trace the development of particular models.[18] Other works have focused on local community efforts to shape plant location decisions,[19] the consequences of plant shutdowns for the workers and communities displaced,[20] the impact of new assembly plants on previously rural communities,[21] and the opening of Japanese-owned plants in the United States.[22] In a less academic vein, car enthusiasts have a number of their own magazines, such as *Road and Track, Motor Trend,* and *Car and Driver,* whose combined

Halpern, *UAW Politics in the Cold War* (Albany: SUNY Press, 1988); John Barnard, *Walter Reuther and the Rise of the Auto Workers* (Boston: Little, Brown, 1983); Victor Reuther, *The Brothers Reuther and the Story of the UAW* (Boston: Houghton Mifflin, 1976); William Serrin, *The Company and the Union* (New York: Vintage Books, 1974); Sidney Fine, *Sit-Down: The General Motors Strike of 1936–1937* (Ann Arbor: University of Michigan Press, 1969).

[15] See, for example, Peter Drucker; Alfred Sloan, *My Years with General Motors* (New York: Anchor Books, 1972); Alfred D. Chandler, *Strategy and Structure* (Cambridge: MIT Press, 1962), chapter 3.

[16] One of the best biographies on Henry Ford is Keith Sward, *The Legend of Henry Ford* (New York: Rinehart & Company, 1948). For a short fictional account of the early history of Ford, see Upton Sinclair, *The Flivver King* (Chicago: Charles Kerr Publishing, 1984 [1937]). See also Allan Nevins and Frank Hill's three-volume study, *Ford: The Times, the Man, the Company* (New York: Charles Scribners Sons, 1954); *Ford: Expansion and Challenge, 1915–1932* (New York: Charles Scribners and Sons, 1957), *Ford: Decline and Rebirth, 1933–1962* (New York: Charles Scribners and Sons, 1962). More recent accounts can be found in Robert Lacey, *Ford: The Men and the Machine* (Boston: Little, Brown, 1986); David Halberstam, *The Reckoning* (New York: William Morrow and Co., 1986).

[17] See, for example, Paul Ingrassia and Joseph White, *Comeback: The Fall and Rise of the American Automobile Industry* (New York: Simon and Schuster, 1994); Maryann Keller, *Rude Awakening: The Rise, Fall and Struggle for Recovery of General Motors* (New York: William Morrow and Co., 1989).

[18] See, for example, Mary Walton, *Car: A Drama of the American Workplace* (New York: Norton, 1997); Brock Yates, *The Critical Path: Inventing an Automobile and Reinventing a Corporation* (Boston: Little, Brown, 1996).

[19] See, for example, Bryan Jones et al., *The Sustaining Hand* (Lawrence: University Press of Kansas, 1986).

[20] See, for example, Kathryn Marie Dudley, *The End of the Line* (Chicago: University of Chicago Press, 1994); Jeannie Wylie, *Poletown: A Community Betrayed* (Champaign: University of Illinois Press, 1989).

[21] See, for example, Joe Sherman, *In the Rings of Saturn* (New York: Oxford University Press, 1994).

[22] See, for example, Robert Perrucci, *Japanese Auto Transplants in the Heartland: Corporatism and Community* (New York: Aldine de Gruyter, 1994); David Gelsanliter, *Jump Start: Japan Comes to the Heartland* (New York: Farrar, Straus and Giroux, 1990).

circulation is in the millions. Fictional works have placed cars and highways at the center of a romantic culture of the road, as well as using them as symbols of the alienation of modern society.[23] Yet, amidst this automania, political scientists have largely neglected the study of government policy directly affecting the nation's largest industry and have made few attempts to assess the industry's political power.

Impact of the Automobile

To begin to outline the significance of the auto industry, it is essential to sketch a few of its impacts on American society, including some historical background on its rise to prominence. It is difficult to overestimate the importance of the industry because, as Peter Drucker noted, "The automotive industry . . . is to the twentieth century what the Lancashire cotton mills were to the early nineteenth century: the industry of industries."[24] Alongside the railroad and steam engine, cars, Baran and Sweezy wrote, are one of the epoch-making inventions of modern times, which "shake up the entire pattern of the economy and hence create vast investment outlets in addition to the capital which they directly absorb."[25] Throughout their history, automobile companies have been instrumental in shaping changes in the labor process, corporate structure, labor relations, and consumer spending patterns. For decades, mass production industries modeled themselves after the auto industry, and in the post–World War II era the industry's management–labor relations set a standard for the rest of the nation.[26] Automobile companies have long been among the largest of all corporations. On a worldwide basis, the industry is the largest manufacturer and GM is the largest corporation. American producers dominated world auto production for most of the twentieth century, from before World War I until 1980, when Japanese automakers took the lead. (American producers regained that distinction in 1994.) The industry has been the largest in the nation since the early 1920s.

Sitting at the center of the American economy, the automobile industry exerts enormous influence on economic events at home and abroad. A 1981 Department of Transportation report summed up the importance of the industry.

Because of its scale and reach, the auto industry has played a central role in the definition and accomplishment of our broadest national goals: work for Americans;

[23] See, for example, Jack Kerouac, *On the Road* (New York: Viking Press, 1955); J. G. Ballard, *Crash* (New York: Vintage Books, 1985); J. G. Ballard, *Concrete Island* (New York: Vintage Books, 1985).
[24] Drucker, p. 176.
[25] Paul Baran and Paul Sweezy, *Monopoly Capital* (New York: Monthly Review Press, 1966), p. 219.
[26] Stephen Amberg, *The Union Inspiration in American Politics* (Philadelphia: Temple University Press, 1994), p. 5.

energy security; and, perhaps most important, national security. In the future direction of this industry, then, will lie critical answers about America at home and in the world: about the number and kinds of jobs for our people; about our strategic position in the world defined by our economic power; about our competitive position in an evolving international economy.[27]

And the industry continues to have a major impact on the American political economy. Accordingly, the Commerce Department observed in 1996 that "without question, a successful and growing automobile industry is critical to the overall strength of the U.S. economy."[28] This point is all the more remarkable considering the growth of the service sector and "information revolution" that has transformed much of the economy in recent decades.

Typical histories of the automobile in America emphasize mass production and the rapidly widespread ownership of cars. Comparisons are then drawn with European nations, where the auto long remained a luxury item. Yet, in its earliest years in this nation, the auto was the preserve of the wealthy. In fact, Woodrow Wilson wrote in 1906, "Nothing has spread socialistic feeling in this country more than the automobile" because it offered "a picture of the arrogance of wealth."[29] Within a few years, however, cars were commonly available in the United States, and within a generation they were transforming both the economy and the society. "Without the new automobile industry," the historian William Leuchtenburg has argued, "the prosperity of the Roaring Twenties would scarcely have been possible." In less than thirty years, car production went from 4,000 (1900) to 4,800,000 (1929).[30] And as early as 1929, sociologists Robert and Helen Lynd recognized that cars were having a profound impact on social relations and cultural practices. According to their work *Middletown,* a pathbreaking community study of a typical U.S. city of the day, one working-class wife told the Lynds: "We'd rather do without clothing than give up the car." Another said: "I'll go without food before I'll see us give up the car." A teenage boy, when asked in Sunday school to name a temptation we have today that Jesus did not have, responded: "Speed!"[31]

[27] U.S. Department of Transportation, Report to the President, "The Auto Industry 1980," (1981), p. 2.

[28] U.S. Department of Commerce, International Trade Administration, Office of Automotive Affairs, "Industry Sector Report: U.S. Automotive Industry" (September 1996), p. 3.

[29] Cited in Frederick Lewis Allen, *The Big Change* (New York: Harper and Brothers, 1952), p. 121.

[30] William Leuchtenburg, *The Perils of Prosperity* (Chicago: University of Chicago Press, 1958), pp. 185–6.

[31] Robert and Helen Lynd, *Middletown* (New York: Harcourt, Brace & World, 1929), pp. 255–6, 258. For a general collection of writings examining the car and American culture, see David Lewis and Lawrence Goldstein, eds., *The Automobile and American Culture* (Ann Arbor: University of Michigan Press, 1983).

There are currently more than 200 million motor vehicles in the United States; cars comprise approximately three-quarters of this total. More than half of American households own two or more cars, and overall there are 1.77 vehicles for every household in the country. Between 1969 and 1995 the vehicle population grew six times faster than the human population. In 1994, Americans drove their vehicles for a total of 2.4 trillion miles and collectively spent 8 billion hours stuck in traffic. Estimates of the cost of this quagmire range from $43 billion to $168 billion.[32] Accommodating the ever-increasing car population has had an enormous impact on the physical landscape of America. One estimate suggests that "up to 10 percent of the arable land in the United States is taken up by the auto infrastructure."[33] Moreover, over half of the urban space in the United States is devoted to cars. In Los Angeles, the quintessential car city, this figure rises to two-thirds. How can this occur? Zoning regulations, designed for the car, separate residential, commercial, and industrial uses. As a consequence, the number of parking spaces continues to mushroom because social activities (shopping, eating out, going to work, recreation, etc.) are so widely separated that a car is required to get to the location of each activity; in Los Angeles it is estimated that there are eight parking spaces for every car.[34]

Cars affect more than the constructed landscape. Motor vehicle production absorbs significant percentages of industrial and material output in the United States. In the mid-1990s the industry accounted for 77 percent of all U.S. rubber consumption, 60 percent of malleable iron, 40 percent of machine tools, 25 percent of glass, and 20 percent of semiconductors. Supplier and manufacturing activity was spread out over more than 4,000 plants in forty-eight states and the District of Columbia.[35] In 1996, the Big Three (GM, Ford, and Chrysler) generated over $372 billion in revenue.[36] Altogether the auto industry directly employs 800,000 people, with 30,000 dealer franchises employing another 900,000 people. Employment of those who are indirectly related to the industry reaches almost seven million. The industry also has an enormous impact on the media. In 1995, for example, the automakers spent over $10 billion on advertising, more than any other industry, product, or service in the nation. Each of the Big Three ranks among the top ten advertisers in the nation.[37]

---

[32] Kay, p. 121.   [33] Freund and Martin, p. 19.

[34] Freund and Martin, p. 19.

[35] Walter Adams and James Brock, "Automobiles," in Adams and Brock, eds., *The Structure of American Industry,* 9th ed. (Englewood Cliffs: Prentice-Hall, 1995), p. 65.

[36] With the 1998 merger of Chrysler and Daimler-Benz, the "Big Three"—the long-time designation of the three largest U.S. firms – became a thing of the past.

[37] "Total Measured U.S. Ad Spending by Category and Media," *Advertising Age* (September 30, 1996), p. S54.

Death and Injury on the Road

Motor vehicles also affect public health and the environment. Over 3 million Americans have died in crashes, a number that is three times the combat deaths suffered by the United States in all wars since 1776; over 100 million have been injured. Motor vehicle crashes are the leading cause of death for those under thirty-five, and are the primary cause of quadriplegia and paraplegia. In 1994, there were 40,716 traffic fatalities, 5.2 million individuals were injured, and 27 million vehicles were damaged.[38] Crashes are the second leading cause of hospitalized and nonhospitalized injury, and half of all injury deaths result from motor vehicle collisions, as do half of all brain injuries. Motor vehicle crashes are either the fourth or fifth leading cause of death in the United States, depending on how death categories are combined. Another way to depict these losses is to calculate the number of years of life lost before the age of sixty-five. Vehicle crashes account for the fourth leading number of years of life lost, 62 percent of years lost from injury, and more than twice the number of years lost than result from acquired immunodeficiency syndrome (AIDS).[39] The economic costs of vehicle collisions parallel these human losses. In 1994, for example, the economic loss to society from motor vehicle crashes was estimated by the Department of Transportation at $150.5 billion. In addition, in 1993 the cost of automobile insurance was $110 billion.[40] Needless to say, any recitation of these bare figures can never come close to capturing the impact of vehicle crashes because of the pain and suffering inflicted upon the victims and their families.

Autos and the Environment

The automobile has a tremendous impact on the environment. Cars are largely responsible for smog and toxic air pollutants, not to mention the nation's increasing dependence on foreign oil. They are a major contributor to acid rain, which destroys forests, wildlife, and aquatic resources. The burning of gasoline is also a major contributor to global warming. Cars and light trucks account for about two-thirds of the carbon dioxide (CO_2) emissions that stem from transport sources and over 20 percent of overall CO_2 emissions. In addition, for each gallon of gasoline used, 19 pounds of CO_2 are produced. Over its lifetime, the average American car emits 57 tons of CO_2.

---

[38] U.S. Department of Transportation, National Highway Traffic Safety Administration, *The Economic Cost of Motor Vehicle Crashes 1994* (Washington, D.C.: NHTSA, July 1996).

[39] U.S. Department of Transportation, National Highway Traffic Safety Administration, "Saving Lives and Dollars: Highway Safety Contribution to Health Care Reform and Deficit Reduction" (Washington, D.C.: NHTSA, September 1993), p. 1.

[40] U.S. Bureau of the Census, *Statistical Abstract of the United States 1995* (Washington, D.C.: Government Printing Office, 1996), p. 538.

The seemingly unquenchable thirst for oil accounts for much of the oil tanker traffic across the oceans. Because of "normal accidents"[41] that result from oil tanker traffic, thousands of oil spills annually dump millions of gallons of oil into the nation's waterways. Between 1973 and 1997 the Coast Guard recorded over 200,000 oil spills onto U.S. waterways alone that dumped over 200 million gallons of oil, and in 1989 there was, of course, the 11 million gallon spill from the Exxon *Valdez*. The need for more domestic sources of oil has led to the consideration of drilling in increasingly remote and fragile ecosystems such as the Arctic National Wildlife Preserve and expanded drilling of the outer continental shelf.

Because approximately half of the nation's oil is imported, its usage has a large impact on the trade deficit. Forecasts predict increasing imports as the nation's drivers use more gasoline and domestic drilling continues to decline. The dependence on foreign oil also transforms energy policy into a national security issue. Given the political instability of the Middle East, oil imports "require" our continued military presence there. Thus, oil imports bring with them hidden expenses in continued military outlays that need to be factored into a full accounting of the costs of auto dependence. If military expenses for the 1991 Gulf War are factored into the cost of oil, for example, Amory and L. Hunter Lovins estimate that the price at the time would have been in excess of $100 per barrel, approximately five times the actual market price.[42]

Public health risks associated with auto-related air pollution are extensive, affecting healthy children and adults, and with an even greater impact on those with respiratory ailments. Auto emissions are the main source of urban smog, and car-related air pollution is responsible, according to one estimate, for 30,000 deaths a year.[43] Mobile source air pollution causes more than half of all cancers due to air pollution. In 1995, EPA estimated that road vehicles were responsible for 79 percent of carbon monoxide (CO), 73 percent of volatile organic compounds (VOC), and 72 percent of nitrogen oxides (NOx). Passenger cars account for 48 percent of CO, 43 percent of VOC, and 34 percent of NOx. Light duty trucks, an increasingly popular family purchase, account for most of the difference. These pollutants are not the only ones that vehicles produce. "The average car emits a toxic cocktail of more than 1,000 pollutants."[44] And little is known about the effects of the interaction of these chemicals in the human body. In addition, vehicle traffic, a leading cause of noise pollution, has its own significant health consequences, including high blood

---

[41] Charles Perrow, *Normal Accidents* (New York: Basic Books, 1984).

[42] Amory Lovins and L. Hunter Lovins, "Make Fuel Efficiency Our Gulf Strategy," *New York Times* (December 3, 1990), p. A15.

[43] Kay, p. 111.

[44] Greenpeace, *The Environmental Impact of the Car: A Greenpeace Report* (New York: Greenpeace, 1991), p. 19.

pressure and stress. Driving itself is not a benign activity either. It has been shown to raise levels of stress hormones, blood sugar, and cholesterol, as well as heart rates and blood pressure.[45]

Despite substantial reductions in the emissions of new cars, the percentage contribution from mobile sources to total emissions, except lead, has remained largely unchanged despite federal standards in place since the 1970s. Several factors explain this paradox including inadequate testing protocols, malfunctioning pollution control equipment, and, most important, increasing miles driven. This fact is easily explained: Americans are forced to rely on cars for ground transportation.

Transportation Policy

The dominance of the auto is often assumed to be the result of the unforeseen consequences of an infinite number of private decisions. Simply put, many believe that Americans became dependent upon cars because they preferred them to any public transportation alternative. However, the dependence on automobiles was not a natural process that occurred by itself. Unbridled highway development and other subsidies for cars have been the primary focus of public policy instead of balanced transportation planning for a variety of modes (e.g., light rail, heavy rail, buses, as well as cars). Indeed, the American "love affair with cars," the stuff of endless myth, is more akin to an arranged marriage.[46]

Two initiatives spurred by the auto industry were instrumental in ensuring the overreliance on automobiles: federal support for road building and the dismantling of urban rail transportation. Beginning as early as 1916, the federal government subsidized state road-building efforts. By the 1930s, the automakers realized that future growth of the industry required an extensive network of highways. Thus, GM, already the dominant firm in the industry, established the National Highway Users Conference, bringing together over 3,000 businesses from a range of industries tied to the auto to lobby for highways. No other group or set of interests could match the lobbying juggernaut GM had assembled. These efforts eventually culminated in 1956 with the 42,000-mile Interstate Highway System (IHS), which routed extensive portions of highways directly through cities, facilitating suburban sprawl. Funding of the federal highway system was accomplished by a method that insulated it from subsequent political scrutiny. Gas and other user taxes were earmarked exclusively to fund the system. As a result, highway advocates did not have to compete in the annual budget process to obtain continued federal funding. Road construction became the predominant focus of federal transportation policy for decades, with over $220 billion spent by the federal government

---

[45] Freund and Martin, p. 33.   [46] Greenpeace, p. 1.

over the past thirty years. (Aggregate state and local highway spending far exceeds this amount.)

Meanwhile, federal spending for public transit has never approached this amount. From 1956 to 1970, the initial years of the IHS, the federal government spent $70 billion for highways and only $795 million for rail transit. Although mass transit subsidies increased during the 1970s, they never reached parity with highway spending and were dramatically cut back during the Reagan–Bush years. During the 1980s federal highway spending increased by 85 percent, while mass transit spending declined by 50 percent. Slashing public transit subsidies and increasing highway spending are trends that continued in the Newt Gingrich–led 104th Congress.

The decline of public transit was not simply the result of subsidized highways. To crush alternatives to motor vehicles, a large number of light rail public transportation systems were dismantled in the 1930s and 1940s by a GM-led conspiracy in conjunction with Standard Oil, Firestone, Greyhound, and Mack Truck (a bus manufacturer). This effort was directed at the extensive network of interurban trolley lines in the United States, which by 1917 had 45,000 miles of track. In the 1920s, 20 billion passenger trips were taken on these public lines. To remove these rail systems, a semi-independent holding company was established, purchasing trolley lines, dismantling them, and substituting diesel buses.[47] (GM was the largest producer of diesel buses at the time.) Once this was accomplished, the new transit systems were sold off, with contractual prohibitions against bringing back trolleys. The diesel fleets were more expensive and operated at slower speeds, contributing to the collapse of public transit systems across the nation. With no other viable alternative, commuters were diverted to cars. In 1949 a federal jury convicted GM, Standard Oil of California, Firestone Tire, and others of conspiring to dismantle trolley lines throughout the country. The fine was a meager $5,000, the action too little, too late. By 1949, over 100 electric trolley systems in more than forty-five cities had been dismantled, and 90 percent of the trolley network was gone.

Road construction – and the "deconstruction" of alternatives to driving – are not the only reasons cars dominant ground transportation. Driving is encouraged in our society because much of the cost is borne by either government or society as a whole. The World Resources Institute estimated, for example, that in 1992 "auto-related subsidies – including road construction, tax deductions, and employer-provided parking, plus military expenditures to keep gasoline prices low – add[ed] up to $300 billion a year, equivalent to an additional gas

---

[47] U.S. Congress, Senate, Committee on the Judiciary, *American Ground Transport: A Proposal for Restructuring the Automobile, Truck, Bus and Rail Industries,* by Bradford Snell, presented to the Subcommittee on Antitrust and Monopoly (February 26, 1974), 93rd Cong., 2d sess. Committee Print.

tax of $2 a gallon of gas."[48] And in a 1993 report, the National Resources Defense Council estimated that the hidden annual cost of automobile transportation was even larger: between $380 and $660 billion, equivalent to a real cost of $3.70 to $6.50 per gallon of gasoline. To reach this figure, government costs, including direct construction, maintenance, and traffic control services, were added to indirect societal costs, including building damage and air and water pollution.[49] Another way to depict the hidden costs of auto transportation is to look at the percentage of local police costs that are auto-related. One estimate suggests that for a city such as Pasadena, California, this figure is almost 40 percent.[50]

Organization of the Study

This book argues that there are four periods in government policy toward the industry, each with its own pattern of power relations. The first period extended from the birth of the industry to the mid-1960s, a time of corporate hegemony over government policy. This pattern was broken by the passage of the National Traffic and Motor Vehicle Safety Act, which inaugurated government regulation of the automobile; the second period, from 1967 to 1978, was one of bargaining and compromise, during which time government regulation expanded to include pollution emissions and then fuel economy. While the industry failed to prevent the extension of regulation to these areas, it was often able to delay or modify new standards; the third period, from 1979 to 1988, was a time of resurgence and triumph of industry influence over government as policymakers responded to the industry's first systemic economic crisis by subordinating public policy to the industry's economic interests. The fourth period dates from 1989 to the present, an interregnum of crosscutting trends from which no clear pattern of industry–government relations has emerged.

Chapter 1 examines the theoretical issues involved in the study of power and presents the perspective used in this study. Chapter 2 examines the structure of the industry, including the history of economic concentration, the GM–Toyota joint venture, and labor relations. Chapter 3 begins the historical narrative, tracing the issue of occupant safety from the inception of the industry through the passage of the federal safety act in 1966. Chapter 4 (covering the years 1967 to 1978) examines the three major areas of auto regulation – safety, emissions, and fuel economy – as well as the shift in the industry's political strategy to take advantage of its central economic position. Chapter 5 analyzes the resurgence of the industry's political power during the Carter administra-

[48] James MacKenzie, Roger Dower, and Donald D. T. Chen, "The Going Rate: What It Really Costs to Drive" (Washington, DC: World Resources Institute, June 1992).
[49] Peter Miller and John Moffet, "The Price of Mobility: Uncovering the Hidden Costs of Transportation" (New York: Natural Resources Defense Council, October 1993), p. ii.
[50] Freund and Martin, p. 133.

tion and includes an examination of the Chrysler bailout. Chapters 6 and 7 further develop the analysis of this period by examining the regulatory and trade policies of the Reagan administration, when the industry's power was triumphant. Chapter 8 turns to the most recent developments in the relationship between the industry and the federal government, and covers the major issues of the Bush administration and those of the first term of the Clinton administration, focusing on the Clean Air Act of 1990, the unsuccessful congressional effort to increase fuel economy standards, and trade relations with Japan. The book concludes with a discussion of the implications of this study for understanding corporate power and democratic accountability.

1

Studying Power in America

Political science is concerned with the study of social governance, or how societies are organized and how they change. A corollary to these issues is the question of power: Who in society shapes change, who benefits, and who does not. The classic encapsulation of this approach was made by Harold Lasswell, who wrote that politics is the study of who gets what, when, and how.[1] Accordingly, the study of power is essential if political scientists are to respond to these issues, and such a study must include the economic power of business because of the central role it plays in the distribution of who gets what, when, and how. Unfortunately, most political scientists neglect these areas, in part because of the narrow focus on political behavior and the internal operation of government institutions that dominate research.

Among those political scientists who continue to study social organization and historical change, the concept of power remains contested. Debates have raged decade after decade, generating a voluminous literature, with little hope for any resolution. For years battle lines have been drawn over questions concerning what is actually meant by power, where power is located, how to study power, and how to evaluate the results of such inquiries. Sometimes the conclusions of a study tell us more about the perspective and assumptions of the researcher than about the material presented. Grappling with the issue of power is particularly complex in a liberal democracy where a political system based on formal equality is coupled with an economic system based on inequality of resources. While economic resources clearly present a tremendous political advantage to their holders, those with limited economic resources have also succeeded in shaping public policy because power held in one sphere is not automatically or completely translated into the other. Thus it is not axiomatic who will be triumphant in any particular political battle. For this

[1] Harold Lasswell, *Politics: Who Gets What, When, and How* (New York: McGraw-Hill, 1936).

reason, Franz Neumann argued almost fifty years ago that in a liberal democratic society the translation of economic power into political power should be the crucial concern of political scientists.[2]

In the first decades after World War II, political scientists and sociologists debated power from two main positions: pluralism and elitism. More recently, neomarxism and state-centered theory have framed much of the debate. The earlier set of opposing positions, pluralism and elitism, each offers a different conclusion concerning the nature of power in part because each holds to a different analysis concerning the translation of economic resources into political influence. For pluralists, those with significant economic resources do not dominate politics, while for elitists, a relatively small number of individuals who control society's economic resources, and with them other key social institutions, direct the course of change. Yet, despite this difference, each perspective offers an unchanging description of who holds power that does not adequately account for variations over time. And this, indeed, has been a major problem in the debate over the translation of economic resources into political power. Typically static, albeit conflicting, descriptions are given. This is not to suggest, however, that there are no discernible patterns to power, only that there has been inadequate attention to the variations within broad interpretations.

Of the two more recent additions to the debate on power, state-centered theory has become the most fashionable in the social sciences today. Rejecting each of the preceding theories as society-centered, state-centered theorists argue that public policy and political development are best explained as the result of the actions of state officials acting autonomously from social pressures. The importance of state-centered theory to this discussion is reinforced by its close identification with another recent trend in political science: the "return to history." While there seems to be promise in this approach, its practitioners offer a truncated understanding of history that fails to take into account changing class relations or specific economic conditions, due, in part, to an uncritical acceptance of state-centered theory.

The other addition to the power debate is neomarxism. By focusing on the combined pressures of "accumulation" (the need to maintain a healthy economy) and "legitimation" (the need to maintain public support), neomarxists remain theoretically sensitive to variations in power. Yet, neomarxist scholars have concentrated on abstract issues such as how to evaluate the functions of state actions and how to describe the bias of the state in a capitalist society. When efforts have been made to analyze particular historical events, typically the focus has been on interpreting broad swathes of history such as the New

---

[2] Franz Neumann, "Approaches to the Study of Political Power," *The Democratic and the Authoritarian State* (New York: Free Press, 1957), p. 12.

Deal or the origins of the welfare state. As a result, there has been insufficient development and application of this perspective to specific policy battles of narrower scope.

With so many theoretical options for the study of power, researchers typically choose one camp over another. This study takes a different route. It presents a three-part framework for understanding power that combines elements from a number of different perspectives. It focuses on the dynamics of interest group activity in the context of the events and social structures that shape the ability of political actors to influence policy outcomes. In this way, it is possible to remain sensitive to three realms of explanation that most scholars usually hold apart: political behavior (interest group activity), social structure (state dependence on large corporations for economic activity), and historical change (variation in socioeconomic conditions within the broader dynamics of the political economy). Joining together these three elements of analysis facilitates unraveling "the factors behind the facts."[3] Otherwise, analyses of politics remain either on the level of observable behavior, without attention to the contexts and structures that, in turn, shape the very activities being studied, or they present functional analyses that ignore all contingent factors. The importance of adding a structural component to the study of power needs to be emphasized because it stands in contrast to the standard approach in political science, which reduces the study of politics to "behavior" studied apart from the social structural forces that enable human action to occur and through which human actions take their particular shape.

To elaborate this framework, it is useful to review the long-standing debate over the study of power. The purpose of this discussion is not to present a comprehensive analysis of all the issues that have been debated on power, a task well beyond the scope of one chapter of a book, or to offer a wholly new framework for the study of power, but rather to explain the theoretical perspective that guides this study and to show its intellectual roots.

Behavior

Studying observable behavior remains the dominant concern among political scientists. Most work in the discipline is preoccupied with the study of those topics that lend themselves to statistical manipulation, for example, voting results, campaign contributions, public opinion polling, and the behavioral patterns within government institutions. At the same time, most political scientists subscribe to the pluralist account of power, which stresses that there is no inherent structure or matrix of power within American society. Nelson

---

[3] Herbert Marcuse, *One-Dimensional Man* (Boston: Beacon Press, 1964), p. 100, cited in Sidney Plotkin, *Keep Out: The Struggle for Land Use Control* (Berkeley: University of California Press, 1987), p. 7.

Polsby, an unreconstructed pluralist long involved in these debates, uttered the classic pluralist dictum, contending, "Nothing categorical can be said about power. . . . If anything, there seems to be an unspoken notion among pluralist researchers that at bottom *nobody* dominates. . . ."[4] Instead, pluralists have emphasized that there are multiple "power resources" and that none of these uniquely or unfairly empower their holders. These resources include money and credit, control over jobs, control of information, social status, expertise, charisma, ethnic solidarity, time, and energy.[5] Power may be tied to issues, but issue networks do not overlap. Hence, power is broadly distributed, not concentrated in the hands of a few.

While pluralist scholars claimed that they assumed nothing about power and were open to accepting proof of elite dominance, empirical studies repeatedly came to the same conclusion: power was in flux, open-ended, and widely dispersed. Yet the pluralist tradition was by no means monolithic when it came to evaluating the centrality of interest groups.[6] One camp, led by Arthur Bentley and David Truman, stressed that group pressures were the central ingredient in understanding power.[7] Government was largely neutral, simply reflecting the physics of group forces. This, however, did not imply that all groups had an equal potential for influence. Truman acknowledged from the beginning that business was in a "favored position," with "superior status" to other groups, but he emphasized several factors that reduced the political effectiveness of business: problems with internal group cohesion, overlapping membership that diluted loyalty, and the time-bound nature of coalitions.[8]

Other pluralist writers, most notably the early Robert Dahl, as well as Bauer, Pool, and Dexter, emphasized that studying group pressure was not enough. One must also attend to the role of political leadership and political parties in shaping and mediating group conflicts, thereby widening the pluralist model of the dynamics of policy making.[9] Yet, pluralists were still confronted by the obvious fact that there was a range of inequalities among political actors, such as inequalities of income, status, and access. In perhaps the most celebrated pluralist study, *Who Governs?*, Dahl directly confronted this problem by rejecting the view of "cumulative inequalities," which characterized a variety of elite theories. Instead, Dahl argued, there was a dispersal of resources or

[4] Nelson Polsby, *Community Power and Political Theory,* 2nd enlarged ed. (New Haven: Yale University Press, 1980), p. 113 (emphasis in the original).

[5] Robert Dahl, *Who Governs?* (New Haven: Yale University Press, 1961), p. 226.

[6] For a review of the debates within pluralism, see G. David Garson, *Group Theories of Politics* (Beverly Hills: Sage Publishers, 1978).

[7] Arthur Bentley, *The Process of Government* (Chicago: University of Chicago Press, 1908); David Truman, *The Governmental Process* (New York: Alfred A. Knopf, 1951).

[8] Truman, pp. 248–61.

[9] See, for example, Robert Dahl; Raymond Bauer, Ithiel De Sola Pool, and Anthony Dexter, *American Business and Public Policy* (Cambridge: MIT Press, 1963).

"inequalities" that enabled different groups to dominate different issues.[10] For Dahl, the dispersal of resources meant that no *one* group dominated, a claim that became the sine qua non of the entire pluralist camp. While some groups clearly had greater financial resources to use in influencing political decisions, other groups had resources such as "people power" at their disposal. In this way, Dahl was able to downplay the political advantages of those with concentrated economic resources and argue that power in American society was not stratified or concentrated in the hands of an elite. Pluralists who specifically studied the power of business came to the same reassuring conclusion on the grounds that business did not possess a "monopoly over political access or influence."[11]

These conclusions were made, in part, in response to earlier community power studies done by sociologists that emphasized a stratified or elite view of social power. Beginning with Robert Lynd and Helen Lynd's 1929 study *Middletown,* a host of scholars mapped local power structures and found that economic elites, who had the power to shape the course of their community's economic life, dominated political decision making as well. Because these same individuals also directed local cultural life, a true elite existed. Taking the analysis of elitism to the national level in the 1950s, C. Wright Mills argued that power in American society was being concentrated in increasingly fewer and fewer hands. Gone were the days when fate or blind drift seemed to alter the course of society. Now, Mills argued, history was made by the decisions of those key individuals who, through their institutional positions, commanded the resources of society. For Mills, the higher circles of power could be found in the bureaucratic hierarchies of three key institutions: the military, the large corporation, and the executive branch of the federal government. Sitting atop these command posts of power were a few thousand individuals who were able to shape the direction of change in our society.[12]

Power elite theory made several notable contributions, among them attention to the array of institutions through which power in American society is exercised. However, it did not analyze why public pressures were sometimes successful in shaping political outcomes, nor did it scrutinize the dynamics of the policy process. For Mills, this followed the logic of his outline of power: the higher levels of power were in the hands of an elite who made society's key decisions. Congress, part of the middle level of power and the arena of public attention, was subordinate. Another shortcoming of power elite theory that radical critics pointed out was its failure to sufficiently analyze the connection between capitalist social structure and the institutions that were identified as

[10] Dahl, p. 228.
[11] Edward Epstein, *The Corporation in American Politics* (Englewood Cliffs: Prentice-Hall, 1969), p. 304.
[12] C. Wright Mills, *The Power Elite* (New York: Oxford University Press, 1956).

exercising power.[13] More recent versions of elite theory have been developed that focus on public policy and root their analysis of institutions in their structural context. G. William Domhoff, for example, emphasizes the role of class segments and protest to explain policy changes.[14] Nevertheless, the tendency of many elite theorists has been to map power structures by demonstrating the overlapping networks among elites, thereby downplaying how these elites use their positions of power.

The long-standing gap between the conclusions of elite theories and pluralists was based, in part, on a pivotal difference in how each defined the subject to be examined. Sociological studies focused on a range of key institutions to document the existence of an elite shaping community life. Pluralist writers, regardless of the importance they placed on interest groups, narrowed the focus of the study of community power to an examination of government decisions. While this approach had obvious advantages – it limited the field of study to more easily managed dimensions, and the decisions studied were readily accessible to researchers – it assumed that studying government decisions was sufficient for evaluating community power. As a result of this methodological narrowing, pluralists ignored a wide range of decisions and relations outside of government. And by definitional fiat, the broader concerns of power elite theorists were ruled irrelevant. This constricted conception of power was illustrated by Polsby, who argued that only when a banker explicitly attempts to influence government decisions does he become worthy of attention. When a banker performs his normal activities, he does not affect the community and therefore does not exercise power.[15] Obviously, this contention ignores the tremendous power that banks wield through their loan decisions to shape economic development, and thus indirectly the political agenda, as well as their structural power to redistribute income to the holders of capital. Yet for pluralism, all of this was irrelevant because it did not directly and observably involve government decisions.

As pluralism came to dominate political science, volumes were written challenging its assumptions, methods, and conclusions. Some critics stressed that all too often pluralists were willing to embrace the concept of "dispersed inequalities" without realizing that what appeared from the top as multiple group conflicts appeared from the bottom as the narrow divisions among a few select elites.[16] Pluralist scholars were also vulnerable to the charge that they

---

[13] Robert Lynd, "Power in the United States," in G. William Domhoff and Hoyt Ballard, eds., *C. Wright Mills and the Power Elite* (Boston: Beacon Press, 1968), pp. 103–15.

[14] See, for example, G. William Domhoff, *The Power Elite and the State* (New York: Aldine de Gruyter, 1990).

[15] Polsby, p. 117.

[16] John Gaventa, *Power and Powerlessness* (Urbana: University of Illinois Press, 1980).

ignored so-called nondecisions.[17] Critics pointed out that power could be manifested in the ability to prevent challenges from emerging, whether through control over the rules or through ideological dominance.[18] At the same time, power may be evident when dominant groups are not challenged due to fear of the consequences.[19] Accordingly, E.E. Schattschneider pointed out that group theory failed to understand the bias of the system of the whole, and in particular how the rules of the game shape the terrain on which political battles are fought to the advantage of some over others.[20]

But perhaps the most frustrating shortfall of pluralism, aside from its narrowed definition of politics, was the repeated divorce of political influence from its economic roots. This weakness continues to appear in pluralist accounts of power, such as David Vogel's *Fluctuating Fortunes,* where he attempts to explain changes in business influence over public policy from the 1960s through the 1980s.[21] Vogel at first appears to go beyond an exclusive emphasis on observable political behavior, but like his pluralist colleagues, he ultimately relies on this level of analysis to explain policy change. For example, to explain the resurgence of corporate political influence in the context of the 1970s recessions, Vogel argues that "the 'new class' of college educated professionals, now worried about their own economic prospects, became more sympathetic to the demands of business to reduce taxes, to slow down the growth of government spending and regulation, and to weaken the power of unions."[22] In this formulation, changing economic conditions are no more than a backdrop shaping elite opinion and the preferences of the "new class" of educated middle-class voters who are offered as the true source of policy change. Indeed, Domhoff notes, for Vogel, "changes in the public's 'perceptions' of the long-term health of the economy explain the 'fluctuating fortunes' of business."[23] No attempt is made by Vogel to analyze the unique form of political influence that large corporations have because of the dependence of government on the performance of the business community for a healthy economy. At the same time, he downplays the impact of protest and social turmoil in realigning the political agenda.[24]

---

[17] Peter Bachrach and Morton Baratz, *Power and Poverty* (New York: Oxford University Press, 1970).

[18] Steven Lukes, *Power* (London: Macmillan Publishing Co., 1974).

[19] See, for example, Matthew Crenson, *The Un-Politics of Air Pollution* (Baltimore: Johns Hopkins University Press, 1971).

[20] E. E. Schattschneider, *The Semi-Sovereign People* (New York: Holt, Rinehart and Winston, 1960).

[21] David Vogel, *Fluctuating Fortunes: The Political Power of Business in America* (New York: Basic Books, 1989).

[22] Vogel, 1989, p. 9.   [23] Domhoff, p. 259.

[24] Domhoff, p. 262.

Another shortcoming of pluralism has been to overlook the interplay between economic conditions and interest group influence. David Vogel's work, once again, illustrates this problem. In examining the politics of clean air legislation in the 1970s, he argues that the auto industry's political victories in weakening emissions standards were due to its alliance with the auto worker's union.[25] This explanation, focused on the level of interest group alliances, leaves a number of issues unexplored, such as how faltering economic conditions restructured the options seen as available to policy makers, and how these conditions shaped the strategies and alliances among contending groups and were often invoked for political advantage. (These issues are examined in Chapter 4.)

To analyze these issues, it is essential to add a structural concern to the study of power. For the purposes of this study, the key structure that will be analyzed is capitalist economic relations, and in particular the state dependence on large corporations for tax revenue and economic vitality. This element is chosen because of the primary role economic relations play in the reproduction of society. Also, the importance of linking this element to studies of public policy was articulated by Robert Lynd when he wrote that "Capitalism means and has always meant that the whole institutional system has become weighted so that, like loaded dice, events tend to roll with a bias that favors property."[26]

Structure

The notion of state dependence, or the so-called privileged position of business, is typically associated with the development of neomarxist theories of the state in the 1970s because it was the subject of extensive internecine debate. However, this concept has a much longer and varied history, as evidenced by its appearance in works across political perspectives. Frances Fox Piven and Richard Cloward have pointed out that the conservative economist Joseph Schumpeter discussed state dependence on large corporations for tax revenues as a constraint on policy makers early in the twentieth century.[27] Even David Truman, one of the most widely read pluralists of the 1950s, made this point when he wrote that "the favored position of 'business' is furthered by the existence of an economic system under which businessmen's confidence and expectations of profit are of crucial importance to the health of the econ-

---

[25] David Vogel, "A Case Study of Clean Air Legislation 1967–1981," in Betty Bock et al., eds., *The Impact of the Modern Corporation* (New York: Columbia University Press, 1984), p. 344.

[26] Lynd, p. 111.

[27] See Frances Fox Piven and Richard Cloward, *The New Class War,* revised, expanded ed. (New York: Pantheon Books, 1985), pp. 88–9; Joseph Schumpeter, "The Crisis of the Tax State," *International Economic Papers* (New York: Macmillan Publishing Co., 1954, [1918]), no. 4, p. 20.

omy."[28] In fact, G. William Domhoff, who remembers first encountering this idea in Michael Reagan's 1963 work *The Managed Economy,* goes so far as to argue that in the 1960s this view was obvious and "taken for granted."[29]

True or not, Charles Lindblom, one of the deans of postwar pluralism, created a tremendous stir in the mid-1970s when he, along with Robert Dahl, reconsidered their original conclusions concerning power and the role of business by embracing the notion of state dependence. Today, both acknowledge business to be more than just one of many interests, having a more powerful influence than the designation "interest group" would imply.[30] Central to Lindblom's new understanding of power is the privileged position of business within market societies. Because "jobs, prices, production, growth, the standard of living, and the economic security of everyone" rests in the hands of business, he wrote, "government officials cannot be indifferent to how well business performs its functions. Depressions, inflation, or other economic distress can bring down a government."[31] As a result, businessmen are not mere representatives of special interests. "They appear as functionaries performing functions that government officials regard as indispensable."[32] Thus, Lindblom notes that government officials do not have to be "bribed, duped, or pressured" to grant businessmen their privileged position, nor do they have to be "uncritical admirer[s] of business." It becomes plain to see "that public affairs in market-oriented systems are in the hands of two groups of leaders, government and business, who must collaborate and that to make the system work government leadership must often defer to business leadership. . . . Businessmen cannot be left knocking at the doors of the political systems, they must be invited in."[33]

From this new structural position, Lindblom needed to explain those obvious instances when business lost its political battles or, in other words, when its privileged position was insufficient to triumph over other interests. To do so, he divided policy issues into two categories: primary issues, those business cannot afford to lose and are typically not contested – basically private ownership – and secondary issues, those that business can afford to lose and are debated – such as tax reform and environmental regulation. This typology, however, does not allow for evaluations of modifications of business power that stem from the welfare state or from legislation strengthening the rights of workers and unions, for example, because all losses except the socialization of ownership

---

[28] Truman, p. 255.

[29] William Domhoff, p. 189; Michael Reagan, *The Managed Economy* (New York: Oxford University Press, 1963), pp. 86–7.

[30] For an analysis of this transformation and its shortcomings, see John Manley, "Neo-Pluralism: A Class Analysis of Pluralism I and Pluralism II," *American Political Science Review* vol. 77, no. 2 (June 1983), pp. 368–82.

[31] Charles Lindblom, *Politics and Markets* (New York: Basic Books, 1977), pp. 172–3.

[32] Lindblom, p. 175.   [33] Lindblom, p. 175.

are labeled as secondary. In this way, Lindblom's understanding of the privileged position of business does not allow for an analysis of the consequences of what Andre Gorz describes as "reformist reforms" and "nonreformist reforms." For Gorz, the difference between the two hinges on whether or not the reform conforms to or changes the structural relations of power[34] – in other words, whether reforms leave untouched the overall relations of power or transform them into something fundamentally different.

A better handling of the privileged position concept can be found within the neomarxist tradition. Scholars working within this tradition emphasize that since government, for the most part, does not directly engage in economic activity (particularly in the United States), it can only attempt to stimulate economic growth. Corporations must be induced to invest. As a result, the control over capital provides corporations with an unparalleled form of leverage over policymakers: the withholding of investment and withdrawal of economic activity.[35] In simple terms, corporate officials can choose not to use their capital, or to relocate it, or they can simply threaten to do these things. Thus, the neomarxist scholar Claus Offe concludes, "The entire relationship between capital and the state is built not upon what capital can do *politically* via its association, as the critical theory of elitism maintains, but upon what capital can *refuse* to do in terms of investments. . . ."[36] However, Offe adds that the dependence of the state is "fine tuned" by business lobbying. Jeffrey Isaac summarizes what the privileged position of business means for the neomarxist tradition in terms of the options considered by policymakers:

[I]t does not mean that the state is incapable of acting against the politically expressed preferences of capital. Nor does it mean that every policy pursued by the state is undertaken with an eye toward short-term economic prosperity. It simply, but crucially, means that successful capital accumulation is an essential policy consideration due to the state's dependence on economic prosperity for revenues and stability.[37]

The consequence of state dependence is not, however, a uniform resource over time. In general, this kind of leverage will be enhanced during periods of economic contraction as concerns over the economy accelerate. It is also likely to increase in an era when capital has become increasingly mobile because the prospect of investment flight places government officials under constant pressure to maintain a positive business climate.

This structural limitation became central to the neomarxist claim that the state in capitalist society is, inevitably, a capitalist state. Public policy cannot

[34] Andre Gorz, *A Strategy for Labor: A Radical Proposal* (Boston: Beacon Press, 1974), pp. 7–12.
[35] Claus Offe, *Disorganized Capitalism* (Cambridge: MIT Press, 1984), p. 166.
[36] Offe, p. 192 (emphasis in the original).
[37] Jeffrey Isaac, *Power and Marxist Theory* (Ithaca: Cornell University Press, 1987), p. 180.

be understood simply as the result of open-ended interest group conflict and electoral politics. Class inequality reproduces itself throughout society, including the political system. And in this class society, the business class is privileged. Yet, within neomarxism the idea of structural dependency spurred a continuing debate.[38] Did it mean that regardless of who served in government, the results of public policy would always favor business? Or did it mean that state dependence was just one of many advantages that propertied interests wielded over nonpropertied interests? Answering these questions became further complicated because these issues were caught up in the larger theoretical discussion of the relationship between structure and agency. At one extreme, theories that emphasize structure view human action as determined by the settings and institutions of social life. Individual behavior, according to this view, is merely the result of external circumstances. At the other extreme, theories of agency view individual action in terms of unconstrained choice. Individuals have the ability to act, or not act, as they wish, dependent largely on their own volition.[39]

Emblematic of this dichotomy was a much-publicized debate in the late 1960s and early 1970s between the British scholar Ralph Miliband and the French theorist Nicos Poulantzas.[40] Without rehashing its details, the debate indicates in retrospect the balancing act that is required to avoid the pitfalls of either divorcing behavior from its social context or ruling out the ability of human actors to make social change. At the time, Miliband's position was identified as merely "instrumentalist," and he was unfairly criticized for presenting nothing more than a reworked power-elite theory that ignored any force impinging on the state beyond the direct actions of the capitalist class. Poulantzas, on the other hand, was seen as clinging to a relentlessly structural argument. In his early work, for example, he argued that the capitalist state was forced to undertake policies conducive to the reproduction of capital, regardless of its personnel or existing political coalitions.[41] Although the debate was often described as a battle between instrumentalism and structuralism, this caricature shortchanged Miliband's position from the start and never captured the evolving complexity of Poulantzas's work. Indeed, from the beginning, Miliband noted the structural forces of state dependence and the "pressure" on

[38] For surveys of these debates, see Bob Jessop, *The Capitalist State* (New York: New York University Press, 1982); Martin Carnoy, *The State and Political Theory* (Princeton: Princeton University Press, 1984); Clyde Barrow, *Critical Theories of the State* (Madison: University of Wisconsin Press, 1993).

[39] Steven Lukes, "Power and Structure," in *Essays in Social Theory,* (London: Macmillian Publishing Co., 1977).

[40] For a review of this debate see Carnoy, pp. 104–7.

[41] Nicos Poulantzas, *Political Power and Social Classes* (London: New Left Books, 1974).

governments to maintain business confidence, and Poulantzas came to see the state as a site of class struggle.[42]

By the mid-1970s, many scholars trying to develop critical theories of the state embraced various versions of structuralism because it was perceived as presenting a new form of critique, one that offered a more sophisticated view of the political dynamics of advanced capitalism. As its practitioners claimed to have reached a higher theoretical plane, they dismissed as mundane the research of those who studied the details of business participation in the state because all such studies could offer was evidence to debunk pluralist claims of power being open-ended and in flux; they could not develop a more theoretically grounded critique of advanced capitalism. In recently reviewing this debate, Frances Fox Piven argues that those on the structural side of the debate appeared to have prevailed simply because their work was perceived as new in the "intellectual fashion contest." "Structuralism," she observed, "also lent itself to wondrous excesses of theoretical elaboration, which could entirely avoid the actual empirical muddiness of class politics in postwar capitalist societies, where real-world capitalists were fragmented and fractious, and real-world workers were often on the wrong side of the class conflict."[43]

In the two decades since this debate, Piven points out, the so-called instrumentalist side of the debate has, in fact, held up quite well. An extraordinary political mobilization of the business community has obtained new accommodations from the state by dismantling welfare-state protections and by weakening unions, if not destroying them outright. Put another way, if the capitalist mode of production automatically produced state structures oriented toward furthering capital accumulation, this tremendous increase in corporate political activity would have been unnecessary. Yet, by the late 1970s, for example, total corporate spending on advocacy advertising and grass-roots lobbying reached, according to Ferguson and Rogers, $1 billion annually.[44] And since that time, corporate political spending has increased. Clearly, business officials have considered this money well spent, and much evidence vindicates their belief. But, Piven adds, the structural dependence of the capitalist state made this all the more possible. There was widespread awareness among political elites that the American corporate community had been toppled from world dominance, profits were suffering, and political solutions were needed.

---

[42] Ralph Miliband, *The State in Capitalist Society* (New York: Basic Books, 1969), pp. 146–52; Nicos Poulantzas, *State, Power and Socialism* (London: New Left Books, 1978).

[43] Frances Fox Piven, "Reflections on Ralph Miliband," *New Left Review,* no. 206, (July–August 1994), p. 24.

[44] Thomas Ferguson and Joel Rogers, *Right Turn: The Decline of the Democrats and the Future of American Politics* (New York: Hill and Wang, 1986), p. 88.

A closer examination of Miliband's understanding of state dependence offers a perspective that balances a focus on interest group activity with that of the privileged position of business. Miliband observed that governments using their vast powers against business soon confront "perils" that are "best epitomized in the dreaded phrase 'loss of confidence.'"[45] He saw this form of pressure as "more important and effective" than any other and one that exerted a "permanent pressure" on government. "The existence of this major area of independent economic power is a fact which no government, whatever its inclinations, can ignore in the determination of its policies. . . ."[46] State dependence on business, while an important pressure, does not automatically mean that government officials know how to respond to each particular policy battle. Indeed, Miliband insisted, the active goodwill and support inside the state system "does not remove the need for [businesses] to exert their own pressure for the achievement of their immediate and specific goals."[47] Since achieving specific political goals requires active pressure on state officials, Miliband saw it necessary to focus, as Piven notes, on the "capitalist class as a power elite."[48] As a result, he felt compelled to examine the composition of the state elite and their ideological inclination to support business to describe the advantages capitalists had within the state.

From this perspective, state dependence is an essential policy consideration, not a force that automatically shapes specific state actions to the benefit of business. Domhoff, writing from the perspective of someone who has long examined the empirical muddiness of class politics, stresses that business officials have never been so confident of their structural position as to feel that they do not need to dominate the state, given the potential for other interests to use government policy.[49] In light of this understanding of structural advantage, it is important to analyze precisely how business takes advantage of its privileged position, and how the combination of the political behavior of business and its structural position shape public policy.

This approach is also necessary because government officials cannot simply ignore citizens' demands if they wish to maintain legitimacy in the eyes of the electorate. Winning elections requires citizen support. Moreover, evolving social norms, such as environmentalism, further constrain the attentiveness of state officials to corporate interests. Thus, Offe argues that the relative weight of these different pressures depends on "cyclical and conjunctural variations which may allow a group to exploit its specific social power to a larger or smaller extent at different points in time."[50] In other words, particular policy outcomes are shaped by the larger structures of power, as well as by how

---

[45] Miliband, p. 150.   [46] Miliband, p. 147.
[47] Miliband, p. 145.   [48] Piven, p. 25.
[49] Domhoff, p. 194.
[50] Claus Offe, *Contradictions of the Welfare State* (Cambridge: MIT Press, 1984), p. 160.

groups mobilize their resources in the context of the ever-shifting vulnerability of policy makers to these pressures.

History

While focusing on the interrelationship between political behavior and structural advantage provides two key elements to the study of power, these two broad considerations, individually or together, still offer an overly abstract description of political change. To explain policy change more fully, it is essential to add a third element: sensitivity to how historical variations in socioeconomic contextual conditions shape the power of political actors. For example, cyclical variation in the economy or periods of social turmoil will each affect the dynamics of policy making. In addition, the impact of these variations is affected by the broader historical dynamics of the time in which they occur. Because discussions of the importance of studying history have been framed lately by state-centered theory, it is important to turn to this perspective. Although state-centered theory appears to represent an advance by emphasizing historical analysis, the selective focus on only certain elements of history undercuts its value.

A number of political scientists have been involved in the "turn to history" as part of an effort to reconceptualize the issues involved in studying the origins and evolution of political institutions, often described as "state building." State-centered theories of social change reject the "society-centered" views of both pluralism and neomarxism, and in their own way add a structural dimension to the analysis of political change. By "structure," however, state-centered theory focuses almost exclusively on political structures. Statists contend that despite the differences between pluralism and neomarxism, each of these perspectives characterizes government decisions as a reflection of societal power relations, whether they are understood as group pressures or framed by the language of class conflict. Statist approaches, on the other hand, do not believe that state actions are reducible to or determined by social forces. Instead, they result from the autonomous actions of state officials who, in attempting to resolve conflict, make society-shaping decisions. Indeed, for Stephen Skowronek, one of the leading statist practitioners, creating new political institutions is a uniquely political process that follows a logic of state actors, institutional resources, and policy legacies.[51] To test their theories and to rescue the interpretation of past events from society-centered perspectives, state-centered theorists have been at the heart of the movement to "return to history." But by "history," statists offer a reading of the past that does not consider the interaction between economic factors and political activity. Instead, by history they simply mean the history of policy legacies and political

[51] Stephen Skowronek, *Building the New American State: The Expansion of Administrative Capacities* (New York: Cambridge University Press, 1982).

institutions, which is why this turn to history is sometimes referred to as the "new institutionalism."[52]

This orientation can be found in the opening editorial statement of *Studies in American Political Development,* one of the flagship forums for statist work. In 1986, Karen Orren and Steven Skowronek wrote, in what surely was not an oversight, that *"Studies'* institutional perspective is defined broadly to encompass the social and cultural institutions that impinge on government as well as government institutions themselves."[53] Glaringly absent from this formulation was a concern for economic relations of any sort. This criticism is not a quibble over terminology. Orren and Skowronek contend that the study of history is "the natural proving ground for the claim that institutions have an independent and formative influence on politics."[54] By this they mean that institutions are independent of societal pressures. They see their focus as an antidote to "a long season in which social forces and processes were the predominant topics of study."[55] The narrowness of this "political" orientation is one of the many criticisms lodged against state-centered theory.[56] Although few disagree with the statist claim that public policies shape social action, or with the point that political structures imprint on current debates legacies from the past, the contention that state actors resolve conflict through autonomous actions suggests that the state and society are separate from and independent of each other. Bob Jessop criticizes this view, in part, because it "implies that both [state and society] exist as independent entities which are fully constituted, internally coherent and mutually exclusive and that one always unilaterally determines the other. This would reify and absolutize what is really an emergent, partial, unstable, and variable social distinction. . . ."[57] Another shortcoming of state-centered research has been a proclivity to study past political patterns in order to discern whether or not there are parallels between past practice and current trends. Although this effort can uncover some interesting commonalities, this tendency, as Thomas Ferguson emphasizes, "also abstract[s] seriously from

[52] For an analysis of this relationship, see David Brian Robertson, "The Return to History and the New Institutionalism in American Political Science," *Social Science History* vol. 17, no. 1 (Spring 1993), pp. 1–36.

[53] Karen Orren and Steven Skowronek, Editors' Preface, *Studies in American Political Development* vol. 1 (1986), p. vii.

[54] Orren and Skowronek, p. vii.

[55] Orren and Skowronek, p. vii.

[56] For a summary of the major criticisms, see Bob Jessop, *State Theory* (University Park: Pennsylvania University Press, 1990), pp. 278–88.

[57] Jessop, p. 287. For an empirical critique of the state-centered approach, see, for example, Brian Waddell, "The Dimensions of the Military Ascendancy During U.S. Industrial Mobilization for World War II," *Journal of Political and Military Sociology* vol. 23 (Summer 1995), pp. 81–98.

the historically specific concatenation of events and forces" that shape current politics.[58]

While state-centered theory was developed to go beyond society-centered perspectives, a strong commonality remains between state-centered theory and pluralism: each downplays the political influence of the large corporation and those with significant financial resources. State-centered theory and pluralism also share a set of assumptions on the relationship between society, economy, and the state.[59] Statists and pluralists assume the separation of society, economy, and the state. For marxism, on the other hand, capitalist society is understood as a totality – albeit a contradictory one – whereby the state is located within the basic economic contradictions and conflicts of capitalism. The task of research is to study the political and socioeconomic forces shaping state actions. This theoretical difference may help explain why there are unending disagreements between these two basic approaches to power.

A more complex understanding of history than the one offered by state-centered theory requires attention to how specific socioeconomic conditions shape the dynamics of policy making. For example, the auto industry's economic losses have enhanced its lobbying clout. In other words, there are political advantages to economic downturns. Jim Johnston, GM's vice president of industry–government relations, noted this situation in 1994 on retiring after thirty years as one of the industry's main political liaisons: "When there is a recession, people listen more closely to what we're saying because they are wary about doing things that might keep the recession going. So they listen better in times of trouble."[60] From a very different perspective, Ralph Nader criticized this same fact. When the economic condition of the nation deteriorates, the guiding philosophy of our political institutions, he wrote, is that "we should leave the wealthy and powerful alone, or succor them with the fruits of the public treasury."[61] While economic downturns generally amplify the state's dependence on capital as the policy makers increasingly worry about economic stability, an economic collapse like the Great Depression can weaken the power of business as these same officials attempt to meet the crisis.[62]

---

[58] Thomas Ferguson, *Golden Rule* (Chicago: University of Chicago Press, 1995), p. 283.

[59] Rhonda Levine, "Bringing Classes Back In: State Theory and Theories of the State," in Rhonda Levine and Jerry Lembcke, eds., *Recapturing Marxism* (New York: Praeger Publishers, 1987), p. 99.

[60] Cited in Max Gates, "GM's Johnston Knows Washington Ins and Outs," *Automotive News* (July 18, 1994), p. 10.

[61] Ralph Nader and William Taylor, *The Big Boys: Power and Position in American Business* (New York: Pantheon Press, 1986), p. 506.

[62] Fred Block, "The Ruling Class Does Not Rule: Notes on the Marxist Theory of the State," *Socialist Revolution* vol. 7, no. 3 (1977), p. 24.

For the purposes of this study, the socioeconomic conditions that will be focused on include general economic conditions, such as prosperity or recession; the industry's economic situation (profits or losses); and whether social movements are mobilizing, protesting, or on the wane. To analyze the impact of socioeconomic conditions properly, one must locate these specific conditions within the broader and longer-term dynamics of the political economy so that researchers remain sensitive to how these specific conditions were experienced at the time they occurred. Major losses by a large corporation, for example, can have a different impact if these losses are an isolated event, part of a pattern, or part of a societywide downturn. The same holds true for the impact of a particular protest or riot.

A brief example will illustrate the different impact that the industry's downturns have had on its political fortunes. During the early 1980s, when the auto industry experienced its first major crisis in the post–World War II era – and record losses – a number of major policy changes were made to aid the industry. In the early 1990s, when the industry experienced another round of losses that dwarfed this earlier episode, industry officials mounted a more elaborate political campaign but achieved far more mixed results. Explaining the differences between these two sets of policy responses to industry losses requires attention to the broader historical context of the post–World War II political economy. The first round of losses was not only unprecedented for the industry but came at a time of nationwide restructuring as manufacturers responded to new global economic forces. With the end of the "American century," the political compromises of the past were reopened in an attempt to restore economic growth. The industry's second crisis, by contrast, followed soon after a period of record profits in the middle to late 1980s. Many saw this later round of losses as either self-inflicted by the automakers themselves or simply as cyclical. Either way, they were less deserving of a major political response. (This issue is taken up in Chapter 8.)

It is important to emphasize that the elements of behavior, structure, and history are not independent of each other, with each having its own separate effect. While they can be separated for analytical simplicity, scholarship must try to capture the complex interaction among the three. Contingency and agency do not begin where structure ends. Nor does a historical conjunction of events determine the outcome of a particular political battle. The task for researchers is to explain how these factors interact and affect one another. While the power resources of interest groups are shaped by their economic position in society, changing macroeconomic conditions influence how lobbying efforts are strategically organized and their relative political impact.

A focus on behavior, structure, and contextual conditions facilitates analysis of variations in political influence over time. This is essential because, while ceteris paribus (all things being equal) is a necessary convention of analytical argument, in simple terms the ceteris is virtually never paribus; in the real world, all other things are never really equal. Similar-seeming recessions or protests, for example, do not have the same impact at different points in time. To emphasize the indeterminacy of this relationship is not to suggest, however, that no regularities can be found in the exercise of power. The long-term inequality that characterizes American society indicates something quite to the contrary. Combining a sensitivity to the realms of behavior, structure, and history provides the opportunity to capture the complex interaction that shapes social change. It avoids the pitfalls of having to choose one level of social explanation over another, artificially abstracting the dynamics of political conflict. Most important, it allows an analysis to go beyond an exclusive focus on the contestants and their actions.

2

The Structure of the Auto Industry

In recent years the American automobile industry has undergone a fundamental transformation. Beset by foreign competition, it has reorganized operations and reduced capacity in response to new competitors using new production methods. The industry's restructuring is part of the larger phenomenon of U.S. companies responding to global competition by shifting investments, closing plants, and seeking greater flexibility in labor relations. The economic history of the U.S. auto industry is briefly reviewed here to lay the groundwork for the subsequent discussions of changing political patterns. This discussion also serves to highlight the more strictly economic side of corporate power.

Recent Changes

Although the U.S. auto industry has always seen its ups and downs in sales and profits, lately these ebbs and flows have resembled tidal waves. In 1980, for example, U.S. automakers sustained losses of $4.2 billion – a record at the time. GM, one of the most profitable companies in the twentieth century, experienced its first loss since its 1921 reorganization. (Even during the Great Depression it never lost money.) Meanwhile, Chrysler found itself on the verge of bankruptcy, saved only by a government bailout. In stark contrast, during each year of the previous two decades prior to 1980, the industry never returned less than $2 billion in combined profits (1980 dollars).[1]

By 1983, the industry's fortunes turned around and it earned profits of $6.7 billion. And in 1984 its profits grew to $10 billion. Each of these years set new industry records. Since that time, sales and profits have continued to seesaw. Annual sales of cars and light trucks by the U.S. automakers climbed to

---

[1] U.S. Congress, Senate, Committee on Finance, *Issues Relating to the Domestic Auto Industry. Hearings before the subcommittee on International Trade,* Part 2, 97th Cong., 1st. sess. (January 14–15, 1981), p. 170.

9.3 million in 1983, up from less than 8 million in 1981 and 1982. By 1986 sales surged to 11.8 million, only to fall back to 8.7 million in 1991. In the mid-1990s, sales hovered around 11 million. Because of one-time charges and accounting changes, it is problematic to compare directly actual profits and losses throughout the industry year to year. However, the magnitude of historic profits and record losses suggests an industry in tremendous flux. Combined, the Big Three lost $7.5 billion in 1991 and $30 billion in 1992 while earning almost $14 billion in profits in 1994 and approximately $13 billion in both 1995 and 1996. However, alongside recent rebounds in profits have come large dislocations in employment. During the past twenty years, 300,000 workers have been displaced, and production capacity has been downsized by 1.7 million vehicles.

In many respects, to speak of the U.S. auto industry is to speak of GM. If GM were a sovereign state, its economic size would place it ahead of all but nineteen nations.[2] GM is the largest corporation in the world in sales and in share of economic output. Its financial subsidiary, the General Motors Assistance Corporation (GMAC), is the largest consumer finance company in the world. In 1995, GM had assets of $191 billion and sales of $170 billion. Its sales were larger than those of AT&T, IBM, Microsoft, and Federal Express combined. It has 700,000 employees worldwide, with over 347,000 in the United States, which is twice the number of employees in the Postal Service.[3] Its sales are equal to the combined total of the two largest Japanese producers: Toyota and Nissan. However, while GM remains an industrial behemoth, over the past thirty years its impact on the American economy has greatly diminished. Its North American workforce is now half of what it once was, and its overall share of the economy has also shrunk. In 1970, GM was responsible for 2.3 percent of the nation's economic output; by 1997 this figure had declined to 1.5 percent. This figure is still significantly larger than that of the next largest company in the United States, Ford, at 1.2 percent. In contrast, Microsoft, one of the leading information-age companies, accounts for only about 0.1 percent of the U.S. gross national product.[4]

In its post–World War II heyday, the auto industry was a simple triopoly insulated from foreign competition. Today GM, Ford, and Chrysler share the U.S. market with a number of companies from abroad and account for approximately three-quarters of domestic sales compared to the 95 percent of sales that once were in Detroit's hands. In addition, "American" cars contain many

---

[2] Walter Adams and James Brock, "Automobiles," in Adams and Brock, eds., *The Structure of American Industry,* 9th ed. (Englewood Cliffs: Prentice-Hall, 1995), p. 69.

[3] Keith Bradsher, "What's New at G.M.? Cars, for a Change," *New York Times* (September 8, 1996), Section 3, p. 1.

[4] Keith Bradsher, "Forget Microsoft. G.M. Is Still the Biggest Kid on the Block," *New York Times* (July 24, 1998), Section 4, p. 4.

foreign-made parts, blurring the distinction between domestic and offshore vehicles. Cars are produced in the United States by eleven companies: two American, two German, and seven Japanese. For many contemporary car buyers, it is foreign manufacturers, whether their assembly plants are located in the United States or abroad, that have come to symbolize quality. First with small cars and now with luxury vehicles, Japanese car makers have taken a significant proportion of younger car buyers away from Detroit. The prominence of the Japanese car industry is remarkable, considering that it hardly existed in 1960. In twenty years it rose from obscurity to sell more cars worldwide than U.S. car makers. Not until 1994, when the Japanese economy was ailing, did American car makers regain their leadership in sales. At the same time, German car makers have continued to hold on to a segment of the luxury market, also embodying an image of quality and workmanship. With the recent entrance of Korean car producers into the U.S. market, the largest in the world is becoming further fragmented.

On the surface, it seems that those critics who once spoke of American "monopoly capitalism" to describe the structure of the post–World War II economy have been proven wrong. International competition and global corporations seem to rule the day instead of the domestic oligopolies of the past. Yet the appearance of international competition masks a countertrend in which auto companies are linked together in various ways to create global networks. Indicative of this trend, *Ward's Automotive International,* a leading industry trade publication, now issues a special annual edition entitled "How the World's Automakers are Related." The 1995 edition ran to thirty pages, detailing the "equity arrangements, joint ventures, deals to supply parts or components, marketing or distribution arrangements, technology agreements or manufacturing tieups" among the world's car makers. The U.S. automakers, for their part, have bought large shares of both Japanese and European car manufacturers. Examples of this trend include Ford's ownership of the British Aston Martin and Jaguar, GM's 50 percent stake in Saab, and Chrysler's ownership of Lamborghini. In addition, the U.S. automakers have entered into joint ventures with Asian car companies. GM has two such relationships: one with Toyota in California and the other with Suzuki in Ontario. Ford has a joint venture with Mazda in Michigan, and Chrysler had one with Mitsubishi in Illinois.

Casting a shadow over all of these arrangements is the 1998 merger of Daimler-Benz (Mercedes) and Chrysler. The $36 billion acquisition by Daimler was historic for a number of reasons. It was the largest merger in automotive history, the largest industrial takeover in history, and the largest acquisition of any American company by a foreign buyer. Commentators hailed the move as the beginning of a massive consolidation wave that will inevitably transform the worldwide automotive industry.[5] In light of these trends, competition among firms today bears little resemblance to the standard economics textbook version of competitive markets. Instead, it suggests that there is an evolving trend toward a concentrated industry on a larger scale, with limited competition among a small number of firms. See Figure 1 for some Big Three partnership arrangements in place with other automakers before the Daimler-Chrysler merger.

Lean Production

Underlying these financial arrangements is a new system of production. In fact, the most widely discussed study of auto production, done by an international team at the Massachusetts Institute of Technology (MIT) in the late 1980s, argues that changes in the production process are turning every car maker upside down and represent an historic advance in manufacturing methods.[6] Pioneered by Toyota, these changes are so significant that a new term is used to describe them: "lean production." Moreover, it is claimed that lean production is as significant a development beyond mass production as the latter was in its day over craft production. With craft production, highly skilled workers used simple but flexible tools to produce custom products that were expensive. With mass production, a system of narrowly skilled design professionals, orchestrating the activities of unskilled or semiskilled workers tending capital-intensive machinery, can turn out high volumes of standardized products at relatively low cost. Lean production, on the other hand, uses fewer inputs, produces higher-quality products, and "reskills" labor.

Despite the claims by its proponents, however, some have questioned whether lean production represents something qualitatively new or is simply a speedup of labor.[7] The issues involved in this debate are extensive and raise a number of significant questions beyond the scope of this discussion. Yet, for the manufacturers of cars, one thing seems certain. Lean production is the direction they need to take to stay competitive. Thus, for the sake of this discussion, the claims of lean production will be accepted as they are presented by its leading spokesmen and deserve closer attention.

Lean production is characterized by teams of multiskilled, or at least multi-tasked, workers producing a greater variety of products. The term "lean" is used because the process cuts in half the number of inputs used in the produc-

---

[5] "The First Global Car Colossus," *Business Week* (May 18, 1998), pp. 40–3.

[6] The following summary of lean production is taken from James Womack, Daniel Jones, and Daniel Roos, *The Machine That Changed the World* (New York: Rawson Associates, 1990).

[7] See, for example, Steve Babson, ed., *Lean Work: Empowerment and Exploitation in the Global Auto Industry* (Detroit: Wayne State University Press, 1995).

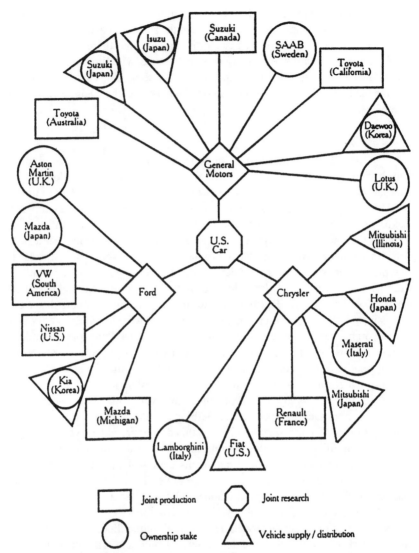

Figure 1. Some recent Big Three partnership arrangements. (*Source: Structure of American Industry* 9/E by Adams/Brock, eds. © 1995. Reprinted by permission of Prentice-Hall, Inc., Upper Saddle River, NJ.)

tion process: labor, manufacturing space, engineering time, investment in tools, and development time for new products. With a goal of zero defects, lean production is able to produce higher-quality products, at lower cost, and responds more quickly to consumer demand than traditional mass production. Teamwork is considered to be at the heart of this new system. As such, lean production turns on its head the twentieth-century history of Taylorism, sometimes known as "scientific management," which eschews teamwork and treats workers as incapable of thinking.[8]

Lean production originated in the early 1950s during the birth of the postwar Japanese auto industry. Toyota officials realized that they could not pattern their factories after those of American manufacturers. They did not have the markets, the capital, or the physical plants that the American automakers had. Over the next twenty years the Toyota system evolved by organizing workers into teams, with attention to continually enhancing their skills. In this way, labor was treated as a resource to be developed instead of a variable cost to be shed during downturns. Because of storage limitations and lack of capital, just-in-time inventories were a necessity. This required that greater attention be given to quality, since there were no spare parts available if defects were discovered. Thus, lean producers were forced to correct defects immediately, requiring constant interaction with suppliers to improve quality. With mass production, on the other hand, the preeminent goal was to keep the assembly line going. Large inventories of parts were kept, and as a result, by the time defects were discovered, thousands of defective parts had already been produced. Ignoring these errors became commonplace, resulting in mounting defects, which either had to be corrected at the end of the line, thereby raising costs, or passed on to consumers.

The various aspects of lean production function together to produce a system that is more efficient and better able to produce quality products. Increasingly, American manufacturers inside and outside the automobile industry have adopted lean production, resulting in dramatic improvements in productivity and quality. Chrysler's productivity, for example, practically doubled between 1980 and 1992, and today the most efficient plants of Chrysler and Ford are estimated to assemble cars almost as efficiently as the most efficient Japanese producers. GM, on the other hand, remains less efficient.

History of Concentration

During the industry's early years there was competition among a large number of firms, reaching a high of eighty-eight companies in 1921. (These firms were sheltered from foreign competition by tariffs. From 1913 to 1922

---

[8] See Stan Luger, "The Team Concept and the New Global Economy," in Lawrence Flood, ed., *Unions and Public Policy: The New Economy, Law, and Democratic Politics* (Westport: Greenwood Press, 1995), pp. 39–51.

tariffs on imports ranged from 30 to 45 percent, and from 1922 to 1934 tariffs ranged from 25 to 50 percent.) The trend toward concentration in the domestic industry began in the mid-1920s, when forty-three firms left the industry between 1923 and 1926. By 1935 only ten firms were left, and by the late 1950s just three firms accounted for virtually all domestic production and sales.[9] (In 1987 American Motors [AMC], long the industry's marginal member, merged with Chrysler.) Commenting on this overall consolidation long before AMC's demise, Bradford Snell, a critic of the industry's structure, concluded that "the trend toward concentration in the automobile industry is unequalled in the history of American manufacturing."[10]

For Snell, the industry's concentration was due in large part to the annual style change, which first appeared in 1923, effectively eliminating smaller manufacturers unwilling or unable to restyle each year. GM led the market in emphasizing styling changes, and its market share increased from 13 percent in 1922 to 43 percent in 1927. After entering the market in 1923, Chrysler followed GM's lead and captured 6 percent of the market by 1927. Ford initially resisted this trend and quickly lost its position as the industry's dominant firm. From 1922 to 1927 Ford's market share fell from 51 percent to 9 percent. In 1928 it adopted the annual style change, and within two years its sales were back up to 31 percent of the U.S. market. Collectively, the Big Three increased their market share from less than 65 percent in 1923 to over 90 percent in 1935.

Prior to the introduction of the annual style change, when entry into the industry was relatively easy, scale economies were not a deterrent to new entrants. Continual style changes forced smaller firms to change tools and dies before they were worn out, while larger firms were able to spread the cost of these changes over more vehicles, thereby lowering their unit cost. Redesign also required large-scale advertising to alert consumers to the "new" cars being produced each year. Moreover, style changes brought with them the need for extensive forward integration into franchised dealer networks with specialized maintenance abilities and parts inventories. Previously, parts had been standardized and interchangeable.

As early as the 1930s, the role of the annual style change in driving out competition was noted by the Federal Trade Commission (FTC). Commenting on the declining number of vehicle manufacturers, the FTC's 1939 *Report on the Motor Vehicle Industry* stated, "The introduction of yearly models, and the increasing importance of the style factor, the large amount of capital required to finance new models in good and bad years, all favored the large manufactur-

---

[9] See Bradford Snell, "Annual Style Changes in the Automobile Industry as an Unfair Method of Competition," *Yale Law Journal* vol. 80 (1971), p. 577.

[10] Snell, p. 577.

ing company with huge capital and equipment resources."[11,12] By the early 1960s the overall cost of annual style changes, with 1948 as a baseline, was estimated to account for 25 percent of the cost of a new car.[13]

In the two decades after World War II, the auto industry was a tightly knit, joint-profit-maximizing oligopoly, earning profits well above the average for all manufacturers.[14] This situation led to a number of antitrust investigations by the Justice Department and the FTC, almost all of them involving anticompetitive behavior rather than monopoly structure. Few of them culminated in decisive action.[15] There were also several major hearings on the industry's concentration held by the U.S. Senate Subcommittee on Antitrust and Monopoly in 1955 and 1957.[16] The reports generated by these hearings exposed Detroit's oligopolistic behavior. Few doubted that GM was the price leader – raising prices first, with the others to follow. The committee was chaired by Sen. Estes Kefauver (D-TN), an antitrust crusader. Its 1958 report stated: "In all of their testimony, officials of Ford, Chrysler, and American Motors – sometimes explicitly and more often implicitly – made clear that their basic approach to the pricing of their products was in terms of meeting the price setting by General Motors."[17] Instead of cutting prices to stimulate demand when sales lagged, output was cut and prices were raised. At the time, GM had

[11] Cited in Snell, p. 607, from FTC report, p. 26.

[12] Snell argues that the failure in the early 1950s of Kaiser, the only serious entry of a domestic car maker since 1923, was a consequence of its inability to afford annual styling changes due to insufficient volume. Kaiser first entered the market in the late 1940s and captured 5 percent of the market in 1948. Yet, retooling and advertising costs were too much for the small firm, which continued to sell its 1948 model in 1949 and 1950. In 1951 the company did restyle, but its volume was too low for efficient production. As a result, Kaiser's unit costs and prices were higher than those of the Big Three, and it was forced to withdraw from the market in 1954.

[13] Franklin Fisher, Zvi Grilliches, and Carl Kaysen, "The Costs of Automobile Model Changes Since 1949," *Journal of Political Economy* vol. LXX, no. 5 (October 1962), pp. 433–51.

[14] Lawrence White, *The Auto Industry Since 1945* (Cambridge: Harvard University Press, 1971).

[15] George Heaton, Jr., "Government Structural Policies and the Automobile Industry," *Policy Studies Review* vol. 2, no. 4, (May 1983), p. 765. For an additional examination of the industry's antitrust history, see Simon Whitney, *Antitrust Policies,* vol. 1 (New York: Twentieth Century Fund, 1958).

[16] U.S. Congress, Senate, Committee on the Judiciary, *A Study of the Antitrust Laws: Investigation of General Motors. Hearings before the Subcommittee on Antitrust,* 84th Cong. 1st sess. (November 1955); U.S. Congress, Senate, Committee on the Judiciary, *Administered Prices. Hearings before the Subcommittee on Antitrust and Monopoly,* 85th Cong., 1st sess. (1957).

[17] U.S. Congress, Senate, Committee on the Judiciary, *Administered Prices: Automobiles, Report of the Subcommittee on Antitrust and Monopoly,* 85th Cong., 2d. sess. (1958), p. 74.

the ability to target its financial returns, a consequence of its market dominance, not traditional business acumen. The 1956 report of the Senate's antitrust subcommittee emphasized this point. "Efficiency to General Motors is apparently its ability to achieve its planned return on investment. This is not economic efficiency and General Motors' return is more a reflection of its market power than its economic efficiency."[18]

A decade later, Ralph Nader pointed out that GM's rate of return seemed unaffected by taxes, which apparently had become simply another cost of production to be passed on to the customer. After taxes, for example, the 1929 rate of return was 36.2 percent, while the 1950 rate of return was 37.5 percent. The 1929 rate of return was attained with pretax earnings of 38.5 percent on the average stockholder's investment, while in 1950 GM made a pretax profit of 77.4 percent, earning 37.5 percent after taxes.[19] For the other two members of the Big Three the pattern was similar. As a result, the combined rate of return for all three between 1947 and 1967 was nearly twice the average for all manufacturers in the United States.[20] (Today, returns, even during years of record profits, are a fraction of the rate of this profitable past.)

In part because of its high returns during this period, GM was seen by many as the prototype of the modern corporation. Others were impressed by its reach well beyond manufacturing passenger cars. In the 1950s, GM not only was the leading car maker, selling almost as many cars as all other automakers in the United States combined, it was also the world's leading producer of trucks, automotive parts, buses, and locomotives. At the same time, GM sold significant numbers of refrigerators, ranges, washers, and food freezers. To sell all these products, GM had the largest advertising budget of any corporation in the nation. In addition, during World War II and through the mid-1950s, GM was the single largest prime contractor for defense equipment.

With a stable oligopoly in place led by GM, the U.S. automakers became technologically stagnant. There were no important product innovations by the Big Three from 1949, when power steering and the automatic transmission were introduced, until the mid-1970s.[21] Over the same period, foreign firms took advantage of Detroit's lethargy and, as noted by long-time auto journalist

[18] U.S. Congress, Senate, Committee on the Judiciary, *Bigness and Concentration of Economic Power — A Case Study of General Motors Corporation. Report of the Subcommittee on Antitrust and Monopoly,* 84th Cong., 2d. sess. (1956), Report 1879, p. 8.

[19] U.S. Congress, Senate, Select Committee on Small Business, *Planning, Regulation and Competition: Automobile Industry — 1968. Hearings,* 90th Cong., 2d. sess. (1968), p. 208.

[20] Davis Dyer, Malcolm Salter, and Alan Webber, *Changing Alliances* (Boston: Harvard Business School Press, 1987), p. 33.

[21] J. Patrick Wright, *One a Clear Day You Can See General Motors: John DeLorean's Look Inside the Automotive Giant* (New York: Avon Books, 1979), p. 4.

Brock Yates, led the introduction of a long list of new technologies, such as "fuel injection, disc brakes, rack and pinion steering, radial tires, quartz head-lights, ergonomically adjustable bucket seats, five-speed manual transmis-sions, high-efficiency overhead camshaft engines, independently sprung sus-pensions, advanced shock absorbers, and strict crash-worthiness standards."[22]

During this "golden era," GM became an organization where loyalty and obsequiousness replaced competence and competition as the dominant traits of the managerial elite. Pleasing one's superiors, by carrying their bags or picking them up at an airport, for example, became an obsession. John DeLorean, the now notorious former GM vice president, who was the youngest divisional manager when he headed Pontiac in 1962, recounted one story that illustrates the lengths to which executives went to ingratiate themselves with their supe-riors, in this case a Chevrolet sales official:

The boss liked to have a refrigerator full of cold beer, sandwiches, and fruit in his room to snack on at night before going to bed. They [junior managers] lined up a suite in one of the city's better hotels, rented a refrigerator and ordered the food and beer. However, the door to the suite was too small to accommodate the icebox. The hotel apparently nixed a plan to rip out the door and part of the adjoining wall. So the quick-thinking zone sales people hired a crane and operator, put them on the roof of the hotel, knocked out a set of windows in the suite, and lowered and shoved the refrigerator into the room through this gaping hole.[23]

When the sales official left the next day the refrigerator was removed, having provided what DeLorean describes as the most expensive midnight snack eaten by a GM executive.

While ignoring technological innovation, Detroit also resisted meeting the demand for small cars; for the Big Three, small cars meant small profits. Yet by the late 1950s, Volkswagen's success in selling a small car was a harbinger of the import barrage that would soon engulf the industry. By 1959 imports comprised 10 percent of the domestic market. Although the import share declined to 5 percent by 1962, after Detroit introduced a smaller domestic vehicle, the next import challenge, this time from Japan, permanently trans-formed the U.S. car market. By the early 1970s, imports accounted for 15 percent of the market. And by the end of that decade, when consumer demand for small cars dramatically increased, in large part due to the oil shock of 1979, in one year the import share of the market increased from 15 percent to 23 percent. The following year, 1980, it increased to 28 percent.

---

[22] Brock Yates, *The Decline and Fall of the American Automobile Industry* (New York: Vintage Books, 1983), p. 149.
[23] Wright, p. 45.

Era of Foreign Competition

As demand for small cars grew and foreign automakers established themselves as permanent players in the American market, domestic producers faced a new challenge. Traditionally, Detroit had viewed small cars as a low-profit market. However, changes in domestic demand forced the Big Three to rethink this position, and in the 1970s a number of domestically produced small cars were sold; none succeeded in stopping the import challenge. More recently, another approach to reach a portion of this market segment has been to import foreign-made cars for sale under domestic labels, the so-called captive import. In 1988, for instance, the Big Three sold 363,000 small cars in the United States that were made in Japan or Korea. By 1994, however, the number of captive imports dropped to approximately 70,000.[24] Joint-venture transplant factories – plants owned by American and Asian car makers with operations in North America – have taken up some of the slack.

By the late 1990s Detroit had expanded its operations outside the United States, especially in Mexico. Since 1978 GM has opened more than fifty parts factories in Mexico, which by 1997 employed almost 75,000 workers, making it the largest private employer in the country. Ford had eleven plants, while Chrysler has none. In 1997, auto and auto parts imports from Mexico reached $19.2 billion, up from $7.2 billion in 1992. Altogether, there were 360,000 workers in Mexico involved in auto-related production and approximately 1 million vehicles were exported, almost all of them to the United States.[25]

Before 1998, when Chrysler merged with Daimler-Benz, the Big Three continued to produce the majority of cars sold in the United States and were still able to behave in an oligopolistic manner. They realized that price cutting by one firm would be followed by similar cuts by the others, leading to unchanged market shares but smaller profits. Given this situation, the industry needed one firm to act as its price leader, a role long fulfilled by GM. Today GM remains the leader in establishing the pricing patterns for large cars. There is no equivalent price leader for small cars. Yet, these market segments are not completely separate. Price increases in one can lead to price increases in the other. One indication of this interplay is the fact that when currency exchange rate changes have led foreign car makers, which generally sell smaller cars, to raise their prices, the Big Three, which generally sell larger cars, are quick to follow.[26] Another indication of the oligopolistic behavior of Detroit's automakers is their continued practice of annually raising prices, even when sales

---

[24] Lindsay Chappell, "GM Leads Effort to Stem Tide of Captive Imports," *Automotive News* (December 12, 1994), p. 3.

[25] Sam Dillon, "A 20-Year G.M. Parts Migration to Mexico," *New York Times* (June 24, 1998), p. C1; "Why Mexico Scares the UAW," *Business Week* (August 3, 1998), pp. 37–8.

[26] Adams and Brock, 1995, p. 78.

have declined. Adams and Brock describe this as "characteristic of a tightly knit oligopoly, [where] the industry's prices behave in a perverse, administered fashion over the course of the business cycle."[27]

Even though the American automakers now share the U.S. market with international competitors, they still remain powerful companies, extensively integrated horizontally, vertically, and internationally.[28] By the mid-1990s, GM produced approximately 70 percent of its own parts; equivalent figures for Ford and Chrysler were 50 percent and 30 percent, respectively. A new aspect of the industry's vertical integration occurred in the 1980s when each of the Big Three purchased ownership stakes in car rental firms. GM bought minority stakes in Avis and National; Ford acquired Hertz and Budget Rent-a-Car; and Chrysler purchased Thrifty, Dollar General, and Snappy.[29]

The international reach of Detroit, while extensive, often goes unnoticed. In 1995 Ford was the largest auto producer in Australia, Britain, Mexico, and Argentina; the second largest in Canada; and the third largest in Brazil and Spain. GM was the second largest auto firm in Canada, Australia, and Germany; it was the third largest in Britain. The role the U.S. automakers play in Canada is an international aspect of the industry that is often overlooked. If 1995 U.S. sales of cars, minivans, and light trucks made in Canada were counted as imports, GM, Ford, and Chrysler, would rank as three of the four top importers of vehicles to the United States, ahead of Nissan, Honda, and Mazda.[30]

Meanwhile, fearing import restrictions, Japanese and South Korean car makers have opened a number of assembly plants in North America. Honda operates plants in Ohio and Ontario. Toyota runs factories in Kentucky and Ontario. Nissan has a plant in Tennessee. Hyundai manufactures cars in Quebec. Subaru and Isuzu jointly operate a plant in Indiana. Production from these transplant factories increased rapidly from 138,000 in 1984 to 1,119,000 in 1989. At the same time, domestic car production by the Big Three declined from 7,368,000 to 5,703,000.[31] By 1992, transplant production reached 1.4 million vehicles, accounting for 25 percent of new car production, which equaled the entire output of Ford. Transplant production reached a maximum of 2.3 million vehicles in 1994. The opening of transplant factories in the United States is not limited to Asian car makers. In 1995 BMW began producing cars in South Carolina, and in 1997 Mercedes began operations in Alabama.

---

[27] Adams and Brock, 1995, p. 82.   [28] Adams and Brock, 1995, p. 70.
[29] Adams and Brock, 1995, p. 70.   [30] Adams and Brock, 1995, p. 70.
[31] Rebecca Morales, *Flexible Production* (Cambridge: Polity Press, 1994), p. 68.

Joint Ventures

As noted earlier, one way the domestic automakers have responded to the challenge of international competition has been to enter into joint ventures with other firms. The most significant joint venture has been between GM and Toyota, bringing together the largest and the third largest car companies in the world. In 1983, the companies announced a fifty–fifty joint venture, forming New United Motor Manufacturing, Inc. (NUMMI), to produce small cars in an unused GM plant in Fremont, California. The joint venture car, at first essentially a Toyota Corolla, was initially marketed by GM as a Chevrolet Nova. Later the venture produced Toyota Corollas or Geo Prisms. Although it was met with a storm of protest from industry critics, as well as from Ford, Chrysler and AMC, the deal was sanctioned by the FTC. The implications of this agreement made it one of the most important auto policy decisions of the 1980s and gave official sanction to joint ventures between the world's largest firms under the banner of competitiveness. Accordingly, it deserves further attention.

In 1984 the FTC voted 3–2 to approve the deal, claiming that there would be "procompetitive" benefits from allowing the largest American and Japanese car companies to work together. (Together the two firms sold more cars in the United States than all the other car makers combined.) Writing for the majority, Chairman James Miller III, made three basic points about the joint venture: (1) it would increase the total number of small cars available in the country, giving consumers greater choice at lower prices, despite the import quotas on Japanese cars that were in place at the time; (2) the joint venture car would cost less to produce than if GM were forced to rely on some other production source; (3) and it "offers a valuable opportunity for GM to complete its learning of more efficient Japanese manufacturing and management techniques [and thus] the venture should lead to the development of a more efficient and competitive U.S. industry."[32] The potential for anticompetitive collusion was prevented, according to Miller, by a consent decree limiting the exchange of information to joint venture business and requiring that all communication be logged.

In addition to the intrinsic controversy of allowing two dominant firms to join together, the FTC's decision-making process was also controversial. The commission held no public hearings to provide an adversarial forum in which the factual and legal contentions made by GM and Toyota could be challenged. Until Chrysler petitioned for the release of information, all materials submitted by GM and Toyota were kept from public review. Still, the FTC allowed the joint venture partners to withhold any information they deemed confidential. Meanwhile, the two firms waived the requirement that the FTC's decision contain a finding of fact and conclusions of law, as well as the right to judicial

---

[32] U.S. Federal Trade Commission Decisions, vol. 103, p. 374, (1984), *General Motors Corp. et al.*, Docket C-3132, pp. 387–8.

review. As a result, the decision was a brief outline of conclusions that were difficult to challenge. With a Reagan-appointed majority uninterested in questioning the actions of these corporate giants, the joint venture partners could afford to waive these rights because there was little doubt as to the outcome of the decision.

Other aspects of the case brought the legitimacy of the proceedings even further into question. Chrysler charged that GM and Toyota had timed their compliance with the FTC's request for information to wait out the term of Commissioner David Clanton, who it was thought might vote against the plan. After months of delay, certain key documents were turned over after he left the FTC and two days before Senate approval of his replacement, Terry Calvani, who voted for the plan. Ralph Nader also challenged the objectivity of FTC Chairman Miller, a private consultant to GM until November 1980, a mere 16 months before the consideration of the plan was announced.

The benefits to the two auto giants were significant. With an initial price of $6,000 per car, the projected sales of 250,000 vehicles had a retail value of $1.5 billion, vaulting the Fremont plant to the top half of the Fortune 500 and exceeding AMC's total sales in 1983. GM and Toyota also benefited in more ways than their expected profits. GM obtained the ability to sell small cars without having to make a major investment, and the Freemont plant was already idle. Toyota, for its part, increased its share of the American market at a time when import limits existed for Japanese cars, and they had yet to open their own plants in the United States. In addition, Toyota gained firsthand experience in managing American workers before the firm invested in its own U.S. plant.

Despite the gains for GM and Toyota, the agreement had a number of immediate drawbacks. With a new small car to sell, GM was able to phase out its Chevette model. Meanwhile, the joint venture vehicle, as initially conceived, was basically a knockdown kit, designed and engineered by Toyota, with a predominance of high-technology components made in Japan. It was simply assembled in California. Thus, Toyota maintained control of the technology and the highest-value-added components, while GM became, in effect, a car retailer. The new plant was slated to hire 2,500 auto workers, the overwhelming majority of them out-of-work United Auto Workers (UAW) members. However, these gains did not begin to offset the loss of 17,000 jobs associated with the demise of the Chevette.

Given the magnitude of the issues involved, the closed decision-making process used, and the fact that the Democrats controlled the House of Representatives at the time, an extensive hearing was held on the FTC's ruling, providing the closest thing to an official public record.[33] At this hearing,

---

[33] U.S. Congress, House, Committee on Energy and Commerce, *The Future of the Auto-*

Patricia Bailey and Michael Pertschuk, the two Carter-appointed members of the FTC, likened the joint venture to a partial merger. Pertschuk charged that "Battalions of neo-classical economists dancing on the head of a pin cannot obscure the threat that this marriage of competitors poses to the American consumer, nor the fact that this joint venture is a plain and unambiguous violation of the antitrust laws."[34] He argued that the price of new cars would very likely continue to rise above competitive levels. He also emphasized that a whole series of government policies in the 1980s, including regulatory rollbacks (see Chapter 6) as well as the import quotas on Japanese cars (see Chapter 7), were geared to helping American manufacturers compete on an even footing with foreign companies. The joint venture would allow GM to sell small cars, not by manufacturing them itself, but by selling cars made primarily in Japan. Bailey, for her part, saw the venture as a harbinger for an industry already undergoing concentration. The FTC's approval would accelerate this process, she argued, "almost inevitably touch[ing] off a reactive pattern of strategic pairing between car manufacturers" and "a decrease in the overall number of market participants, leading to the increased likelihood of tacit, if not actual collusion."[35] Bailey believed that the FTC had swept aside generally recognized antitrust law principles and concluded, "If this joint venture between the world's first and third largest automobile companies does not violate the antitrust laws, what does the Commission think will?"[36]

Ralph Nader argued at the hearing that the FTC's approval was a "watershed issue in the history of antitrust enforcement."[37] The venture, he argued, fit all of standard criteria for nonpermissible ventures. It was a fifty-fifty venture that involved selling a standardized product; the new product would compete directly with those currently sold by the respective corporations; and the joint venture parents accounted for a substantial share of the market.[38]

The other American car companies also argued against the plan. Ford urged the FTC to enforce the antitrust laws and not try to cure the self-inflicted wounds of GM. If GM could not sell a small car on its own, that was its own doing. Chrysler had its high-profile chairman, Lee Iacocca, testify. He criticized the venture as bad for American consumers because of what he saw as the inevitable collusion that would result from GM and Toyota sitting down together to set prices. Iacocca added that because GM and Toyota were the respective domestic and import price leaders, higher prices would result throughout the industry. While Iacocca was hardly a disinterested observer, he

mobile Industry. Hearings before the Subcommittee on Transportation and Tourism, 98th Cong., 2d sess., February 8, 1984, Serial No. 98–117. Hereafter referred to as Joint-Venture (J-V) Hearings.

[34] J-V Hearings, p. 513.   [35] J-V Hearings, pp. 60–70.

[36] J-V Hearings, p. 81.   [37] J-V Hearings, p. 190.

[38] J-V Hearings, p. 209.

noted that if this deal was not illegal, the antitrust laws had lost all meaning. And in response to GM's claim that it wanted to learn Japanese management techniques from Toyota, Iacocca drew attention to a statement made by GM Chairman Roger Smith: "I know what the Japanese management system is. We have had a 34 percent interest in Isuzu for 12 years. But I don't know if the Japanese management will work in the United States."[39] (GM also had an ownership stake in Suzuki. It was not alone in owning shares of Japanese car makers. Ford, at the time, owned 25 percent of Mazda, and Chrysler owned 15 percent of Mitsubishi.)

Amid the acrimony among the automakers, the UAW was largely silent. The UAW's low-profile stance on the joint venture was emblematic of an organization adrift in a sea change. While others were calling the ruling one of the most significant policy decisions affecting the industry and a watershed antitrust case potentially costing thousands of jobs, Owen Bieber, the union president, did not attend the hearing, sending instead a short statement in which the union offered no opinion on the agreement: "Because we cannot predict the net effect on competition, the UAW has not taken a position on this issue before the FTC."[40] However, the union stated its general approval of joint ventures as a way to apply innovative approaches to the production of small cars.

John Kwoka, Jr., a consultant to the FTC on the proposed joint venture, and until 1980 the commission's chief economist for auto industry matters, stated that an alternative venture with a smaller Japanese company – Isuzu, for instance – would pose no anticompetitive threat. His report to the FTC concluded that the GM–Toyota venture, by contrast, was a substantial threat to competition in the small car market. Although efficiencies are easy to argue and hard to assess, Kwoka calculated the possible efficiencies to be gained and suggested that it was "overwhelmingly likely" that any possible savings would be offset by price increases.[41]

Many saw the joint venture as symbolic of the crisis of globalization and deindustrialization gutting domestic manufacturing jobs. As Robert Reich (later secretary of labor in the Clinton administration) testified at the time, the long-term survival of firms like GM, Ford, and Chrysler was not at stake; what was in question were the number and quality of jobs that would remain as the industry reorganized itself:

Despite the name plate that graces the exterior of these automobiles, they will be assembled and produced all over the world from components which are sourced all over the world; and they will be assembled from those components on the continents and in the jurisdictions where they are going to be distributed, partly because of economies of scale and efficiency, but also because of certain political exigencies.[42]

---

[39] Cited in J-V Hearings, p. 154.   [40] J-V Hearings, p. 170.
[41] J-V Hearings, pp. 273–99.   [42] J-V Hearings, p. 244.

Reich suggested that the Japanese strategy was to establish joint ventures around the globe in order to keep the highest-value segments to themselves, thereby gaining dominance in engines, transmissions, and transaxles, the high-technology components of production. Although Reich himself no longer thinks that foreign investments like these represent a threat to jobs in the United States, and thus should be welcomed,[43] Candace Howes, in a 1993 study, provides considerable evidence that Japanese transplants are indeed costing U.S. workers jobs.[44] Moreover, she argues that the transplant strategy is more accurately seen as a subterfuge for increasing import penetration of the U.S. market. Although cars assembled in the United States appear to be domestically built, only 15–20 percent of a car's value is related to assembly. Transplant factories continue to import key high-value components.

Chrysler subsequently filed a suit in federal court against the venture but settled out of court. The settlement was considered by many a face-saving move allowing Chrysler to bow out of a suit it had little chance of winning after the FTC approval, as well as a public relations necessity to clear the way for its own joint venture with Mitsubishi.

Diversification

Joint ventures have been just one of the strategies that the nation's automakers have pursued in their effort to respond to new market conditions. During the 1980s, the Big Three also spent billions of dollars acquiring businesses unrelated to the automotive field. In fact, *Automotive News,* the industry's leading trade journal, selected as its 1985 "Story of the Year" the "buying spree" of the Big Three.[45] These acquisitions were in three basic areas: financial services; high technology, in particular computers, robots, and artificial intelligence; and defense contracting. In the mid-1990s, many of these acquisitions were spun off as, once again, industry officials reorganized. The two most prominent examples of this trend were GM's $2.5 billion acquisition of EDS – Ross Perot's data processing services firm – and its $5 billion acquisition of Hughes Aircraft, both of which were subsequently spun off.[46]

Labor Relations

Labor is, of course, one of a number of costs of production calculated in any business. However, labor is also unique among the factors of production, as political economists remind us, since it represents the activity of living

[43] See Robert Reich, *The Work of Nations* (New York: Vintage Books, 1992).
[44] Candace Howes, *Japanese Auto Transplants and the U.S. Automobile Industry* (Washington: Economic Policy Institute, 1993).
[45] John Teahen, Jr., "Top Story: Big 3 Buying Binge," *Automotive News* (December 30, 1985), p. 1.
[46] For an account of Perot's tempestuous relationship with GM, see Doron Levin, *Irreconcilable Differences: Ross Perot versus General Motors* (Boston: Little, Brown, 1989).

individuals. Unlike other factors of production, workers have consciousness and will. Obtaining their cooperation is essential for efficient, high-quality production. The history of labor struggles by autoworkers, from the bitter and violent battles of the 1930s, through the peaceful and profitable arrangements of the 1950s and 1960s, to the era of givebacks and decline of the 1980s, is often seen as emblematic of the evolution of organized labor in the United States. It is worth remembering that the 1930s' fight for the right to unionize took on many of the trappings of war. GM, for example, spent over $1 million on espionage and munitions between 1933 and 1936 to prevent its workers from unionizing. Other auto companies were scarcely more cooperative.[47] As a result, the struggle over unionization, which included the now famous episodes of The "Battle of Overpass" and the sitdown strikes in Flint, Michigan, are still considered high-water marks in labor militancy of this period.[48] Yet, in the twenty-five years after World War II the union settled into peaceful relations with the industry, leading journalist William Serrin, author of *The Company and the Union,* to subtitle his book "The 'Civilized Relationship' of the General Motors Corporation and the United Automobile Workers."[49]

This civilized arrangement developed in the aftermath of the pivotal 1945–6 strike, thereafter seen as establishing the pattern for postwar labor relations. The UAW demanded that GM open its books so that the union could base wage demands on the company's ability to pay. GM, of course, refused the request, citing its managerial prerogative to keep this information privileged. Many in the business community saw the union demand as a direct challenge to business autonomy and the right to make investment and other economic decisions. At stake, many thought at the time, was the future of labor relations in the postwar world because a UAW victory might establish a pattern that other unions would follow. Despite President Harry S. Truman's appointment of a panel to arbitrate the issue, providing neutral observers to examine GM's books, after a 119 day strike the union felt compelled to abandon its demand. The union continued its attempts to shape the economic direction of the industry, calling on automakers in 1949, for instance, to manufacture small cars. However, with the contract of 1950, henceforth known as the "Treaty of

---

[47] For an account of the battle to unionize Ford, see Keith Sward, *The Legend of Henry Ford* (New York: Reinhart and Co., 1948), pp. 370–429; See also U.S. Congress, Senate, Committee on Education and Labor, *Violations of Free Speech and Rights of Labor: Industrial Espionage,* 75th Cong., sess. 1–3, 1937–8, Report No. 46.

[48] For a detailed account of the Flint sit-down strike, see Sidney Fine, *Sit-Down: The General Motors Strike of 1936–1937* (Ann Arbor: University of Michigan Press, 1969).

[49] William Serrin, *The Company and the Union* (New York: Alfred A. Knopf, 1973). For a different view that examines shop floor worker dissatisfaction, see Steve Jefferys, *Management and Managed* (New York: Cambridge University Press, 1986).

Detroit," the union abandoned attempts to intercede in managerial decision making and focused instead on negotiating higher wages and benefits.

The automakers, in turn, were glad to facilitate this change in union demands in order to buy labor peace. They negotiated contracts that made auto employees among the highest-paid workers in America. Pioneering benefits packages were implemented – ones that soon became the goal for most workers in the country – which included pensions, cost-of-living allowances, productivity raises, supplemental unemployment, profit sharing, early retirement, and health insurance.

The transformation of the UAW from its more overtly political days during the 1930s and 1940s to a junior partner of big business can also be seen in its changing attitude toward industrial planning. Beginning in the 1930s and continuing until after World War II, Walter Reuther, who headed the union from 1946 until his untimely death in 1970, led efforts to extend labor's role in industrial governance. As the head of the union's GM division during the war, Reuther's proposals for wartime conversion of the auto industry received widespread attention. After the war, he called for a Peace Production Board to direct the conversion of industry back to civilian production in a manner that would ensure full employment. He also recommended that housing be the first priority of postwar industry, believing that government-owned aircraft plants could be used to manufacture prefabricated, mass-produced, low-cost homes. However, with the turn toward business unionism soon after the war, broader proposals such as these were shelved.

Despite its turn toward business unionism, the UAW retained its progressive political reputation. In part this image was maintained by Reuther's public stances on a variety of social issues, as well as by participation in the civil rights movement, symbolized by his marching with Martin Luther King, Jr., in Selma, Alabama. Reuther's political activities involved testifying before Congress almost 100 times on the major social and economic issues of the day.[50]

As the industry began losing money in the early 1980s, autoworkers were forced to negotiate givebacks, a turn of events previously unthinkable. Although many of these benefits were subsequently won back, the focus of the recent contracts has been job security, not economic benefits. Nevertheless, hundreds of thousands of workers have lost – and continue to lose – their jobs. Another indication of the union's declining power is the end of pattern bargaining among the Big Three. In fact, even within the same corporation, different labor contracts are now negotiated among the different divisions. Historically, the union was unable to gain control over the labor process or to impinge on management's unilateral control over investment decisions. Instead, it ac-

---

[50] Victor Reuther, *The Brothers Reuther and the Story of the UAW* (Boston: Houghton Mifflin Co., 1976), p. 434.

cepted steadily increasing economic benefits. Now the gains embedded in the compromises made in the past are eroding in response to new technology and shifting international investments. Today, while the auto companies may continue to make profits, autoworkers are the big losers in a market reorganized by global relationships and new methods of production.

Prospects for the Future

By all forecasts, the worldwide automobile industry is currently undergoing a dramatic transformation that will reduce the number of firms and create a much smaller number of truly global giants. One of the underlying factors leading to consolidation is worldwide overcapacity, a problem that has continued to worsen since the mid-1980s. In 1985, the world's automakers could produce 25 percent more vehicles than the market demanded. By 1995 this figure reached 30 percent, and the U.S. automakers predicted that year that by 2000 capacity would exceed demand by 36 percent. This translated into a capacity to produce 79 million vehicles, with a demand for only 57 million. This excess is greater than the total sales of all domestic and imported cars and light trucks in the United States.[51] Faced with this situation, the world's automakers continue to invest in low-wage countries in an attempt to shore up profits. Globalization threatens to bring ever larger swings of boom and bust to an industry already prone to cycles of profits and losses. The political consequences of globalization are unclear. But as the rest of this study will show, the industry's economic cycles have reverberated throughout the nation and are integral to understanding its political position.

[51] William Greider, *One World, Ready or Not: The Manic Logic of Global Capitalism* (New York: Simon and Schuster, 1997), pp. 111–12.

3

Corporate Political Hegemony and Its Decline: 1916–1966

Before 1966 the automobile was the only form of transportation without federal safety standards. Railroads, trucks, planes, and ships were all subject to federal regulation. At the same time, auto crashes were the leading cause of death and injury in the transportation sector, accounting for 92 percent of all deaths and 98 percent of all injuries.[1] This anomaly was the result of efforts by auto industry officials who, seizing the initiative on safety with their superior resources, deflected attention away from the contribution of vehicle design to injuries. By being able to shape the public perception of traffic safety issues, industry officials prevented governmental scrutiny of their design decisions and preserved their managerial autonomy.

Public interest advocates, eventually led by Ralph Nader and supported by members of the medical community, ended the industry's unilateral control over vehicle design through the passage of the National Traffic and Motor Vehicle Safety Act of 1966.[2] This concerted effort, however, was not enough to weaken the industry's political preeminence. The advent of safety regulation also required one of the most liberal Congresses in American history – the 89th, responsible for much of the Great Society legislation – as well as a series of shocking revelations concerning the industry's disregard for occupant safety. At this time, there was a growing environmental and consumer movement targeting the practices of the nation's corporations; riots, demonstrations, and protests concerning civil rights and the Vietnam War were also commonplace, all of which functioned to strengthen the hand of public interest forces. Meanwhile, the industry was enjoying year after year of healthy sales and profits, and when challenged could not plausibly claim that it could not afford federal regulations. Notwithstanding the alignment of all these factors,

[1] Ralph Nader, *Unsafe at Any Speed,* updated ed. (New York: Bantam Books, 1972), p. 146.
[2] P.L. 89–563.

54

the early advocates of a federal role in traffic safety had an additional hurdle to overcome: the long-held belief – itself the achievement of industry efforts – that traffic safety was a state and local responsibility. However, by 1966 this obstacle was gone. Sen. Warren Magnuson (D-WA), who played an important role in the final passage of the safety act, attributed this particular shift to the Interstate Highway System, which legitimized a federal role in traffic safety. In this sense, an expression of the industry's unchallenged strength a decade earlier had sowed the seeds of its own political decline.

The lack of safety standards before 1966, as Ralph Nader pointed out, was the result of "a political and propaganda machine directed by the traffic safety establishment."[3] Supported and directed by the auto industry, the highway safety establishment was a series of overlapping public and private groups carrying out the industry's political agenda, which for decades had no organized challenge. Thus, in 1966 journalist Elizabeth Drew observed: "The interlocking directorates and mutual dependence of virtually all safety groups on the same sources of revenue – the automobile industry and commercial allies – produced a remarkably harmonious point of view."[4] Concern for car-related injuries and deaths repeatedly was directed to the single factor of driver behavior and the "nut behind the wheel" thesis: highway deaths and injuries were the result of poor driving. In this way, the industry and its design practices were protected from public scrutiny. As early as 1914, this position was encapsulated in what later became the holy trinity of highway safety, the three E's: engineering, education, and enforcement. Engineering referred to highway design, education to driver education, and enforcement to traffic regulations.[5] Organization after organization repeatedly invoked this same triumvirate. Although seemingly objective, this approach was in reality a political strategy used to insulate the industry from government regulation; its intent was not to save lives but to shape how the problem of highway deaths was defined.[6]

Capture of the Safety Movement

At the end of the nineteenth century, early proponents of the automobile argued that cars were safer than horse-drawn vehicles. Horses were seen as "willful and wild," while cars did not "shy or run away."[7] However, in 1899, the danger of cars was made vividly apparent when the first recorded fatality attributed to a motor vehicle occurred after a New York real estate dealer was run over near Central Park.[8] As the auto population grew, so did the death and injury toll. By 1909 motor vehicle crashes killed and injured

---

[3] Nader, p. 207.

[4] Elizabeth Drew, "The Politics of Auto Safety," *Atlantic Monthly* (October 1966), p. 97.

[5] Joel Eastman, *Styling vs. Safety: The American Automobile Industry and the Development of Automotive Safety, 1900–1966* (Lanham, MD: University Press of America, 1984), p. 7.

[6] Nader, p. 202.   [7] Eastman, p. 115.

more people than horse-drawn vehicles. Growing numbers of casualties brought mounting concern about traffic safety and with it criticism of the car itself. (By 1913, annual traffic fatalities had reached approximately 6,800.) Newspaper and magazine articles appeared with titles such as "Menace of the Automobile," "Curbing of the Automobile Danger," and "Slaughter on the Highways."[9]

In response, industry officials established a safety committee in 1916, which by the early 1920s was chaired by Paul Hoffman of the Studebaker Corporation. (Hoffman, a founder of the Committee for Economic Development, a wartime offshoot of the Business Advisory Council, later headed the Marshall Plan.[10]) He was one of the first in the industry to argue that safety problems could be a deterrent to the car's popularity. In 1923, C. W. Price, former president of the National Safety Council (NSC), also argued that the industry should be more involved in shaping public thinking about traffic safety. He emphasized that "The whole problem of public safety is still in the formative stage, awaiting the leadership of some group of interests — such as the automobile industries — having more invested capital, wider contacts, greater influence, and more aggressiveness than have thus far been available for this movement."[11] Price acknowledged that there were sound economic reasons for the industry to take over the safety movement: a public reaction against the use of automobiles had set in because of the increasing death toll on the nation's roads and high insurance costs. (By the mid-1920s, annual traffic fatalities surpassed 20,000.) He also argued that if positive actions were not taken, legislation would be passed regulating vehicle design.[12]

A year later, Commerce Secretary Herbert Hoover organized a national conference on street and highway safety, the first official government acknowledgment that motor vehicles presented safety problems. The major result of the conference was the subsequent approval of uniform traffic rules for the nation. Given this limited response, most industry officials saw little reason to be concerned about government-mandated safety standards. In the early 1930s, for example, when Hoffman asked the board of directors of the Automobile Manufacturers Association (AMA) to allocate $10,000 to study the best method for involving the industry in the highway safety movement, his request was rejected since there was no imminent threat of legislation. But just three years later this decision was reversed after a sudden jump in public concern for the problem of vehicle safety, sparked by a *Reader's Digest* article entitled " — And Sudden Death." Describing in detail the "pain and horror" of different

---

[8] Eastman, p. 115.   [9] Eastman, p. 116.

[10] For an analysis of Hoffman's role in the CED and the Marshall Plan, as well as overall activities of the Business Advisory Council, see Kim McQuaid, *Big Business and Presidential Power* (New York: William Morrow and Co., Inc., 1982).

[11] Cited in Eastman, p. 136.   [12] Eastman, p. 136.

kinds of car crashes, the article was reprinted in approximately 2,000 news-papers and magazines. Total printed circulation reached an estimated 35 million copies by the end of 1935. (Meanwhile, annual traffic fatalities were escalating, reaching over 30,000 by the mid-1930s.)

In 1936, Congress responded to this mounting interest when it requested that the Bureau of Public Roads survey motor vehicle traffic conditions. The growing focus on traffic safety led the AMA not only to fund Hoffman's request, but also to form the Automobile Safety Foundation (ASF) to carry forward the industry's position.[13] The narrow solution it fashioned to the safety problem was guided by the "classic three" – education, engineering, and enforcement. In Hoffman's hands this boiled down to several elementary recommendations: "Train safe drivers. Make penalties for unsafe driving certain – but not punitive. Engineer hazards off the right-of-way. . . ."[14] A full-scale program was outlined by Hoffman in the *Saturday Evening Post.*[15] Hoffman's recommendations conveniently overlooked the role of the vehicle itself, something he admitted years later was a conscious move to avoid harming sales.[16] Of the three parts of the program, the primary focus of the safety establishment was driver behavior. Nader summarized the logic of the industry's position. "Most accidents are in the class of driver fault; driver fault is in the class of violated traffic laws; therefore, observance of traffic laws by drivers would eliminate most accidents."[17]

A central flaw in this formulation, however, is that no distinction is made between "accidents" – a term that has been replaced by "crash" – and injuries. While the former maybe unpreventable, the latter can be mitigated by appropriate vehicle design. The distinction between car crashes and injury forms the basis for the concept of the "second collision," the one between the passenger and the vehicle. It is this collision that determines the nature and extent of injuries, as compared to the first collision, between the vehicle and another object. Injury-prevention scientists have shown that the human body can survive significant decelerating forces inflicted during crashes if the forces are spread over time and space. In essence, the damage from a crash is done not by the force, but by how the force is dissipated. For example, falling on a surface that "gives," like a haystack, spreads the force over a large area, unlike falling on a sharp object like an ice pick.[18] Emphasizing driver behavior as *the* cause of injuries oversimplifies a complex process because most automobile crashes

---

[13] Eastman, p. 140.   [14] Cited in Eastman, p. 141.

[15] A year later it was published in an expanded form: Paul Hoffman in collaboration with Neil Clark, *Seven Roads to Safety: A Program to Reduce Auto Accidents* (New York: Harper and Brothers, Publishers, 1939).

[16] Eastman, p. 135.   [17] Nader, p. 202.

[18] Nader, p. 71.

result from an interaction among the driver, the vehicle, the road, and the environment.

The ASF took the lead in directing the issue of traffic safety, ensuring that the industry's interests would be protected. During its first years, the ASF's funding came exclusively from the AMA. Financial support eventually broadened to include oil, rubber, steel, glass, cement, and asphalt companies, as well as auto dealers, advertising agencies, and banks. The list of officers and trustees of the ASF was a veritable Who's Who of the automotive industry. There were no members affiliated with any independent safety group, no medical doctors, and no academic researchers.[19] By 1963, the AMA contributed half of the ASF's income, $764,086 out of a total of $1,528,173, the foundation's approximate budget for the twenty previous years. Overall, 90 percent of its funds came from the auto industry and its suppliers.

On the eve of federal regulation, the ASF spent roughly $700,000 on research and action programs in areas such as safety education, traffic law enforcement, driver education, and highway improvement. Virtually nothing was spent on the issue of the design aspects of the car.[20] A publication from the early 1960s not only repeated the industry's long-held view on traffic safety but elevated the position to a philosophical principle. "Being inanimate, no car, truck or bus can by itself cause an accident any more than a street or highway can do so. A driver is needed to put it into motion – after which it becomes an extension of his will."[21] To further shape societal thinking about vehicle safety, the ASF supported the promotion of drivers education in the nation's high schools. The manufacturers, in turn, made special provisions for dealers to donate or loan cars to schools. For the driver education movement, the solution to the traffic safety problem was simple: to improve drivers' behavior, stress individual responsibility. That driver education increased the number of drivers, and thereby contributed to the escalating number of crashes, was ignored. At the same time, the contribution of driver education programs to improving traffic safety was itself questionable inasmuch as students who enrolled in them may have been less prone to be involved in crashes in the first place.

Paralleling the ASF's position, the NSC functioned as another arm of the industry. Individuals migrated between the two groups, and each group reinforced the industry's position on traffic safety. The NSC, however, was concerned with a wide variety of issues, not just traffic safety, and received the majority of its funding from across the corporate sector. But as with the ASF, industrial and commercial executives dominated its board of directors. The

---

[19] Hoffman, pp. 77–83.

[20] David Klein and William Haddon, "The Prospects for Safer Cars," *Consumer Reports* (April 1965), p. 176.

[21] Cited in Nader, p. 209.

NSC did more than avoid the issue of vehicle design; during the legislative battle over the safety act, the organization insisted that the research and standards pertaining to the operation and crashworthy qualities of vehicles were already adequate. Its evidence for this claim was a letter from the car manufacturers' trade association.[22] The NCS's close corporate connections did not prevent it from contending, during the first congressional auto safety hearing, that the organization was nonprofit, nonpolitical, and noncommercial.[23]

The public came to know the NSC through its compilation of traffic injury statistics. The strangeness of this arrangement often escaped notice: a private organization, with a vested interest in the data it collected, provided what seemed to be official public information. In the late 1950s, there was already telling evidence that the council was acting as the auto industry's publicity arm even when it came to compiling traffic injury data. Daniel Patrick Moynihan, later a New York U.S. senator and one of earliest advocates of a government role in vehicle safety, pointed out at the time that there was an enormous discrepancy between the NSC's estimates of injuries from car crashes and the Public Health Service's (PHS) estimates. In 1957 the NSC claimed there were 1,400,000 injuries from car crashes, while the PHS estimated that the number was 4,880,000.[24]

The centerpiece of the NSC's traffic safety activities during the late 1950s and early 1960s was promoting the "Action Program" of the President's Committee on Traffic Safety (PCTS). This committee grew out of a 1954 industry-sponsored White House Conference on Traffic Safety. An unusual mix of private power and public authority, the PCTS was given wide discretion in deciding its own role. The importance of the body was stressed in a 1959 report by the secretary of commerce. "There is no parallel group within government circles that has responsibility for developing official programs of equal breadth and for encouraging their application at all levels of government. . . ."[25] Nader put the unique blend of private and public power in perspective in 1965 when he remarked that the committee "is a federal institution quite without parallel in the history of American government. . . . There has never been another agency created by and then leased back outright to private enterprise."[26]

---

[22] Nader, p. 226.

[23] U.S. Congress, House, Committee on Interstate and Foreign Commerce, *Traffic Safety. Hearings before the Subcommittee on Traffic Safety,* 84th Cong., 2d. sess. (1956), p. 237. Hereafter referred to as the Roberts hearings.

[24] Daniel Patrick Moynihan, "Epidemic on the Highways," *Reporter* (April 30, 1959), pp. 16–23.

[25] U.S. Congress, House, Committee on Public Works, "The Federal Role in Highway Safety," letter from the Secretary of Commerce (March 3, 1959), 86th Cong., 1st sess., House Document Number 93, p. 8.

[26] Nader, p. 231.

Originally, the PCTS was entirely funded by private industry, but by 1961 the federal government paid three-quarters of the budget. The PCTS was staffed by civil servants paid by the federal government; its executive director and his two assistants were selected and paid by the automakers. By the mid-1960s corporate interests supplied $50,000 a year to the PCTS, a rather modest fee for maintaining an agency that, according to Chairman W. R. Hearst, Jr., "by virtue of its identification with the Office of the President, provides the traffic safety movement with the prestige of the President, which no other organization could accomplish."[27] When John Kennedy became president, the future of the PCTS appeared to be in doubt. But Kennedy soon reappointed Hearst as chairman, changing the makeup of the committee only slightly by adding representatives from the Departments of Commerce; Labor; Health, Education and Welfare; and Defense to sit as ex-officio members. However, their role remained secondary. Daniel Patrick Moynihan, at the time the Labor Department's representative, said of the PCTS:

I served as a departmental representative on the body for a year before learning that the executive director was neither chosen [n]or paid by the Federal Government, but rather by the industry. This man presided over the expenditure of public funds, . . . and generally disported himself as the head traffic safety man in government although, in fact, he was a paid agent of the interests he ought at least to have been keeping an eye on.[28]

The PCTS, of course, exploited its appearance as the official voice of the federal government. A 1962 episode is revealing. In the decades before federal regulation, there was a periodic debate on whether traffic safety was the responsibility of the federal government or the states. The industry, fearful of federal regulation, maintained that it was a local concern. To support this position, a pamphlet entitled "Vehicle Equipment Safety Compact," with the presidential seal prominently displayed on the cover, was circulated by the PCTS. It emphasized that traffic safety was entirely the responsibility of states, not the federal government. The pamphlet was printed and paid for by the AMA. Although it appeared to be an official government document, there was no record of any federal agency approving it.[29]

With all these organizations in place and with no strong challengers, industry officials would have been well served if they had quietly attended safety issues in order to preempt critics from mobilizing around the position that the automakers had a callous disregard for the public. However, industry officials viewed themselves as above such matters, manifesting an arrogance that would soon contribute to their defeat.

[27] Cited in Nader, p. 232.   [28] Cited in Eastman, p. 164.
[29] Nader, p. 237.

Built-in Design Failings

Before turning to a discussion of the passage of federal safety legislation, it is useful to examine a few examples of the industry's early design practices to illustrate how its behavior contributed to its own undoing. This detour from the main narrative is also important because it illustrates how corporate behavior shapes social life, creates social problems, and sets the public agenda.

Intimately intertwined with the industry's antipathy toward the safety issue was its long-standing stress on marketing. It is simply impossible to separate the automakers' long-held aversion to safety from their concern for sales. Throughout the history of the industry, fast cars and "performance" have been used as marketing strategies. Discussing vehicle safety was taboo for almost all of the industry's history because it was feared that such talk would tarnish the image of cars as fun. (Only in the 1990s, after the mandatory installation of air bags, was this taboo partially overcome.) Lee Iacocca, a top Ford executive in the mid-1960s, expressed the industry's long-held view: "Styling cars sells cars and safety does not."[30]

While there were many examples of unsafe design, including dangerous instrument panels and steering columns that impaled drivers in collisions, one of the most visible instances of disregard for safety was the style of tail fins in the 1950s, now nostalgically recalled for their identification with American postwar excess. Although they increased pedestrian injuries, marketing hoopla led to ever larger and ever more dangerous designs. Meanwhile, no engineer employed by the industry ever did an analysis of the consequences of this design feature for pedestrian injuries.[31] Frivolous features were not the only problems with vehicle design. As early as the 1930s and continuing throughout the 1950s, there were criticisms of poor braking and steering.[32] Steering problems were not unusual in the 1930s due to the adoption of smaller-diameter, low-pressure balloon tires and a change in weight distribution. Auto stylists promoted these tires for their appearance and softer ride. However, the tires created steering problems due to increased road friction. These problems were compounded by the style-related placement of the engine over the front wheels for the sake of creating interior room. Although engineers opposed this move, it went ahead anyway, increasing the danger of blowouts.[33]

The fixation on styling also hampered the ability of drivers to see the road. Stylists pushed for the wraparound windshield, which GM subsequently hailed as "increasing the vision of the driver." Critics disagreed. At the annual meet-

---

[30] Cited in Jeffrey O'Connell and Arthur Myers, *Safety Last: An Indictment of the Auto Industry* (New York: Random House, 1966), p. 5

[31] Nader, p. 194.

[32] See Eastman, pp. 60–6.

[33] See Eastman, pp. 62–3, for a lengthier discussion of this episode.

ing of the American Medical Association in 1956, Dr. Dupont Guerry, chair of
the Department of Ophthalmology at the Medical College of Virginia, attacked
the new feature because of its detrimental effects on vision. Roy Haeusler,
director of auto safety at Chrysler, admitted that the industry did not consult
any authority in optics when designing the wraparound windshield and reluctantly agreed that it caused distortion.[34] Complaints also arose over the effects
of tinted glass on night vision and the obstruction of vision, causing blind
spots. The industry argued that the negative effects of tinted glass were minor,
although tests published in the *Journal of the Optical Society of America*
claimed that the glass was unsafe. In response to the problem of blind spots, in
the 1930s industry officials claimed that "there are no statistics showing that
blind spots cause accidents."[35] Glare was another problem related to field of
vision. It was often a common complaint of drivers who claimed that they did
not see pedestrians. Nader reported the results of tests done in 1963 by Prof.
Merrill Allen of Indiana University demonstrating the inherent defects in
windshield design. When the color of the dashboard was alternated from white
to black during broad daylight pedestrians fifteen feet away were either completely invisible or easily seen. Allen studied a wide range of American cars
and found that not one of them provided a suitable visual environment.[36]

GM's stance on dashboard padding is another example of disregard for
safety and an imperious attitude toward public health concerns. In 1955, a New
York bank official wrote to GM explaining how after he braked to avoid hitting
a kitten, his eight-year-old son was thrown against the dashboard and broke his
tooth. He suggested that GM pad the dashboard to avoid such injuries in the
future. GM's vehicle safety engineer, Howard Gandelot, wrote back: "Driving
with young children in an automobile always presents some problems. As soon
as the youngsters get large enough to be able to see out when standing up, that's
what they want to do – and I don't blame them." He described how he trained
his sons to brace themselves by putting their hands on the dashboard when he
gave the command "Hands"! and how he practiced it with them. The banker
wrote back to GM's customer research department, suggesting that perhaps he
had not made himself clear and that the engineer's advice was not practical in
an emergency situation. He added, "For safety's sake the danger should be
removed by making the dash safer to bounce into." Gandelot replied, "A lot of
people are hurt in bathtubs, too, aren't they? Do you hear anybody demanding
that they take the bathtubs out of homes?"[37]

Part of the explanation for the industry's behavior in this instance was its
conviction, which took the form of an iron law of marketing, that safety did not

---

[34] Eastman, p. 53.   [35] Eastman, p. 56.

[36] Nader, p. 51.

[37] Harold Mehling, "Big Three Fight Over How Safe to Make Your Car," *Bluebook
Magazine* (October 1955), cited in the Roberts hearings, p. 41.

sell. In 1955, at the urging of Robert McNamara, a Ford vice-president (and U.S. defense secretary in the 1960s), Ford decided to, in effect, test this suspicion and used safety themes in a number of advertisements. When sales lagged, industry officials took this as proof that they had been right all along. Yet a closer look at the popularity of the safety options revealed a different picture. Ford offered consumers the option of having padded dashboards, deep-dish steering wheels, padded sun visors, and lap belts. A company press release indicated that safety did sell. In the section entitled "Public Will Buy Safety" it stated:

Since two of the five features – crash padding and seat belts – were optional with the customer, it was possible to measure demand by totaling up the number sold. The demand surprised even the optimistic Ford staff. No optional feature in Ford history caught on so fast in the first year. For example, 43% of all 1956 Fords were ordered with safety padding. When tinted glass was first produced in 1952, only 6% of the customers wanted it. Even Fordomatic [automatic transmission], one of the most popular options, was ordered by only 23% of the customers when it was introduced in 1951. Power steering, introduced in 1953, was ordered by only 4%. During the first year, one of every seven buyers ordered seat belts.[38]

Why, then, did Ford drop its emphasis on safety and discontinue offering most of these options? Nader subsequently discovered that GM expressed its disapproval of the safety campaign directly to Ford's top executives and used the weight of its enormous monopoly power to have it halted.[39] It is important to remember that at the time, GM controlled more than half of the American motor vehicle market, or more than all the other car makers combined. It could easily have engaged in retaliatory pricing and severely damaged, if not bankrupted, Ford by lowering its prices. In addition, GM unsuccessfully tried to push McNamara, on track to become president, out of the company.

The Rise of Opposition
Throughout the 1950s, the industry's view of traffic safety was questioned by a number of different sources. While earlier criticism of the industry had been isolated, now it was the medical and scientific establishment that rejected the industry's point of view. In 1953 the American Medical Association and the American College of Surgeons, for example, recommended to the car makers that safety be given greater attention. Others soon came to be involved in the traffic safety issue. Independent crash research was conducted by the Air Force and a handful of academe-affiliated institutes. (The Air Force's involvement began during the Korean War, when it was discovered that more of their personnel were killed in auto crashes unrelated to combat than in enemy action.[40]) Growing interest in vehicle design led the automakers, one by

[38] Nader, p. xi.   [39] Nader, pp. ix–xiii.
[40] Moynihan, p. 16.

one, to establish safety departments for the first time. This did not represent a sudden transformation of the industry's thinking on vehicle design. Instead, business prudence dictated watching these new developments closely.

As concern with safety increased outside of government, there were few signs of change within Washington. Traditionally, responsibility for traffic safety and roads resided with the states. As late as 1959 the Commerce Department supported this view, arguing: "The direct projection of federal authority into highway safety functions that have been the responsibility of state and local governments is concluded to be impractical, and would only weaken state and local authority."[41] By the late 1950s, those federal government activities in traffic safety that did exist were scattered and disorganized. At least sixteen different federal agencies were involved, but there was virtually no coordination or cooperation among them.[42] Of the sixteen, ten engaged in or sponsored research affecting highway safety; four were concerned with engineering standards and specifications; and twelve provided some other type of safety service. About half were involved in a single phase of vehicle safety, while a few worked in four or five different areas.[43] Yet, none were involved in developing standards for crashworthy vehicles.

Congress Responds

The first congressional response to the growing awareness of the built-in safety hazards of cars came in 1956 with the formation of a House of Representatives subcommittee on traffic safety, initiating a ten-year effort for federal regulation. Throughout this period, Congress remained the main arena of this struggle. At first, it was led by Rep. Kenneth Roberts (D-AL), who played a pivotal – and today an underappreciated – role in laying the groundwork for federal safety legislation. Before becoming interested in car safety, Roberts had sponsored legislation regulating refrigerator-door design to prevent the suffocation of children playing in abandoned refrigerators. In the two and a half years directly prior to the legislation, thirty-nine children had died.[44] The carnage from car accidents dwarfed the problems with refrigerators, so Roberts turned his attention to this more pressing issue.

---

[41] Commerce Department, "The Federal Role in Highway Safety," p. 2.

[42] The agencies involved were the Agricultural Extension Service; Air Force; Army; Bureau of Public Roads; Bureau of Standards; Civil Service Commission; FBI; Federal Safety Council; General Services Administration; PHS; Interstate Commerce Commission; National Park Service; Navy; Post Office Department; PCTS; and Commission on Accidental Trauma of the Armed Forces Epidemiological Board.

[43] Commerce Department, "The Federal Role in Highway Safety," pp. 106–20.

[44] Daniel Patrick Moynihan, "The Legal Regulation of Automobile Design," in *Passenger Design and Highway Safety* (New York: Association for the Aid of Crippled Children and Consumers Union of the United States, 1962), p. 266.

The Roberts committee studied five general areas of traffic safety: human factors in traffic crashes, legislation, vehicle design, highways, and enforcement. Sen. Paul Douglas (D-IL), the first witness at the 1956 hearings, dramatically set the stage by reciting a litany of statistics on car crashes: 38,000 people killed in 1955 and 42,000 estimated deaths for 1956; 100,000 disabled in 1955, with estimates of as many as 2 million people involved in crashes; and 100,000 more deaths caused by autos since 1900 than all war deaths in the nation's history. Douglas observed that these grim facts were taken for granted:

[I]f a scheming enemy of the United States were to touch off a series of catastrophes that in each year took the lives of more Americans that were killed in battle in the Korean war and injured from 10 to 20 times the number wounded in that bloody struggle, the people would demand and get protection against this terrible slaughter and these wanton injuries.

The Congress would declare war against such an enemy and the people would mobilize their energies to defeat him and to stop such grievous human losses.[45]

Douglas then targeted the issue the industry had long sought to avoid: the need for government-mandated vehicle design standards to mitigate the traffic death toll.

For their part, industry officials showed no sign of altering their position as criticism of their design practices escalated. Industry spokesmen did not deviate from their usual refrain about driver behavior being the key to safety on the roads. Occasionally their testimony before the Roberts committee was perplexing. GM Vice-President for Engineering C. A. Chayne, for example, gave the relationship between safety and speed a novel interpretation when commenting on the increasing horsepower of the company's vehicles. Instead of admitting that increasing power led to faster driving and greater danger, he asserted that a powerful engine provided the driver with the maximum ability to carry out safe decisions. Thus, the chief reason for engines of greater horsepower was that they were safer.[46]

In issuing its report the following year, the committee made nineteen recommendations, including a call for expanded research on safe vehicles and less emphasis on speed and horsepower. However, the committee concluded that it was not prepared to recommend federal regulatory legislation along the lines of the comprehensive regulatory powers exercised in the field of aviation. Yet, the report added that if state and local governments continued to lag behind the public demand for action, there would be an "increased demand for action by the Congress."[47]

[45] Roberts hearings, p. 3.   [46] Roberts hearings, p. 239.
[47] U.S. Congress, House, Committee on Interstate and Foreign Commerce, *Report of the Special Subcommittee on Traffic Safety,* 84th Cong., submitted January 3, 1957, House Report 2971, p. 4.

Despite signs that the industry's hold over the issue of traffic safety was slipping, its position on safety standards remained the same. In 1958, GM's Lawrence Hofstad, vice-president of the research staff, stated: "I am convinced that more progress can be made in traffic safety by emphasizing the relations between the driver, the signalling system, and the road, than by undue emphasis on the crash-proof car."[48] Nevertheless, pressure for mandatory safety standards did not dissipate, and the issue received further attention when Roberts held another round of hearings in 1959. This time the focus was a bill requiring that the General Services Administration (GSA) establish safety standards for government-purchased cars. Roberts saw the bill as an intermediate step toward requiring safety devices on all cars. The bill on government-purchase standards passed the House even though both the GSA and Detroit opposed it. However, Senate approval was not forthcoming, and the bill died. Not until August 1964 did the Senate agree to the bill (discussed later).

As vehicle safety gradually attracted interest in Congress, state-level efforts also were initiated. The first such effort came in 1959 in New York State, where a joint legislative committee was formed on motor vehicles and traffic safety, which then attempted, unsuccessfully, to require seat belts as mandatory equipment. This step was necessary because until the mid-1950s the industry as a whole resisted installing seat belts. After 1955, Ford and Chrysler offered seat belts, but only as optional equipment. GM continued its opposition to installing seat belts, arguing that they had little merit, not enough was known about them, and the public was not interested. Two years after New York's failed effort, in 1961, Wisconsin passed the first legislation requiring the installation of seat belts. New York State's seat belt law passed the next year, and soon a number of other states followed. Given New York's share of the nation's car market, the law was a major blow to the industry's efforts to stifle concern for safety. (In January 1964, under growing pressure, the industry as a whole agreed to make seat belts standard equipment.)

Roberts never had the opportunity to participate in the passage of the final safety act because of his defeat for reelection in 1964. However, he was instrumental in a crucial step along the way: the 1964 passage of mandatory safety standards for cars purchased by the federal government, effective with the 1967 models.[49] The standards involved seventeen items including dashboard padding, seat belt anchorages, flashers, impact-absorbing steering columns, safety glass, dual braking, and an outside rearview mirror. Nevertheless, Nader criticized the standards as minimal because in some cases they were less than what the industry already offered as standard equipment, and in others

---

[48] Cited in Eastman, p. 119, from *Atlantic Monthly* (February 1958), pp. 20–1.
[49] P. L. 88–515.

they merely required features that were optional. Industry insiders confirmed the gist of Nader's criticism. In May 1965, Arjay Miller, president of Ford, said: "Although some reports may lead the public to believe that the GSA standards will be new, in most instances they are similar to or stem from our current engineering practice."[50] This development resulted from the industry's influence on the GSA, where representatives of the automakers sat on the committee deciding the standards, allowing them, as *Automotive News* pointed out, to "influence the selection of reasonable features."[51]

While the safety standards did not present an engineering challenge to the automakers, because of the way discussions with the GSA were handled they quickly turned into a public relations embarrassment. Throughout the GSA's consideration of a requirement for collapsible steering columns, for example, the automakers argued that it was already too late to initiate changes in the 1968 models since their designs were set and tool-and-die making had begun. The industry persisted in holding to this position as late as January 1966. Yet, two weeks later, with public pressure mounting, both GM and AMC announced that 1967 cars would have the new feature, and disclosed in the process that the telescoping column in fact had been exhaustively tested over the past five years.[52] (Nader argued that the industry's knowledge was ten years old.[53]) For many observers this episode confirmed the suspicion that Detroit was withholding and slanting technical information in its effort to prevent federal regulation, hurting their credibility in the upcoming main battle for mandatory safety standards for all cars.

The National Traffic and Motor Vehicle Safety Act

The decisive fight over federal standards brought together a loose collection of lawyers, doctors, and public health experts and was supported by the UAW and the Teamsters Union. Key members of Congress became involved, as did a tireless advocate who would soon become a household name: Ralph Nader, whose efforts on behalf of auto safety were monumental. In fact, at the time, Elizabeth Drew, described his contribution as "probably unprecedented in legislative history."[54] A potent lobbying force was created. At the same time, a number of independent factors shaped the context of policymaking to the benefit of advocates of federal regulation. There was a mounting

---

[50] Cited in Nader, p. 262.   [51] Cited in Nader, p. 262.

[52] See U.S. Congress, Senate, Committee on Commerce, *Traffic Safety Act. Hearings on S.3005,* 89th Cong., 2d sess. (March–April 1966), Serial No. 89–49, p. 247. Hereafter referred to as the Magnuson hearings.

[53] U.S. Congress, Senate, Committee on Government Operations, *The Federal Role in Traffic Safety. Hearings before the Subcommittee on Executive Reorganization,* 89th Cong., sess. 1–2 (1965–6), pp. 1304–22. Hereafter referred to the Ribicoff hearings.

[54] Drew, p. 96.

death toll on the nation's roads, which lent urgency to the cause of traffic safety. Between 1961 and 1966 the number of annual traffic deaths jumped from 38,000 to 53,000, a 38 percent increase. Some forecasts predicted 100,000 annual deaths. Meanwhile, there was growing public interest in consumer and environmental protection, which made members of Congress sensitive to calls for new legislation. In light of the riots and protests of the time, these issues seemed tame. Moreover, this was a time of substantial industry profits, which made it difficult for industry officials to argue that mandatory safety standards would be a financial burden. In fact, profits in the auto sector were well above the level of the average manufacturing firm in the nation. In addition, with the economy as a whole growing throughout the 1960s and at the apex of the American century, public officials in general felt comfortable establishing new regulations, with few doubts as to whether new environmental or public health standards were affordable.

When the 89th Congress convened in 1965, and with Representative Roberts no longer holding office, the initiative for traffic safety shifted to the Senate. A number of senators moved into the limelight, including Abraham Ribicoff (D-CT) and Warren Magnuson (D-WA). Ribicoff, new to the Senate after having been governor of his state, had already established himself as "Mr. Safety" by sponsoring a vigorous campaign to penalize speeders on Connecticut's roadways. As chairman of the Government Operations Committee's Subcommittee on Executive Reorganization, Ribicoff announced that hearings aimed at curbing the "fantastic carnage" on the highways would begin in February. Bringing the issue of vehicle safety to the front pages of the nation's newspapers, these hearings were instrumental in creating momentum in Congress that soon snowballed, touching off what Elizabeth Drew described as a "political car-safety derby, with politicians jockeying for the position out front."[55]

Media interest was heightened as the industry's disregard for vehicle safety was exposed. A particular exchange between Frederick Donner, GM's chairman of the board, and Sen. Robert Kennedy (D-NY) has come to epitomize both the industry's evasion of the safety issue and its weakening political situation. During the Ribicoff hearings, Kennedy inquired how much money GM spent researching car safety. Donner replied that the company did not account for this research separately. When Kennedy asked how much the company spent on safety outside the company, Donner offered the figure of $1.25 million. (Of this total, $1 million had been given to MIT the week before the hearings.) Kennedy then inquired about GM's profits during the previous year. Donner objected, arguing that it was irrelevant. Kennedy persisted. Donner was forced to turn to his aides for help, in itself an awkward moment. The answer provided was $1.7 billion. Kennedy noted, in response, that if the

---

[55] Drew, p. 96.

corporation had spent only 1 percent of its profits on safety, that figure would amount to $17 million.[56] The *Washington Post* observed: "Kennedy dealt with Donner ($653,000 in salary and bonuses last year and [James] Roche [president of GM] ($482,000) much as if he were examining a couple of youthful applicants for a driver's license who hadn't done their homework."[57] The *Wall Street Journal* called the auto executives' performance "dismal."[58]

As congressional momentum built, President Johnson entered the fray over auto safety with his 1966 State of the Union Address, outlining his intention to propose a Highway Safety Act. However, his administration was divided over the content of the legislation. On one side were Joseph Califano, assistant to the president, and Charles Schultze, director of the Bureau of the Budget, who argued for a bill requiring federal safety standards. On the other side was Commerce Secretary John Connor, who pushed for a bill allowing for the establishment of standards after two years if the industry's voluntary action did not improve. Connor, a former member of GM's board of directors, won the battle for delay. President Johnson also sent to Congress a request for a new Department of Transportation, bringing together eleven different agencies and bureaus. Many saw this as a further attempt to delay the safety movement. In any case, Ribicoff and Magnuson quickly criticized the delaying provisions of the Johnson proposal. Nader dismissed it as a "no-law law."

With increasing public attention on the industry's safety practices, Nader's book *Unsafe at Any Speed,* published at the end of 1965, began to receive its due. It painted the nation's auto executives as callous, if not worse, in their attitude toward safety. Nader documented the built-in design problems of the nation's cars, as well as the industry's longstanding political opposition to vehicle safety standards. For many, though, it was Nader's first chapter on the Covair, whose problems he documented were well known to GM, that convinced them that the automakers were clearly unscrupulous. The plummeting regard for Detroit was accelerated when GM's harassment of Nader became public in March 1966. GM had initiated an "investigation" of Nader that included interviews with friends and associates under the pretext of a prospective job offer. Its investigators also put Nader under surveillance and, according to Nader, attempted to entrap him for the purposes of blackmail. At the time, Nader was an unpaid staff member of Ribicoff's subcommittee and had testified before the committee. In February, Nader was followed into a Senate office building by two investigators who lost him and then asked a guard where he had gone. Suspicious, the guard called Jerome Sonosky, chief counsel of Ribicoff's committee. On being told that Nader was being followed, Sonosky

[56] Ribicoff hearings, p. 780.
[57] July 14, 1965, p. A-2, cited in O'Connell and Meyers, p. 92.
[58] July 20, 1965, p. 14, cited in O'Connell and Meyers, p. 92.

immediately called Ribicoff and exclaimed: "A strong auto safety bill has just been passed."[59]

After Nader informed the press of the surveillance and investigation, GM was forced to acknowledge that it was behind these activities. Later that month, Ribicoff called GM President James Roche to testify under oath about GM's actions. To prepare its response to this growing public relations debacle, GM hired Ted Sorensen, a former Kennedy advisor and speech writer, as special counsel. He advised Roche to apologize. Although Roche went before the committee and apologized to Nader, the testimony subsequently offered, including presentations by a number of Roche's aides, was very vague about who exactly was responsible for various aspects of the investigation. Regardless, GM's apology sent shock waves throughout the industry and further diminished the credibility of the automakers among the public.[60] (In 1970, GM settled an invasion of privacy suit filed by Nader for $425,000.)

While Ribicoff's hearings damaged the industry, the battle for federal safety legislation was finally fought out in the Commerce Committee under the leadership of Warren Magnuson.[61] When Magnuson opened the Commerce Committee's hearings on the Johnson administration's Traffic Safety Act, he announced that the second session of the 89th Congress was likely to be known as the "Automobile Safety Congress." The industry's position at these hearings, summed up by Elizabeth Drew, basically rehashed what its executives had said before: "We are doing a good job on safety, and we will do even better; leave us alone, loosen the antitrust laws so that we can get together on this, and let the states have a larger role in setting safety standards."[62] Industry officials proudly pointed to the recent creation of a President's Safety Committee, within the AMA, as well as a Safety Administrative Committee. John Bugas, vice-president of Ford and chairman of the AMA Safety Administrative Committee, also drew attention to the industry's increased efforts in safety research, as well as to recent grants of $10 million to the University of Michigan for the establishment of a Highway Safety Research Institute and $800,000 to Cornell University for a three-year program of in-depth, on-the-scene crash investigations. Despite these gestures, however, industry officials continued to oppose even the administration's proposals for voluntary action.

The automakers were not alone in fighting against the imposition of federal safety standards. The safety establishment continued its efforts on behalf of the

[59] Cited in Charles McCarry, *Citizen Nader* (New York: Saturday Review Press, 1972), p. 20.

[60] For a full account of GM's surveillance and investigation of Nader, see Thomas Whiteside, *The Investigation of Ralph Nader* (New York: Arbor House, 1972).

[61] For a discussion of Magnuson's role in the consumer legislation of the 1960s, see Michael Pertschuk, *Revolt Against Regulation: The Rise and Fall of the Consumer Movement* (Berkeley: University of California Press, 1982).

[62] Drew, p. 99.

industry. At the Ribicoff hearings, for example, Howard Pyle, president of the NSC, defended the industry, arguing against the idea of a centralized auto safety agency and opposing the creation of a cabinet-level office responsible for auto safety. However, he added that if any new legislation were to pass, it should be administered by the Commerce Department. Pyle also suggested that the already existing organizations involved in safety be moved into the Executive Office of the President. The Business Council, a business lobbying group of top corporate executives, also opposed federal regulation, as did the Insurance Institute for Highway Safety, an organization sponsored by the nation's auto insurers.

Meanwhile, in March 1966, the Senate unanimously passed a tire safety bill, a harbinger of the legislation to come. However, industry officials continued to dismiss the concerns expressed by members of Congress about vehicle safety performance. During the Commerce committee hearings in April 1966, for example, Sen. Vance Hartke (D-IN) asked Harry Chesebrough, vice-president of Chrysler, about a magazine story reporting the braking distance of two cars under identical conditions. One took 138 feet to stop without the driver holding the steering wheel to maintain control; the other took 238 feet to stop and constant attention of the driver to prevent rear wheel lockup. Hartke wondered if the public would be interested in this kind of information. Chesebrough responded: "I don't know why the public would have any concern over it."[63]

As pressure for safety legislation grew, a May 1966 *New York Times* article fueled the mounting public distrust of the auto industry by exposing its obsession with styling, seen at the time as the equivalent of its neglect of safety. The nation's "paper of record" noted:

Chevy offered 46 models, 32 engines, 20 transmissions, 21 colors (plus 9 two-tone combinations) and more that 400 accessories and options; the number of cars that a Chevrolet customer could order was greater that the number of atoms in the universe. This seemingly would put General Motors one notch higher than God in the chain of command.[64]

Perhaps the final blow that shattered the industry's credibility was the discovery of secret recall campaigns. Nader had told Sonosky, chief counsel to the Ribicoff committee, that the industry had been quietly recalling cars because of safety defects. Doubting the extent of the problem that Nader described, Ribicoff asked the automakers to describe their recall efforts. Nader was proved right when the automakers responded that there were 426 individual recall cases between 1960 and May 1966, involving 8 million cars, or

---

[63] Magnuson hearings, p. 468.
[64] Hal Higdon, "The Big Auto Sweepstakes," *New York Times,* Sunday Magazine (May 1, 1966), p. 97.

almost one in five produced during this period.[65] Most were due to problems with brakes, steering, or suspension systems. However, it was impossible to know how many vehicles actually had defects or how many were repaired, in part because notification of the defects were made to dealers and not to car owners. Since this revelation came on the heels of the industry's refusal to support any form of federal regulation, legislators now were inclined to see the industry as not just uncooperative but as unreasonable. Sonosky, for instance, thought this revelation had an even greater impact than exposure of GM's harassment of Nader.[66]

Now even the Commerce Committee's Republicans could not support the industry's position, and the die was cast for auto safety legislation. Given the inevitability of federal standards, the industry shifted its focus to modifying the proposed bill and hired Washington lawyer Lloyd Cutler, who advised the industry to get the story off the front pages and make the bill "bearable."[67] (Cutler has continued to represent different industry interests over the years and served as White House counsel during the Carter and Clinton administrations.) The final version of the bill was hammered out between Cutler, sitting in one room, and Nader in another, with staff members shuttling between the two antagonists.[68]

The Commerce Committee's recommendations removed the discretionary provisions from the administration's bill. From the opening sentences of the committee's report, it was clear that the industry's control over traffic safety politics had ended:

The legislation which the Commerce Committee unanimously reports today reflects the conviction . . . that the soaring rate of death and debilitation on the Nation's highways is not inexorable. [It] also reflects the committee's judgement that the Federal Government has a major responsibility to meet in assuring safer performance of private passenger cars which it has not yet met.[69]

The report asserted that "the compelling need for strong auto safety legislation" was embodied in the statistics of highway deaths. While it acknowledged that the auto industry was central to the national economy, it added: "The committee met with disturbing evidence of the automobile industry's chronic subordination of safe design to promotional styling, and an overriding stress on

---

[65] See Ribicoff hearings, Appendix, pp. 1–153 (following Part 4), for the information submitted by the industry.

[66] McCarry, pp. 82–3.   [67] Drew, p. 99.

[68] Drew, p. 100.

[69] U.S. Congress, Senate, Committee on Commerce, *Report on Traffic Safety Act of 1966* (S. 3005), 89th Cong., 2d sess., Senate Report 1301 (June 23, 1966), p. 1. Hereafter referred to as Commerce Committee Report.

power, acceleration, speed, and 'ride' to the relative neglect of safe performance or collision protection."[70]

The report noted the lack of improvement in safe design until the prod of
heightened public opinion; several examples were provided of safety devices
that were not implemented until years after their feasibility and desirability
were established. Moreover, the industry was described as lax in notifying
owners of defects and taking effective steps to ensure speedy and efficient
repair of those defects. Mandatory safety standards were therefore necessary.
"The promotion of motor vehicle safety through voluntary standards has
largely failed. The unconditional imposition of mandatory standards at the
earliest practicable date is the only course commensurate with the highway
death and injury toll."[71] Industry suggestions that the inclusion of safety equipment in cars should be left to consumer choice was explicitly rejected: "The
individual in the marketplace, upon whom the free market economy normally
relies to choose the superior among competing products, is incapable of evaluating the comparative safety of competing models."[72]

Mandatory safety standards were not established by this legislation, however. Congress delegated this responsibility to a regulatory agency that in 1970
became NHTSA. To guide the promulgation of safety standards, Congress
mandated that regulations be reasonable, practical and appropriate. "Reason-
ableness" involved realistic costs, feasibility, and adequate lead time. (This
vague mandate quickly became the source of endless conflicts over proposed
safety standards.)

There was little controversy during the floor debate over the safety bill,
although several strengthening amendments were proposed in the House. The
respective versions of the bill unanimously passed both houses of Congress.
The only area of serious contention came after Vance Hartke, with Magnuson's
support, introduced an amendment adding criminal penalties for willful violation of the law. Civil penalties by themselves were insufficient, Hartke argued,
"when human life is at stake." He added, "criminal behavior is criminal behavior whether done on a dark road or behind a corporate organization."[73]
Some industry supporters argued that no existing safety laws had both civil and
criminal penalties. Hartke responded that there were several examples of laws
with both: the 1964 Civil Rights Act, and the 1938 Food and Drug Act, the
1933 Securities and Exchange Act. He also pointed out that the Senate had
passed a mine safety bill the previous week containing both penalties. Sen.
John Pastore (D-RI) opposed the amendment, asserting that its spirit was

---

[70] Commerce Committee Report, p. 2.
[71] Commerce Committee Report, p. 3.
[72] Commerce Committee Report, p. 4.
[73] *Congressional Quarterly Weekly Report* (CQWR), July, 1, 1966, "Auto Safety Bill
Passed by Senate 76–0," p. 1365.

"obnoxious" and that the "mere fact [that] it is written in the law, psychologically or otherwise, infers [sic] that the Senate is dealing with Mobsters. To the contrary, the industry was the industrial pride of the country, was the envy of the industrial world."[74] Nader supported the amendment, arguing that without such a provision the new law lacked teeth. Nevertheless, the amendment was defeated by a vote of 14–62. Tip O'Neil (D-MA), sponsor of the House version of the amendment (and speaker of the House in the 1980s), said at the time that to pass a safety bill without a criminal penalties provision invited "the wishy-washy regulatory performance that has caused so much public disillusionment with the processes of government."[75]

After the passage of the safety act, conflicts over safety regulations were propelled into the administrative arena. Of course, the industry would have preferred the comfortable arrangements of the past, but with a president who did not support mandatory standards in the position of appointing the regulators who would implement the new law, the defeat was not as threatening as it might at first appear. Federal regulation had its benefits also. An unnamed industry spokesman explained its advantages to Elizabeth Drew:

. . . [W]e can get some good from this. New York and California were getting into safety, and what they would have demanded probably would have been worse than what the Federal government, after listening to both sides, will come up with. In addition, this law will help us with our product liability problems, and will restore public confidence in our products.[76]

Conclusion

The passage of the National Traffic and Motor Vehicle Safety Act of 1966 brought to an end the auto industry's long-held political hegemony. A new set of political relations was initiated involving a larger number of participants in the politics of auto safety. Industry officials no longer had unilateral control over vehicle design. Government officials became partners at the engineering table, circumscribing the autonomy of corporate planners. Formally, at least, there was now a legitimate public mechanism to hold the industry accountable for vehicle design. Although the vigor of regulators has varied, vehicle design is subject to government requirements, not simply the unilateral decisions of corporate officials. Thus, Elizabeth Drew concluded soon after the passage of the safety act: "The new law, whatever its built-in difficulties – and there are several – is a radical departure from the government's traditional, respectful hands-off approach to the automobile industry, an industry which politician and businessman alike had long considered sacrosanct."[77]

[74] CQWR, July 1, 1966, p. 1365.   [75] CQWR, August 17, 1966, p. 1765.
[76] Drew, p. 102.
[77] Drew, p. 95.

Yet, federal safety policy makers have never questioned the dominance of the automobile itself over the nation's ground transportation. Motor vehicle safety efforts have been directed at making individual vehicles safer, while other government agencies have been involved in engineering roads for safer travel. Providing alternatives to driving and encouraging the use of these alternatives has not been a focus of public policy despite the fact that virtually all other transportation modes are significantly safer. In this respect, the passage of federal safety legislation did little to challenge the position of the auto industry in American society even as it made individual cars less dangerous to operate.

4

The Politics of Compromise: 1967–1978

If auto industry executives thought the worst was over with the 1966 passage of the National Traffic and Motor Vehicle Safety Act, they were wrong. With the rise of the environmental movement, the social consequences of technology increasingly became a contested political issue and attention was focused on the car's impact on the environment. New organizations such as the Center for Auto Safety and Public Citizen, lobbying on behalf of the public interest, expanded the scope of conflict surrounding automotive politics.[1] The results of this new politics was the regulation of pollution emissions in 1970 and fuel economy in 1975.

During this time, automotive politics was characterized by bargaining and compromise, with industry officials resisting each new encroachment on their autonomy, but as battles were lost, new federal mandates were put in place and complied with. Reformist in nature, none of these mandates threatened the centrality of the automobile to American society. Nonetheless, by the late 1970s the reforms of this period were largely over, and by 1979 the industry had recaptured much of its lost political influence. This turnaround resulted from a series of economic events – two oil shocks and a recession – coupled with a change in the industry's political tactics. In response to the turbulent economic events of the 1970s, each of which hurt sales, the automakers altered their lobbying efforts to emphasize the issue of jobs. Because of the industry's central economic position, the argument that government regulation would cost jobs, made at a time of high unemployment, provided leverage that environmental groups were in no position to match. Bearing the brunt of the industry's downturn, the UAW retracted its previous support for extending

---

[1] For an analysis of the importance of the notion of "scope of conflict" for understanding politics, see E. E. Schattschneider, *The Semisovereign People: A Realist's View of Democracy in America* (Hinsdale: Dryden Press, 1975).

federal regulation and joined the industry in calling for modifications in regulatory standards in the hope of arresting declines in auto employment.

The Rise of Social Regulation

Auto industry regulation in this period was part of the larger phenomenon of "social regulation" directed at environmental, public health, and consumer protection. (Traditional business regulation, by contrast, was concerned with more narrowly defined market issues.) Between 1967 and 1973, Congress enacted more than twenty-five consumer, environmental, and other social regulatory laws, as well as developing an extensive regulatory apparatus to administer these laws.[2] Ten major regulatory agencies were created between 1964 and 1977 to administer new social regulations: the Equal Employment Opportunity Commission (1964), the National Transportation Safety Board (1966), the Council on Environmental Quality (1969), the Environmental Protection Agency (1970), the National Highway Traffic Safety Administration (1970), the Occupational Safety and Hazard Administration (1970), the Consumer Product Safety Commission (1972), the Mining Enforcement and Safety Administration (1973), the Material Transportation Bureau (1975), and the Office of Strip Mining Regulation and Enforcement (1977).[3] In contrast, only one agency with responsibility to regulate physical harm from corporate behavior was created between 1900 and 1965, the Food and Drug Administration (1931).

According to another account, by Theodore Lowi, at least 120 regulatory programs were enacted between 1969 and 1979, and in the twenty-year period from 1960 to 1980 the number of federal regulatory agencies grew from twenty-eight to fifty-six. The tremendous expansion of regulatory responsibilities was reflected in the *Federal Register,* the publication that collects the regulatory actions of the federal government. Between 1960 and 1980 the annual number of pages went from approximately 14,500 to 86,000.[4] Of course, federal expenditures for these programs also increased. David Vogel estimates that "between 1970 and 1980, annual governmental expenditures on the enforcement of social regulation increased from $539 million to $5,036 million; the number of personnel staffing these agencies increased from 3,574 in 1970 to 9,707 in 1980.[5]

---

[2] Michael Pertschuk, *Revolt Against Regulation* (Berkeley: University of California Press, 1982), p. 5.

[3] David Vogel, "The 'New' Social Regulation in Historical and Comparative Perspective," in Thomas McCraw, ed., *Regulation in Perspective: Historical Essays* (Cambridge: Harvard University Press, 1981), p. 162.

[4] Theodore Lowi, "Liberal and Conservative Theories of Regulation," in Gary Bryner and Dennis Thompson, eds., *The Constitution and the Regulation of Society* (Provo: Brigham Young University, 1988), pp. 11–13.

[5] Vogel, 1981, p. 163.

This surge in regulatory responsibility reflected the growing public concern for the environment, apparent in virtually every public opinion poll done at the time. One survey showed that while only 1 percent of those polled in May 1969 thought that "pollution/ecology" was an important national issue, by May 1970 the figure was 25 percent. Another survey done in December 1970 found that pollution was regarded as "the most serious problem" facing communities.[6] The growing strength of the consumer and environmental movement was also reflected in the number of nationally oriented public interest groups that were formed at this time, including the Consumer Federation of America (1968), Center for the Study of Responsive Law (1968), Public Citizen (1970), Center for Auto Safety (1970), Common Cause (1970), Center for Science and the Public Interest (1970), and the Public Interest Research Group (1970); on the environmental front there was a similar proliferation: the Environmental Defense Fund (1967), Friends of the Earth (1969), Environmental Action (1970), League of Conservation Voters (1970), National Resources Defense Council (1970), Greenpeace (1971), Sierra Club Legal Defense Fund (1971), and the Environmental Policy Institute (1972). For those groups that already existed, membership seemed to grow overnight. For example, between 1967 and 1971, the Sierra Club's membership almost tripled, going from 48,000 to 130,000, and that of the Audubon Society more than doubled, reaching 150,000.

The surge in formal organization and membership came at a time of cascading social turmoil. Widespread urban riots and antiwar protests enhanced the leverage of liberal/labor groups as political leaders sought to reduce the growing polarization of American society.[7] The environmental movement was a beneficiary of this situation because many in the business community saw it as less threatening than these other movements.[8] The combined effect of these new organizations, ideological shifts, and social disruptions transformed power relations within Washington. With environmental, public interest, and consumer forces ascendant – no one knew when these forces would reach their peak – the business community found itself on the defensive, losing a number of political battles.

---

[6] Cited in David Vogel, *Fluctuating Fortunes: The Political Power of Business in America* (New York: Basic Books, 1989), p. 65; see also Riley Dunlap, "Trends in Public Opinion Toward Environmental Issues: 1965–1990," in Riley Dunlap and Angela Mertig, eds., *American Environmentalism: The U.S. Environmental Movement, 1970–1990* (Philadelphia: Taylor & Francis, 1992), pp. 89–116.

[7] For an elaboration of this argument, see Frances Fox Piven and Richard Cloward, *Poor Peoples' Movements: Why They Succeed, How They Fail* (New York: Pantheon Books, 1977); Frances Fox Piven and Richard Cloward, *Regulating the Poor: The Public Functions of Welfare,* updated ed. (New York: Vintage Books, 1993).

[8] Vogel, 1989, pp. 68–9.

Much of this new legislation delegated responsibility for writing federal mandates to administrative agencies. These agencies were less visible political arenas that corporate officials proved adept at influencing. Regulatory deliberations typically occurred outside the limelight of media attention, making it more difficult for public interest groups to rally public support. At the same time, public interest groups could not marshall anything approaching the scientific and technical resources that regulated industries brought to bear on each new proposal. The lack of public interest participation in administrative proceedings became so apparent that in the late 1970s a Senate committee report commented: "At agency after agency, participation by the regulated industry predominates — often overwhelmingly. Organized public interest representation accounts for a small percentage of participation before Federal regulatory agencies."[9] More often than not, the committee found, there was no public interest participation before regulatory agencies, and when it existed, regulated industries consistently outspent their challengers by a wide margin, not uncommonly by a ratio of 10 to 1. "In every case or agency reviewed," the report concluded, "industry spent many times more on regulatory participation than their public interest counterparts. In some instances industry committed as much as 50 to 100 times the resources budgeted by public interest participants."[10]

Auto regulation is one of shared jurisdiction, with no one agency having total responsibility. Congress delegated authority to promulgate safety standards to the National Highway Traffic Safety Administration (NHTSA). On the other hand, standards on pollution emissions and fuel economy, though established directly by Congress, are implemented separately: the Environmental Protection Agency (EPA) is responsible for administering pollution standards, whereas NHTSA manages fuel economy regulations. EPA is also responsible for certifying the fuel economy ratings of particular vehicles. In each case, the respective agency has some discretion in implementing mandated standards and handling recalls in the event of defects. Since there is no coordinating mechanism to bring these programs together, some promarket critics skeptical of government regulation have charged that government policy often works against itself.[11] Others have rejected this criticism and have pointed to the synergies between safety and fuel economy standards, for example.[12]

[9] U.S. Congress, Senate, Committee on Governmental Affairs, *Principal Recommendations and Findings of the Study on Federal Regulation,* 95th Cong., 1st sess. (September 1979), p. 25.

[10] *Principal Recommendations and Findings of the Study on Federal Regulation,* p. 25.

[11] See, for example, Robert Crandall, Howard Gruenspecht, Theodore Keeler, and Lester Lave, *Regulating the Automobile* (Washington: The Brookings Institution, 1986).

[12] See, for example, Robert Kuttner, *Everything for Sale: The Virtues and Limits of Markets* (New York: Alfred A. Knopf, 1998), pp. 304–8.

Before turning to the safety, emissions, and fuel economy policies of the 1970s, it is useful to briefly examine a 1970 FTC report on automobile warranties. It provides an illustration of how low the industry's political capital had sunk in the late 1960s. The report reflects the new set of political relations in which the industry's political power was constrained, for a time, and government regulation was expanded.

FTC Report

In 1965, the FTC began investigating reports of widespread failures of car makers and dealers to honor new-car warranties. During the public comment period of its review, the agency received one of the largest number of complaint letters from consumers in its history.[13] The agency's report concluded that warranties were being used simply as a gimmick to sell cars. They were "meaningless, voluntary and unilateral."[14] Headed by Caspar Weinberger (defense secretary in the Reagan administration), the FTC suggested that "the automobile industry is no less a public utility industry than the other transportation industries."[15] Accordingly, it should be subject to appropriate government controls.

What the public interest requires from the federal government is enactment by Congress of a new and comprehensive Automobile Quality Act, which would give statutory recognition to the public utility obligations of automobile manufacturers and provide for minimum standards of quality, durability, and performance for new automobiles and all parts thereof, and which would place a statutory obligation on manufacturers to provide consumers with defect-free automobiles in compliance with such standards and to repair defective automobiles and automobile parts which do not conform to such standards.[16]

Safety

While the 1966 safety act signaled the end of the auto industry's political hegemony, it initiated a new set of political battles over the precise standards the automakers would have to meet. With the goal of reducing collisions, deaths, and injuries, Congress delegated to NHTSA authority to hammer out the details. However, the definition of "motor vehicle safety" that Congress wrote into law was vague, and an army of lawyers have haggled over each attempt to implement a safety regulation. Motor vehicle safety was defined as protection against either the "unreasonable risk" of collisions occurring or the "unreasonable risk" of death or injury in the event of a collision.[17] No guidance was given as to the meaning of the phrase "unreasonable risk." In fulfilling its legislative mandate, NHTSA has promulgated over fifty regula-

---

[13] U.S. Federal Trade Commission, *Report on Automobile Warranties* (Washington: GPO, 1970), p. 31.

[14] FTC, p. 68.   [15] FTC, p. 68.

[16] FTC, p. 69.   [17] P. L. 89–563.

tions, which fall into three basic categories: crash avoidance, crash protection and survivability, and postcrash survivability.[18]

The initial safety standards, effective January 1968, provoked a storm of protest from the industry. Henry Ford II complained to reporters that many of the standards were "unreasonable, arbitrary, and technically unfeasible," adding that if they could not be met, "we'll have to close down."[19] When agency officials modified their initial recommendations to temper industry criticisms, William Stieglitz, the new safety agency's chief engineer, resigned in protest, calling the standards "totally inadequate."[20] The eventual standards presented few difficulties to industry officials because the regulations were based on existing industry options and GSA standards. As a result, Nader and other safety advocates criticized these standards as insufficient. However, for Detroit, managerial autonomy was at stake.[21] Having little to do with the limited burden posed by the standards, the industry's reaction was part of a larger battle to minimize government authority over the future direction of auto design. In the end, the new standards forced the automakers to modify their design plans, although tougher standards that would have made cars safer were practical at the time.

The industry's troubles with Congress over motor vehicle safety did not end with the passage of the 1966 safety act. Legislators revisited the issue of NHTSA's authority, expanding it twice during this period. Beginning with the Motor Vehicle Information and Cost Savings Act of 1972, the agency was authorized to issue bumper standards and to develop comparative consumer information on insurance costs and safety.[22] Two years later, Congress passed the Motor Vehicle and Schoolbus Safety Amendments of 1974, which expanded the recall authority of the NHTSA.[23] Prior to this legislation, NHTSA could only require manufacturers to notify car owners of safety-related defects;

[18] Crash avoidance standards involve the braking system, tires, windshield systems, lamps, and transmission controls. Crash protection standards are divided into two basic categories: occupant protection and exterior protection. Occupant protection standards include seat belts, energy-absorbing steering columns, head restraints, high penetration-resistant windshield glass, padded instrument panels, and side door strength. Exterior protection standards require a specific energy absorption capacity of the front and rear bumpers in order to reduce vehicle body damage. Postcrash survivability standards include requirements for fuel system integrity and for flammability of interior materials.

[19] Cited in Ralph Nader, *Unsafe at Any Speed,* updated ed. (New York: Bantam Books, 1972), p. xv.

[20] *Congressional Quarterly Weekly Report,* February 10, 1967, p. 203.

[21] David Bollier and Joan Claybrook, *Freedom from Harm: The Civilizing Influence of Health, Safety and Environmental Regulation* (Washington and New York: Public Citizen and Democracy Project, 1986), p. 73.

[22] P. L. 92–513.

[23] P. L. 93–492.

it could not require a recall or force manufacturers to pay for the necessary repairs. Now recalls of vehicles with safety defects could be ordered and the manufacturers made to pay. Part of the reason this authority was seen as necessary was the large number of recalls that had recently occurred. Between September 1966 and February 1972, 25 million vehicles were recalled by the industry in over 900 recall campaigns.[24] Car makers usually, but not always, paid for necessary repairs. However, the new law did not define a "defect."[25] And because NHTSA itself has chosen not to define a safety-related defect, it relies instead on a case-by-case determination. This practice creates extensive opportunities for the manufacturers to argue about and delay each new case, a practice that continues today.

The new political environment that subjected the automakers to mandatory safety regulations did not lead industry officials to embrace the notion of improving the safety of their vehicles. Rule-making efforts by NHTSA were resisted, voluntary improvements were virtually nonexistent, and cars with serious safety problems continued to be sold. During this period, the most well publicized case of an unsafe car was the Ford Pinto, first sold in 1971.[26]

Internal company memos showed that Ford was aware that when Pintos were rear-ended at moderate speeds, the gas tank ruptured and caught fire. Yet nothing was done to prevent the problem despite the fact that the company could have done so at little cost. Meanwhile, NHTSA was considering a regulation to require that fuel tanks be able to withstand rear-end collisions at a speed of 30 miles per hour (mph). Ford lobbied against the proposal for eight years, delaying its implementation. Not unusual in itself, this effort would have probably gone unnoticed except for one of the arguments Ford used against the proposal, exposed in a *Mother Jones* article by Mark Dowie.[27] The company contended that the costs of the standard far outweighed the benefits in light of the expected number of lives and vehicles saved and injuries prevented. To put this argument in objective terms, Ford calculated the benefits by setting a value of $200,000 for each life saved, $67,000 for each injury prevented, and $700

---

[24] Nader, p. xxxiv.

[25] See Richard Tobin, "Safety Related Defects in Motor Vehicles and the Evaluation of Self-Regulation," *Policy Studies Review* vol. 1, no. 3 (February 1982), pp. 532–45.

[26] For a concise review of the Pinto case, see Russell Mokhiber, *Corporate Crime and Violence: Big Business Power and the Abuse of the Public Trust* (San Francisco: Sierra Club Books, 1988), pp. 373–82; for another case of Ford selling unsafe cars during this period, involving park-to-reverse transmission problems, see pp. 341–50. See also U.S. Congress, House, Committee on Energy and Commerce, *NHTSA's Conduct in the Ford Transmission Case. Hearings before the Subcommittee on Telecommunications, Consumer Protection, and Finance,* 99th Cong., 1st. sess. (August 1, 1985), Serial No. 99–78.

[27] Mark Dowie, "Pinto Madness," *Mother Jones* (September–October 1977), pp. 18–24, 28–32.

for each vehicle not burned, for a total of $49.5 million per year. The cost of complying with the standard was $11 per vehicle, or $137.5 million per year, given Ford's sales.

An injury victim of a Pinto crash seized on this information and won a product liability suit against Ford. A jury found that the company had willfully disregarded the safety of Pinto occupants. In a public relations move a few months later, Ford announced the recall of 1.5 million Pintos but did not send out recall notices to Pinto owners for several more months. In the interim, three teenagers in Indiana died when their Pinto was involved in a rear-end collision that caused the car to catch fire. A local prosecutor took the unprecedented step of filing murder charges against the company, alleging that Ford was guilty of reckless homicide for selling unsafe vehicles.[28]

Ford quickly realized that the case had the potential to do untold harm to the company and marshalled its considerable resources to win the case. The local prosecutor, with a limited staff and budget, was at a disadvantage from the beginning. In addition, the judge in the case, with long-time personal ties to a member of the Ford legal team, consistently ruled in Ford's favor. Although the jury found Ford not guilty, it did not suggest that the Pinto was safe. Its decision, jurors later said, was based solely on the question of whether the company had acted recklessly in handling the recall. One juror lamented: "They got off only through a loophole."[29] Despite the company's court victory, for the public the case came to stand for Detroit's disregard for vehicle safety.

Emissions Control

As air pollution worsened throughout the 1960s, cars were identified as the major cause of urban air pollution. Environmentalists targeted vehicle emissions control as the next aspect of the automobile requiring federal regulation because in 1970 passenger cars alone, as opposed to all vehicles, accounted for 48 percent of carbon monoxide emissions, 32 percent of hydrocarbon (HC) emissions, and 21 percent of nitrogen oxide (NO) emissions. The pattern of policymaking surrounding the Clean Air Act of 1970 resembled the battle over safety: plummeting industry credibility and escalating public support for federal action. Before turning to this issue, a brief examination of California's efforts at pollution control is useful because that is where car-related smog first received public attention.[30] One of the outcomes of California's effort at pollution control was a federal antitrust investigation of the

---

[28] For a detailed study of the case, see Lee Patrick Strobel, *Reckless Homicide?* (South Bend: and books, 1980).

[29] Cited in Strobel, p. 264.

[30] The following summary of events in California is taken from James Krier and Edmund Ursin, *Pollution and Policy: A Case Essay on California and Federal Experience with Motor Vehicle Air Pollution, 1940–1975* (Berkeley: University of California Press, 1977).

automakers for failing to use pollution control devices. Coming to a head in 1969, this case further damaged Detroit's public standing and, in particular, the repeated claim made by auto industry officials that they could be trusted to develop and implement pollution control devices voluntarily.

California's Early Efforts

Worries over smog first emerged in the early 1940s in Southern California. Smog was initially seen as a "mysterious" new form of pollution, different from the smoke troubling urban areas since the 1880s.[31] Scientists in California were baffled in the fall of 1943 when a major smog episode struck the city. Blame was placed on one synthetic rubber plant. As a result, in 1945 the City of Los Angeles passed an ordinance limiting single-source smoke emissions. Needless to say, aggravating episodes of pollution continued. A few years later, the California state legislature took its first step in pollution control when it permitted, but did not require, countywide pollution control districts. Los Angeles established a district immediately. However, pollution problems increased, mainly because cars were ignored as a major source of the problem. While some speculated about the contribution of car emissions to smog, there was little scientific evidence until 1950, when Prof. A. J. Haagen-Smit of the California Institute of Technology suggested that a photochemical reaction converted refinery and motor vehicle emissions into smog. Not surprisingly, oil and auto industry officials rejected Haagen-Smit's analysis. (Independent research confirmed his conclusions in 1954.)

In 1953, the auto industry responded to the growing concern over smog when its trade association established a pollution control committee. A year later, this body announced a joint venture among the vehicle manufacturers to speed development of pollution control equipment. Yet, over the next ten years, little progress was made. Legislative initiatives continued in both California and Washington, D.C., from the late 1950s through the mid-1960s providing for further study of the causes, effects, and control of motor vehicle air pollution. None, however, significantly altered vehicle emissions standards.

---

[31] There are two basic categories of pollutants: primary pollutants, emitted directly from sources, and secondary pollutants, formed in the air by the interaction among primary pollutants and the normal atmosphere. CO and hydrocarbons are essentially primary pollutants, while particulate matter, various sulfur oxides, and NOx exist in both primary and secondary forms. "Smog" results from the reaction among HC, NOx, and sunlight.

The health effects of air pollution are diverse, contributing to a wide range of respiratory and lung diseases. It can reduce the ability of the blood to carry oxygen, and it can harm plants and animals. Motor vehicles emit pollutants in three ways: through tailpipe exhaust emissions (the major source); through evaporative losses from the carburetor and gas tank; and through "blowby" when fumes escape from the pistons into the crankcase and then into the air.

Smog Consent Decree

To observers in the mid-1960s, it was apparent that the auto industry was not progressing in its effort to lessen pollution emissions, and many felt that the industry was intentionally dragging its feet. In 1964, S. Smith Griswold, the Los Angeles County Air Pollution Control Board executive, described the industry's limited accomplishments since its announcement of cooperation among the manufacturers ten years earlier:

What has the industry accomplished in the last years? Until recently, very little. In 1953, the pooling of efforts was announced. Through an agreement to cross-license, progress by one would be progress by all. How has it worked out? Apparently it has served to guarantee that no manufacturer would break ranks and bring into this field of air pollution control the same kind of competitive stimulus that spokesmen for the industry frequently pay homage to as the force that has made them what they are today.[32]

Lawyers told Griswold that what he had described was a classic conspiracy to restrain trade. The following year, the Los Angeles County Board of Supervisors requested that the Department of Justice investigate the matter.

A grand jury was convened and was on the verge of handing down criminal indictments in 1967. However, criminal charges were never filed. Samuel Flatlow, the Justice Department attorney who headed the case, received "an eleventh-hour communication" from the assistant attorney general for antitrust, Donald Turner, instructing him that criminal sanctions were inappropriate. After Flatlow counseled the grand jury against challenging the Justice Department, the grand jury reluctantly terminated its efforts.[33] The case lay dormant for over a year. Finally, civil charges were filed in January 1969, as the Johnson administration was leaving office. The controversial case was quickly settled by the incoming Nixon administration with a court-approved consent decree. A confidential Justice Department memo summarizing the grand jury's investigation was leaked and subsequently reprinted in the *Congressional Record,* leaving little doubt about the industry's illegal behavior. On three occasions the industry had delayed or limited the installation of specific antipollution devices until later model years. In one particular instance, the industry was charged with agreeing to tell California's regulatory officials that installation of proposed equipment was technologically impossible until an agreed-upon date well after it was actually possible.[34]

---

[32] Cited in John Esposito, *Vanishing Air: The Ralph Nader Study Report on Air Pollution* (New York: Grossman Publishers, 1970), p. 42.

[33] Esposito, p. 43.

[34] See the *Congressional Record,* House of Representatives, May 18, 1971, pp. H4063–74.

Instead of challenging these allegations, the industry immediately began negotiating a consent decree.[35] When finally approved, the decree ordered withdrawal of the parties from the cross-licensing agreement of 1955, prohibiting any similar future agreements. Further, the defendants were ordered to grant royalty-free licenses for the use of any pollution control device patents issued during the cross-licensing agreement period. In addition, the manufacturers had to make available the technological reports developed during the time of the agreement to allow other firms to compete on an equal footing.[36] They were also enjoined from exchanging confidential information on research pertaining to pollution control device development, manufacture, sale, or installation and were prohibited from making joint statements before certain regulatory bodies. However, the automakers were allowed to share basic research concerning "the presence, nature, amount, causes, sources, effects or theories of control of motor vehicle emissions in the atmosphere."[37] Finally, the decree contained two renewable ten-year provisions.

The consent decree was seen as a slap on the wrist, and the public reaction was unprecedented. During the thirty-day comment period, 2,000 petitions against the decree were received. According to John Esposito, author of a 1970 Nader report on air pollution, "nothing like this had ever occurred in the history of the consent decree procedure."[38] Fifty-two members of Congress, along with several individual states including Illinois, Connecticut, Maryland, New Jersey, New York, and New Mexico, filed a brief against the decree. Several cities and counties also joined the outcry, including New York City, six cities in California, and the counties of Santa Barbara and Los Angeles. The Air Pollution Control Districts of Los Angeles and the Bay Area, as well as the American Civil Liberties Union (ACLU) of Southern California, also filed complaints. Despite these protests, the court approved the decree with minor alterations. (After it was renewed during the Carter administration, the Reagan administration asked the Justice Department to bring the decree to an end as part of its plan to aid the industry. (See Chapter 6.) The consent decree allowed the industry to avoid criminal prosecution and thus was a victory. However, it demonstrated to many, particularly those supporting or participating in the growing environmental movement, that the auto industry would heed the public interest only if it were forced to by Congress.

---

[35] Stephen Kroll, "The Automobile Pollution Case: Intervening in Consent Decree Settlement," *Harvard Civil Rights, Civil Liberties Law Review* Vol. 5, No. 2 (April 1970), p. 409.

[36] Bennett Goldstein and Howell Howard, "Antitrust Law and the Control of Auto Pollution: Rethinking the Alliance Between Competition and Technical Progress," *Environmental Law* Vol. 10, No. 3 (Spring 1980) pp. 526–8.

[37] Goldstein and Howard, p. 528.

[38] Esposito, p. 47.

Clean Air Act of 1970

The 1970 Clean Air Act (CAA) was a significant departure from past legislation. In 1965, the Motor Vehicle Pollution Control Act, the first step in establishing federal responsibility for emissions control, did not advance beyond what California was already doing.[39] With the CAA, on the other hand, Congress targeted mobile-source pollution, establishing emissions standards in the enabling legislation itself, instead of delegating the authority to do so to EPA.

Pressure for regulating auto emissions came from a broad cross section of American society, reflecting the swelling public interest in ecology that culminated in the first Earth Day (April 22, 1970). Congress, sensitive to this outpouring of support, adjourned for the day to allow members to address local rallies. News reports estimated that 20 million people attended teach-ins or participated in anti pollution protests. In July, the UAW in conjunction with several major environmental groups, including the National Audubon Society Sierra Club, Environmental Action, Friends of the Earth, Wilderness Society and Zero Population Growth, presented a nineteen-point plan to every member of the Senate calling for regulation of auto emissions. The standards were so tough that they would have banned the gasoline engine by 1975.[40]

A number of clean air bills were introduced in Congress as politicians scrambled to be identified with this increasingly popular issue. The final standards in the CAA were the product of political jockeying between Democrats, some of whom were vying for the presidential nomination in 1972 and hoping to capitalize on the growing environmental movement, and President Nixon, who was equally interested in capturing votes. On the Democratic side, the main protagonists were Sen. Edmund Muskie (D-ME), at the time the front runner for the 1972 nomination; Sen. Henry Jackson (D-WA), another presidential aspirant; and Sen. Gaylord Nelson (D-WI), one of the sponsors of legislation to ban the gasoline engine. Muskie, as chairman of the Senate Subcommittee on Air and Water Pollution, eventually became the point man for pollution legislation in Congress. Nixon, not wanting to lose the environmental issue to the Democrats, proposed a 90 percent reduction in emissions by 1980. This reduction, seen as necessary to protect public health, grew out of a report issued by the predecessor of the EPA. Muskie amended an already introduced Senate bill to further tighten pollution restrictions by moving up the deadlines based on information from other studies underway at the time. The final version of the bill passed with unanimous support in Congress, except for a single opposing vote in the House of Representatives. This breadth of support

---

[39] P. L. 87–272.
[40] "Auto Union Urges Ban on Gas Engine," *New York Times* (July 12, 1970), p. 28; John Kifner, "Earth Day Group Zeros in on Autos," *New York Times* (July, 20, 1970), p. 52.

illustrates the extent to which the rise of environmentalism had weakened the influence of business and, in particular, the automakers.

The legislation required a 90 percent reduction in HC and CO emissions by 1975 and a similar reduction for NOx by 1976.[41] Deadlines for compliance could be extended by the EPA if it were essential for the public interest, if the auto companies had made a legitimate effort to comply with the law, and if the required technology was not available.[42] States were preempted from passing their own standards, with the exception of California due to its unique history of pollution control. The law also provided for a $10,000 fine for each car built that did not meet the standards. The severity of the penalty caused William Ruckelshaus, head of the EPA, to compare it to a nuclear deterrent, a weapon so powerful that it would not need to be applied in order to be effective.[43]

The target dates presented the industry with an insurmountable hurdle because they allowed for only two years to develop pollution control devices, whereas the automakers routinely required three years lead time to bring new pieces of hardware into production. Muskie admitted that the targets were technologically unreachable at the time, but he believed that tight deadlines would force the industry to develop the needed technology.[44] Accordingly, Robert Crandall of the Brookings Institution noted some years later that "this 'technology-forcing' strategy was motivated, in part, by a congressional view that the auto industry was implacably opposed to emissions abatement."[45]

Since Congress established performance standards for emissions control, it allowed the industry to select the compliance technology. The industry chose to reduce emissions by adding catalytic convertors to the exhaust system instead of developing a different engine. These devices convert exhaust gases into harmless vapors. However, they have been continually beset by problems. In fact, a report issued as early as February 1973 by the National Academy of Sciences (NAS) called the catalytic system "the most disadvantageous with respect to first cost, fuel economy, maintainability, and durability."[46] By selecting the catalytic converter, with its inherent problems, the industry virtually guaranteed that pollution policy would be an ongoing political battle. In its early years, the problems associated with this devise included reduced fuel economy, engine tuning, and tampering by owners, all of which spurred requests for delays in compliance.[47]

---

[41] P. L. 91–604.   [42] Krier and Ursin, p. 206.

[43] Cited in David Lachman, "The Politics of the Automobile" (unpublished dissertation, New York University, 1979), p. 153.

[44] Bernard Asbell, "The Outlawing of Next Year's Cars," *New York Times,* Sunday Magazine (November 21, 1976), p. 128.

[45] Crandall et al., p. 87.

[46] *Congressional Quarterly Weekly Report* (February 24, 1973), p. 380.

[47] For a brief look at another compliance problem, one that led to a $7 million fine against Ford for providing fraudulent testing data to the EPA, see Mokhiber, pp. 205–12.

Changes in Lobbying Tactics and Delays in Implementing Clean Air Standards

After losing a second major policy battle in just four years, industry officials realized that they were in a fundamentally new political environment and would have to rethink their political strategy. Lobbying practices, which in the past had been either sufficient or often unnecessary, were now inadequate to meet the challenges of the new political climate. Industry officials decided to abandon their traditional low-profile stance. They had long tried to avoid the political spotlight so as not to draw attention to the industry's almost unparalleled economic concentration. GM, the largest corporation in the nation, had been a particularly ripe target for an antitrust breakup for decades. To carry out its political agenda, lobbying activities were often channeled through a variety of front organizations, such as the NHUC, the ASF, and the PCTS. Government regulation of car design forced the automakers to fight more openly for their interests. (However, the use of front organizations continues as a supplement to their more explicit efforts. See Chapters 6 and 8.)

Industry officials also realized that a change in lobbying tactics was needed. In the initial battles over regulation, the automakers had argued that federal regulation violated free enterprise, consumer sovereignty, and managerial autonomy.[48] These broad ideological claims simply did not resonate in an era when corporate behavior was increasingly described as harmful to the public interest. Another approach was to claim that proposed standards were technologically unfeasible; or, if the technology existed, it was not ready for full production; or, if it was ready, the costs were prohibitive.[49] Repeatedly, these claims were proven untrue. Consequently, as standards were met, the industry's credibility suffered. The automakers did not rely solely on either of these two broad sets of arguments. Favors to members of Congress were also provided. As late as 1970, Ford, for example, leased insured Lincoln Continental Sedans to key committee chairmen and ranking minority members for $750 per year compared to the $4,000 it normally charged at the time.[50]

Seeing the failure of their traditional tactics, the automakers honed a new approach. Increasingly, government regulation was painted as detrimental to the public interest, as opposed to serving it, because such mandates hurt job creation and increased inflation. This argument was invoked again and again, and was particularly effective as the industry and the economy in general faltered. Between late 1973 and mid-1975 the nation was plunged into the

---

[48] Kirk Hansen,"The Effect of Fuel Economy Standards on Corporate Strategy in the Auto Industry," in Douglas Ginsburg and Ralph Abernathy, eds., *Government, Technology and the Future of the Automobile* (New York: McGraw-Hill, 1980), p. 154.

[49] Hansen, p. 154.

[50] Carol Greenwald, *Group Power: Lobbying and Public Power* (New York: Praeger Publishers, 1977), p. 82.

worst recession since the 1930s and simultaneously experienced record levels of inflation. Corporate-led attacks that government regulation was at the heart of the nation's economic problems spurred public concern that regulation was, if not the cause of the nation's economic woes, at least a burden that should be lifted from the backs of the nation's businesses. By arguing that government regulation cut into the bottom line, the auto industry came to understand how to use its main weapon, control over investment and employment, in its political battles. Meanwhile, as the social turmoil and protests of the previous decade waned, policymakers worried about reviving economic growth and became less responsive to public interest forces.

The automakers were not alone in redirecting their political tactics and increasing their lobbying efforts. Beginning in 1973 and 1974, corporations throughout the nation mobilized their political resources in what journalist Thomas Edsall described as "one of the most remarkable campaigns in the pursuit of political power in recent history."[51] A broad range of business-sponsored political organizations were formed, such as the Business Roundtable, the Heritage Foundation, and the American Council on Capital Formation, as well as the Center for the Study of American Business at Washington University; other already exiting groups, such as the American Enterprise Institute, were rejuvenated with an infusion of money from the growing number of conservative foundations that also sprang up. The Chamber of Commerce was given new life, with membership growing during the late 1970s by 30 percent per year.[52] Trade associations also increasingly turned their attention to politics. Many moved to Washington. In 1977, for example, an average of one trade association per week moved its headquarters to the nation's capital. And the number of corporations with government affairs offices located in Washington increased from 100 to 500 between 1968 and 1978.[53] Regardless of their location, virtually all of these organizations beefed up their political operations. A primary goal of this political mobilization was to reverse the political defeats of the past decade. In what was to become a mantra for years to come, government regulation came to be blamed for the nation's economic difficulties. Consumer, public interest and environmental groups were overwhelmed by this exercise of political muscle. By the end of the decade, public debate was framed around the costs of regulation, and less and less was heard about its benefits. Corporate political influence was on the rise.

The success of the political mobilization of business in the 1970s can be attributed to a number of factors. To begin with, corporate political spending increased substantially. In addition, corporate political cohesion increased with

[51] Thomas Edsall, *The New Politics of Inequality* (New York: W. W. Norton and Co., 1984), p. 107.

[52] See Edsall, chapter 3, "The Politicization of the Business Community," pp. 107–40.

[53] Vogel, 1981, p. 176.

the formation of a number of classwide lobbying organizations.[54] Much of the energy expended in this political counteroffensive was directed at convincing the public that the economic problems of the 1970s were due to government overregulation, particularly the social regulation of the previous decade. The ideological high ground was captured by these efforts because an explanation was offered for the nation's unprecedented economic woes that no other sector in society had the resources to counter. While government regulation had little to do with the nation's economic stagnation, it was an easy target. In retrospect, the economic problems that developed in the early 1970s were signs of the end of the American century (the period of unparalleled economic prosperity that followed World War II).[55] Coming to grips with its unraveling transformed the political agenda to the advantage of corporate lobbyists.

The turnaround in the auto industry's political influence can be seen in its success in obtaining delays or modifications in clean air rules. From April 1973 to August 1977 the automakers received four delays or modifications in pollution standards. With each of these episodes, industry officials honed their new lobbying approach. One of the opening salvos of this campaign was made in 1972 by Henry Ford II, who went on the offensive against emissions regulations at a stockholders' meeting: "If the emissions standards are not suspended, the result so far as we can see would be to force suspension of most U.S. automotive manufacturing operations in 1975."[56] In granting a one-year extension to the industry in April 1973, William Ruckelshaus justified his actions as avoiding "the potential societal disruptions" if the requirements went into effect on schedule.[57]

Another extension to the emissions standards was made a year later: the Energy Supply and Environmental Coordination Act of 1974.[58] Responding to the "energy crisis" that resulted from the first Arab oil embargo, Congress accepted the automakers' view of the alternatives open to policymakers: cleaner air could be achieved only at the expense of reduced fuel economy, which meant increased usage at a time of unstable supply and rising prices. Simply put, stricter clean air policies would lead to economic destabilization. In the aftermath of the 1973 oil embargo, fuel prices had remained high and the sudden leap in oil prices was blamed for playing havoc with the international monetary system and contributing to a worldwide recession. Treasury Secre-

---

[54] See, for example, Patrick Akard, "Corporate Mobilization and Political Power: The Transformation of U.S. Economic Policy in the 1970s," *American Sociological Review* vol. 57 (October 1992), pp. 597–615.

[55] For an analysis of the economic decline that affected most Americans since 1973, see Wallace Peterson, *Silent Depression: Twenty-five Years of Wage Squeeze and Middle-Class Decline* (New York: W. W. Norton and Co., 1994).

[56] *U.S. News and World Report* (May 22, 1972), p. 61.

[57] *Congressional Quarterly Weekly Report* (April 14, 1973), p. 818.

[58] P. L. 91–190.

tary William Simon went so far as to claim that almost 50 percent of the inflation in the United States was attributable to the rise in energy prices.[59] Meanwhile, "stagflation" entered the public vocabulary to describe the simultaneous existence of inflation and unemployment. By pitting the need for energy conservation against the desire for cleaner air, the industry was able to turn the focus of the debate on emissions standards from environmental concerns to economic recovery – an emphasis that favored its interests.

As the recession continued into 1975, a third delay came in March when the EPA extended existing HC and CO standards for one year. Ostensibly, the cause of the delay was potentially dangerous sulfuric acid emissions from the catalytic converter. Although there was scientific evidence contradicting the EPA claim, the extension was given. A year later, the EPA itself admitted it had been wrong.

By this time it was apparent to a number of observers that the industry's political influence was on the rise, and a shift in lobbying tactics in the context of faltering sales was credited. In 1975, for example, the *Wall Street Journal* ran a front-page story: "Breaking the Rules: Auto Men Use Slump in Seeking Slowdown on Safety, Pollution."[60] It observed that as government passed ever tighter safety and pollution rules, the "automakers, in turn, have resisted almost every new rule, often predicting that production would be disrupted or sales crippled." However, new standards were met and production did not falter. In fact, 1971 to 1973 were record sales years. "Now, however, the auto makers are mounting perhaps their most ambitious campaign yet against federal safety and pollution regulations, and they have been making more headway than ever." Vital to this success was a drop in sales from 9.6 million cars in 1973 to 6.7 million in 1975. The following year the *New York Times* also recognized the industry's new winning set of arguments – jobs and energy – which were posed as the costs of federal regulation.[61]

A similar pattern was evident when Congress permitted additional delays and a permanent weakening of emissions standards with the passage of the CAA Amendments of 1977. The legislative history of this bill illustrates the lengths to which industry officials were willing to go to obtain provisions to their liking. In 1976 both the House and the Senate passed amendments to the CAA extending the emissions deadlines, but because the bills were substantially different, the differences had to be resolved in a conference committee. The stricter Senate version was subsequently chosen. Although it still contained an extension of the emissions standards, on the last day of the 94th

---

[59] *1974 Congressional Quarterly Almanac* (Washington: Congressional Quarterly Press, 1975), p. 723.

[60] John Emshwiller and Albert Karr, "Breaking the Rules: Auto Men Use Slump in Seeking Slowdown on Safety, Pollution," *Wall Street Journal* (January 9, 1975), p. 1.

[61] Asbell, p. 128.

Congress industry officials supported a Senate filibuster on another part of the clean air bill to prevent its passage. As a result, if the law were not amended early in the next session, before the 1978 cars went into production in August 1977, the vehicles slated for production would be out of compliance. Why would the industry put itself in this position?

Industry officials believed that in 1977 they could get more favorable modifications to the law since plant shutdowns and layoffs would then be imminent. Edmund Muskie mimicked the industry's defiant attitude just before the 1976 vote: "Congress would not dare to hold us accountable for failing to meet the law. They wouldn't dare. We are too important. There are too many jobs involved. We are above the law, and unless we can have the law written the way we want it, we will break the present law and dare Congress to do anything about it."[62] E. M. Estes, the president of GM, echoed Muskie's version a few hours later. "They can close the plants. They can get someone in jail – maybe me. But we're going to make [1978] cars to 1977 standards."[63] In August 1977 the gamble paid off.

Coming just weeks before the beginning of the 1978 model year, the passage of the 1977 CAA Amendments averted the threatened plant shutdowns by giving Detroit what it wanted. To achieve this outcome, the automakers did not rely solely on their privileged economic position and the threat of layoffs to convince Congress to meet their demands. They mobilized a coalition of parts suppliers, dealers, and even the UAW to emphasize the economic consequences of failing to amend the law. The UAW urged its 1.5 million members to write or directly contact their senators and representative, telling their members that "Congress must be told *quickly* that your job is as stake. . . . Tell Congress . . . your future depends on protecting air quality without disrupting jobs."[64] A lobbyist from another industry neatly summarized the situation: "The auto companies' success in 1977 was due to one key factor: they employ so many God-damned people."[65] The political advantages of large corporate size, aided by threatened economic hardship, had asserted itself. The CAA of 1977 gave the industry more generous modifications than the 1976 version, allowing the industry to use 1977 standards for its 1978 and 1979 cars. Final compliance with the HC levels was postponed until 1980, and compliance with the CO levels until 1981. The final standard for NOx was permanently changed from the original 0.4 gram per mile to 1.0 gram per mile, going into effect in 1981.[66]

---

[62] Cited in Asbell, p. 126.   [63] Asbell, p. 126.

[64] Cited in David Vogel, "A Case Study of Clean Air Legislation 1967–1981," in Betty Bock et al., eds., *The Impact of the Modern Corporation* (New York: Columbia University Press, 1984), p. 345.

[65] Cited in Vogel, 1984, p. 344.

[66] P. L. 95–95.

Conclusion

The politics of motor vehicle emissions standards in this period, when the automakers both sustained loses and achieved victories, was one of bargaining and compromise. Automakers were unable to prevent the extension of regulation to emissions, as the rising tide of environmental concern constrained their influence and made policymakers sensitive to pressures from the public interest community. Yet, as the industry encountered economic difficulties and as the economy as a whole experienced even larger disruptions, the industry regained some of its lost ground. But even as its political position improved, compromise and delay – not abolition of federal regulation – was the most industry officials could obtain. Still, the industry's turnaround in political influence was insufficient to prevent the extension of federal regulation to fuel economy. In this instance, the national magnitude of disruptions in oil supplies created political momentum that overwhelmed all the efforts the automakers could muster.

Fuel Economy

Fuel economy regulation was established in 1975 by the Energy Policy and Conservation Act (EPCA).[67] Instead of having to meet minimum performance standards for all vehicles, the automakers were required to meet a sales-weighted fleet average. This method allows manufacturers to sell vehicles that do not meet the standards by balancing these sales with those of other vehicles that exceed the standards. Congress set the corporate average fuel economy (CAFE) for new cars at 27.5 mpg for 1985, with lower interim standards beginning in 1978. (In 1974 average fuel economy was 13.2 mpg.) The secretary of transportation had the discretion to increase CAFE requirements after 1985 and to lower the standards to 26.0 mpg if they were unreachable.

As a response to the first oil shock of the 1970s, which disrupted gasoline supplies to the United States for the first time, EPCA involved a wide range of energy issues. The legislation was an amalgamation of five different bills, each targeting a different aspect of energy use, conservation, or security. The final bill, over 100 pages long, involved issues as diverse as the strategic petroleum reserve, rationing authority, auto fuel economy, energy conservation, coal conversion, and oil pricing.[68] The scope of EPCA was so extensive that the Congressional Information Service, which compiles all congressional hearings and reports, noted in its legislative history of the bill that "virtually every

---

[67] P. L. 94–163.

[68] The five bills that became EPCA were the Standby Energy Authorities Act (S.662), the Automotive Fuel Economy Act (S.1883), the Energy Labeling and Disclosure Act (S.349), the Strategic Energy Reserve Act (S. 677), and the Energy Conservation and Oil Policy Act (HR. 7014).

congressional committee can be said to have issued relevant publications during 1974 and 1975."[69]

Congressional debates on improving motor vehicle fuel economy began in 1973 when a number of proposals on the subject began to circulate. These proposals covered a wide range of methods, including gas and motor vehicle taxes, improving fuel economy information, mandated fuel economy standards, and mandated fuel economy labels.[70] Although the industry was experiencing a major drop in sales in 1975, and although industry officials emphasized that any new federal mandate would hurt the already struggling companies, they were unable to prevent the enactment of mandatory standards. Congress discounted the chorus of industry arguments mobilized to stop the extension of federal regulation. The specter of nationwide economic disruption and social disorder due to gas shortages transcended the industry's own claims of economic harm. In this instance, the perceived national emergency easily took precedence over the requests of the automakers. Given an issue of such overriding national concern, the political leverage of the industry was sharply constrained.

EPCA was opposed by GM and Chrysler, as well as by the Ford administration. Others in the industry, the Ford Motor Company, the UAW, and the National Automobile Dealers Association, realized that the energy crisis was such a powerful psychological and economic trauma that mandatory standards were inevitable. As a result, this group supported fleet averaging as an alternative to either excise taxes on less efficient cars, a substantial hike in gas taxes in order to discourage driving, or minimum performance standards for all cars. For many in Congress, fleet-based mandatory fuel economy standards was the most feasible way to lessen consumption and avoid gas price increases that would have antagonized voters.[71] Trying to head off the initiative for legislated standards, President Ford announced in his 1975 State of the Union Address that the car makers agreed to meet voluntarily a gas-consumption target of 18.7 mpg by 1980 in exchange for a five-year postponement in meeting emissions standards. But in a pattern reminiscent of previous safety and emissions debates, many in Congress felt that the industry could not be trusted to improve its vehicles voluntarily. This belief was strengthened by the fact that for a number of years before 1974 the fuel economy of new cars had slowly de-

---

[69] *Congressional Information Service Index* (January–December 1975), p. 1024.

[70] Richard John et al., "Mandated Fuel Economy Standards as a Strategy for Improving Motor Vehicle Fuel Economy," in Douglas Ginsburg and William Abernathy, eds., *Government, Technology and the Future of the Automobile* (New York: McGraw-Hill, 1980), p. 120.

[71] Robert Leone and Stephen Bradley, "Federal Energy Policy and Competitive Strategy in the U.S. Automobile Industry," *Annual Energy Review,* vol. 7 (1982), p. 65.

clined.[72] As a result, the legislation passed, completing the last part of government regulation of the automobile.

Once fuel economy standards were in place, however, industry officials
found a number of ways to mitigate their impact. Loopholes were found in the
compliance regulations, and industry officials were quick to exploit them.
Meanwhile, EPA's testing protocols were often inadequate in measuring on-
the-road performance.[73] As a result, actual fuel economy performance was less
than what official ratings suggested.

Conclusion

This period of bargaining and compromise resulted in the expansion
of government regulation to include emissions and fuel economy and at the
same time, a series of delays and modifications in regulatory standards. Although the scope of auto politics expanded to include new groups critical of the
automobile's impact on American society, the industry redirected its lobbying
efforts and succeeded in molding discussions over regulation to reflect its own
economic interests. Regulatory proposals came to be defined in terms of their
economic impact on the automakers or the nation as a whole, according to the
automakers' own calculations, instead of the benefits to the public. While
industry officials had complained that government regulation harmed their
business since the day the safety act passed in 1966,[74] it was not until the
economic stagnation of the 1970s that these claims became a potent weapon in
their fight against federal regulation. Not only was the government dependence
on large corporations something the automakers stressed in their lobbying,
these lobbying efforts were enhanced by a faltering economy whose problems
signaled the end of the American century.

Notwithstanding the automakers' success in redefining the debates over
regulation, cars became safer, cleaner, and more efficient because of government mandates and enforcement efforts. Future policy battles were conflicts
over reform within the policy framework set down during this period. The
bargaining and compromises of this period lasted for about ten years. When the
industry reeled from record losses in 1980, the entire direction of policy
changed and the automakers' political victories far surpassed those of this
period.

[72] NHTSA, "Automotive Fuel Economy Program," 3rd Annual Report to Congress, 44
FR 5749 (January 29, 1979).

[73] For a report on the initial problems with compliance and implementation of fuel
economy regulation, see U.S. Congress, House, Committee on Government Operations, *Automotive Fuel Economy: EPA's Performance. Report by the Subcommittee on
Environment, Energy, and Natural Resources,* 96th Cong., 2d sess. (May 13, 1980),
House Report No. 96–948.

[74] See Lawrence O'Donnell, "Manufacturers Worry Federal Car Standards May Disrupt
Production," *Wall Street Journal* (September 9, 1966), p. 1.

5

The Resurgence of Corporate Power: 1979–1981

While the auto industry had its political ups and downs during the 1970s, the oil shock of 1979 gave it a jolt. For the second time in six years, oil supplies were scarce and gas prices surged. Inflation rose to over 13 percent for 1979. Making matters worse, in 1980 unemployment rose to over 7 percent, yet the inflation rate remained largely the same. As the nation experienced a recession in 1980, there was an increased demand for small cars and foreign imports, each of which cut into Detroit's longstanding practice of selling large cars for large profits. Chrysler was hardest hit and teetered on the edge of bankruptcy.

The auto industry's problems only increased in the years that followed when the nation sunk into yet another recession in 1981 and 1982, one that set a new post–World War II high for unemployment. Given the industry's central importance to the nation's economy, its financial problems had national repercussions. With concerns over the economy mounting, government officials became increasingly vulnerable to corporate demands for policy changes. Instead of the bargaining and compromises that had characterized the prior decade or so, Detroit's executives gained the leverage to make government policy serve their interests. Government policy, which had previously prodded industry officials to make cars safer, more efficient, and less polluting, was now subordinated to the goal of economic recovery.

The Chrysler bailout was the first initiative in a new pattern of industry–government relations. When the pain of losses spread to the other automakers, President Carter extended government aid to the entire industry. Because the industry's economic crisis came to a head during what turned out to be Carter's final year in office, it is difficult to say what would have been the subsequent course of automotive policy if he had been reelected. What is clear, however, is that taken together, the sequence of measures beginning with the Chrysler bailout and including the plans to aid all the automakers represented a fundamental transformation in the direction of automotive public policy. The federal government was not the only level of government in which this new pattern of corporate power was apparent. In the city of Detroit, a battle involving the destruction of over 1,000 homes to build a GM factory also reflected this new political alignment. Although this episode did not involve the federal government, it is worth reviewing because it provides a dramatic example of the industry's resurgent power.

Chrysler Bailout

The 1979 Chrysler bailout is often presented as an exceptional initiative made possible by the remarkable personality of its chief executive, Lee Iacocca. While this is partially true, the bailout was also made possible by Chrysler's size and its impact on the economy. Chrysler, the smallest and most vulnerable of the Big Three, was also the nation's tenth largest industrial firm. Financial problems were not new to Chrysler, nor was the bailout the first time it had sought federal help. After losing money in both 1974 and 1975, the company unsuccessfully sought federal aid in the form of a tax break. The Senate actually passed a revision of the tax code allowing Chrysler to claim a refund on taxes it had paid during profitable years, extending the normal three year carry-back rule to eight years. However, this provision was deleted in a conference committee. Fears of financial ruin were soon alleviated because during the following two years Chrysler was profitable. Beginning in 1978 and continuing throughout 1980, however, its losses accelerated. The losses for these years were, respectively, $200 million, $1 billion, and $1.7 billion.

By 1978 Chrysler's fortunes were bleak. One of America's largest and best-known corporations, with over 130,000 employees, was edging toward bankruptcy. The banking community refused more loans because lenders had already extended the maximum amount that government regulations or bank polices allowed.[1] With private solutions to its problems precluded, Chrysler sought a public one. Still, before Chrysler could obtain federal help, it had to win over many who believed that the logic of the market dictated Chrysler's demise. In fact, many leaders in the business community, representing some of the nation's blue-chip giants, argued that Chrysler's problems were its own doing and that its faulty management should pay the price.

Yet, market failure had political consequences that transformed the potential bankruptcy into political leverage. The logic was simple: the economic consequences of allowing Chrysler to fail outweighed the cost of the bailout. Indeed, the bailout demonstrated in extreme form that American society was far from resembling a traditional market economy. In reality, large corporations and government exist in a symbiotic relationship beneficial to both; each needs the other to varying degrees. Regardless of the rhetoric of "free enterprise" used by

---

[1] Robert Reich and John Donahue, *New Deals: The Chrysler Bailout and the American System* (New York: Times Books, 1985) p. 111.

the opponents in much of the public debate, there were different rules for the elite of the corporate community. Sen. William Proxmire (D-WI), an opponent of the bailout and chair of the Senate Banking Committee, pointed this out, complaining: "We let 7000 companies fail last year; we didn't bail them out. Now we are being told that if a company is big enough . . . we can't let it go under."[2] However, Chrysler's political influence, while rooted in its privileged economic position, had to be asserted through the exercise of its extensive resources. Chrysler mounted an unmatched lobbying effort by coordinating the efforts of the many groups tied to its fortunes. This kind of lobbying clout, harnessed to the issue of bailing out a giant corporation whose bankruptcy promised to send shock waves throughout the economy, created a virtually unstoppable political force.

Several studies done at the time tried to estimate the economic consequences of a Chrysler collapse. Since no corporation of its size had ever gone bankrupt, estimates of the final economic outcome were speculative. What would happen to the stock market, for instance? How many supplier firms would go under? What about the communities dependent on Chrysler payrolls? The Congressional Budget Office commissioned a study to estimate the economic costs of a failure, which suggested that

[O]ver the three year period from 1979 through 1981, personal income tax revenue would fall by $6 billion, corporate taxes by $4.4 billion, Social Security contributions by $3.4 billion. Government spending for welfare and other programs would rise by $1.4 billion. City governments would lose $75 million in Chrysler property taxes. The federal government would be liable for $800 million in Chrysler pensions it guaranteed. In total [the net loss would be] $16.5 billion over three years. . . .[3]

Another study, this one by the Department of Transportation, claimed that a Chrysler bankruptcy would cause a decline of about 0.5 percent in the gross national product and a rise in the national unemployment rate of between 0.5 and 1.09 percent, and would have a negative impact of $1.5 billion on the balance of trade.[4] While it was unclear how accurate either of these forecasts were, few policymakers wanted to find out.

If nothing else, Chrysler's crisis exposed the dependence of government on the vitality of large corporations. What Chrysler could not get in 1975, when its losses were small, loomed as a necessity in 1979, when bankruptcy seemed

[2] U.S. Congress, Senate, Committee on Banking, Housing and Urban Affairs, *Chrysler Corporation Loan Guarantee Act of 1979. Hearings,* 96th Cong., 1st sess. (November 1979), Part I, p. 2. For additional Senate hearings, see Part II and U.S. Congress, Senate, Committee on Banking, Housing, and Urban Affairs, *Chrysler Corporation Financial Situation. Hearings,* 96th Cong., 1st sess. (October 1979).

[3] Cited in Reich and Donahue, p. 315.

[4] Cited in Michael Moritz and Barrett Seaman, *Going For Broke: Lee Iacocca's Battle to Save Chrysler* (Garden City: Anchor Press, 1984), p. 246.

imminent. In December 1979, while Congress debated the bailout, Lee Iacocca was quick to link the passage of the bailout to a host of larger economic problems: "If government wants to do something about unemployment, if it wants to keep the nation's urban areas and cities alive, if it wants to prevent increased welfare dependency and government spending, if it wants to offset an $8 billion imbalance in automotive trade with Japan, let it approve Chrysler's [request]."[5] The company was not alone in arguing for the bailout. Supporters included the U.S. Conference of Mayors, American Motors, Manufacturers Hanover Trust Company, the National Bank of Detroit, the UAW, the American Federation of Labor–Congress of Industrial Organizations (AFL–CIO), the National Association for the Advancement of Colored People (NAACP), and the Urban League.

Nevertheless, Chrysler had to organize a concerted lobbying effort to impress the doubters, and to overcome the reservations of true believers in the "free market." Many of the leading voices in the business community opposed the bailout, including the Business Roundtable, National Association of Manufacturers (NAM), Citibank, Bank of America, and the *Wall Street Journal.* They feared that this type of government involvement in the marketplace edged too close to nascent public control. The Business Roundtable, the association of the chief executive officers of the nation's top corporations, argued that "Whatever the hardships of failure may be for the particular companies and individuals, the broad social and economic interests of the nation are best served by allowing this system to operate as freely and as fully as possible."[6]

Within the industry, Ford and GM were reluctant to take a prominent stand on the bailout. Each company's chief executive turned down a congressional invitation to testify on the bailout. However, Thomas Murphy, chairman of GM, initially opposed the bailout. At first, Murphy argued that a bailout was counter to the philosophy of free enterprise and would compromise the discipline of the market.[7] He suggested that instead of a bailout, government regulation should be reexamined. Yet the following month, when the NAM took its vote, GM abstained.[8] A few weeks after the vote, Murphy announced that if the bailout was the only way to save the corporation, he would favor it.[9] The reasons for this shift were unclear, and GM never openly explained its change of opinion. Some have suggested that old fears provide a partial expla-

---

[5] Cited in Walter Adams and James Brock, *The Bigness Complex* (New York: Pantheon Books, 1986), p. 302, from the *Wall Street Journal* (December 3, 1979).

[6] Cited in Reich and Donahue, p. 134.

[7] See Reginald Stuart, "G.M. Chairman Opposes Special U.S. Aid Asked by Chrysler," *New York Times* (August 3, 1979), p. 1.

[8] Judith Miller, "Chrysler Aid Is Opposed by N.A.M.," *New York Times* (September 26, 1979), p. D5.

[9] "G.M. Chief Eases Chrysler Aid View," *New York Times* (October 10, 1979), p. D4.

nation: GM may have worried that, without Chrysler, an antitrust suit breaking up the corporation would be initiated. Ralph Nader's opposition to the bailout was based, in part, on the hope that without Chrysler, GM would finally be broken up.

Numerous groups tied to Chrysler directly lobbied on its behalf. In addition to its 130,000 employees, the automaker harnessed its 4,500 dealers and 19,000 suppliers, who were spread throughout virtually every congressional district in the nation. To literally bring home to wavering members of Congress the economic impact of bankruptcy, the company's economic contribution to each congressional district in the nation was tabulated by adding together the volume of business of every Chrysler plant, dealership, or supplier.[10] For example, Rep. Elwood Hillis, (R-IN) received a list of Chrysler suppliers in his district that ran three and one-quarter single-spaced pages and included the names of 436 companies, whose sales to Chrysler totaled $29.52 million for the year. This strategy was particularly useful in demonstrating Chrysler's impact on districts where there were no Chrysler-owned plants. In addition, the plight of Chrysler's local dealers and suppliers elicited sympathy from some members of Congress in a way that the misfortune of a billion-dollar corporation did not. Chrysler also established a team of experts to sell the company on a one-to-one basis to every legislator. By the fall of 1979 the Washington law firm of Pattan, Boggs & Blow (one of the premier legal/lobbying firms in the nation's capital) had put a dozen lawyers on the task. Since partner Tommy Boggs's connections were with Democrats, Chrysler also hired a firm headed by William Timmons, a former aide to Presidents Nixon and Ford, to lobby Republican legislators. In addition, it hired two former Michigan congressmen, Gary Brown and James O'Hara, as well as former Maine Senator William Hathaway. Those opposed to the bailout never mounted a systematic campaign; their stake in the outcome was just not large enough.

The route to the bailout was complicated. It began in late 1978 as an attempt to obtain a $250 million loan from the Indiana office of the Farmers Home Administration, a branch of the Department of Agriculture that helps pay for rural development projects. The money was earmarked for a transaxle plant in Richmond, Indiana. However, the company ran up against a ceiling of $50 million for any single enterprise. Obtaining tax relief was Chrysler's next move. But this option was also foreclosed because Chrysler was losing money, and thus it was not paying any taxes. In spite of these losses, Chrysler was modernizing its plant and equipment to cut costs and produce a more competitive car. As a result, tax credits that normally accumulate from such investments were going to waste. Although the credits could be saved for the future, it was the company's future that was now in doubt. Chrysler proposed that the

---

[10] Reich and Donahue, p. 147.

federal government give it a $1 billion advance against future tax credits, and when the company began earning profits, it would refund the advance. The proposal was crafted, as Reich and Donahue pointed out, to look as little as possible like a handout.[11] Chrysler also wanted a two-year reprieve from environmental regulations.

There were several problems with Chrysler's preferred solution. To begin with, changes in the tax code made for one company might be requested by others. Also, there were no mechanisms to evaluate the actions taken to improve the company's operations. Loan guarantees – the form eventually chosen – on the other hand, were specific and could be supervised. (New York City's experience with federal loans in the mid-1970s was seen as a successful precedent.) But Chrysler wanted to avoid being told by the government what to do and did not want to acquire more debt. Within the Carter administration, support for loan guarantees was solidified when G. William Miller, formerly chairman of the Federal Reserve Board, became treasury secretary in July 1979 when President Carter shuffled his cabinet. Miller argued against the tax plan but lent his support to a loan guarantee.

A number of other alternatives surfaced. Douglas Fraser, president of the UAW, for example, suggested partial government ownership of Chrysler so that the public would share in any future profits. Others wanted to see specific requirements made of Chrysler as a condition for the bailout. Rep. Henry Reuss (D-WI), chairman of the House Banking Committee, wanted to require Chrysler to build energy-efficient cars and mass transit equipment and to guarantee employment as a condition for federal help. Still others suggested a corporate reorganization through the bankruptcy laws. However, Chrysler feared that this option might suggest that the company was going under and would scare away potential customers. In the end, none of these ideas gained much support and the loan guarantees went forward in December 1979.[12]

The bailout, the result of a complicated process replete with amendments and compromises, required eight groups tied to the company to contribute a total $2 billion to the financial rescue as a prerequisite for the federal loan. If any group did not contribute its share, the bailout would collapse, putting pressure on large and small constituent groups alike: (1) the company's union workers had to give $462.5 million in concessions; (2) its nonunion workers had to give $125 million; (3) Chrysler's U.S.-based creditors had to contribute $500 million, 80 percent in loans and 20 percent in concessions to outstanding debt; (4) foreign creditors had to contribute $150 million in new loans; (5) Chrysler had to sell off $300 million in assets; (6) state and local governments had to contribute $250 million in loans; (7) suppliers and dealers had to contribute $180 million; and (8) Chrysler had to sell $50 million in new

[11] Reich and Donahue, p. 101.   [12] P. L. 96–185.

stock.[13] In percentage terms, lenders contributed 32 percent, employees 29 percent, sale of assets 15 percent, other governments 12 percent, suppliers and dealers 9 percent, and sale of new stock 3 percent. A loan guarantee board headed by the treasury secretary was established. Its members included the chairman of the Federal Reserve Board and the comptroller general; the secretaries of labor and transportation sat as nonvoting members, an indication of the fiscal orientation of the bailout. The board had the power to remove management and modify the amounts required by Chrysler's constituents if the corporation failed to meet its obligations. The act forbade dividends on existing stock as long as the loans were outstanding.

Given the visibility of the bailout, it received numerous interpretations. Reich and Donahue noted that opinions ranged from "a loathsome instance of government meddling; [to] an inspiring model of cooperation among business, labor and government; [and] an overblown but routine specimen of the nation's incoherent industrial development policy."[14] Either way, by the summer of 1980 Chrysler had laid off 40 percent of its workforce. Marc Stepp, head of the UAW's Chrysler division, complained that Chrysler's severe layoffs indicated that the loan board was putting pressure on the corporation to strip down its operations. Treasury Secretary Miller demurred, insisting that his sole object was to ensure that Chrysler had a sound plan for recovery. In this way, the rationale for keeping Chrysler afloat that many believed was pivotal – saving jobs – was turned upside down and became a justification for laying workers off. This apparent irony occurred, of course, because the goal of the bailout was measured by the financial health of the company.[15] While it was true that a variety of constituencies were required to make concessions as a prerequisite to obtaining federal loans, there was no question that the biggest losers were the

---

[13] Reich and Donahue, pp. 161–2.   [14] Reich and Donahue, p. 4.

[15] A genuinely ironic twist concerning government policy toward Chrysler came during the Reagan administration. President Reagan went to considerable lengths to distance himself from the bailout throughout 1981, partly due to the company's tenuous future but also because of his dedication to free-market rhetoric. Yet, as Reich and Donahue observed, two actions taken by the Reagan administration – import restraints on Japanese cars, which enabled American producers to raise prices, and changes in the tax laws – funneled public subsidies to Chrysler that were probably larger, though less overt, than the bailout.

The tax changes allowed losing firms, including Chrysler, to take advantage of safe-harbor leasing provisions. Between 1981 and 1983 these alterations allowed Chrysler to obtain tax subsidies of $68 million that would never have to be paid back. Since a money-losing firm could not take advantage of its investment tax credits, the best the automaker could do was to bank them for the future. To Chrysler's good fortune, the Reagan administration made it easier for companies to sell their tax benefits to profitable firms by enabling them to sell – and promptly lease back – plants and equipment to profitable companies that could use the credits.

workers; Chrysler's stockholders, managers, lawyers, and lenders benefited most.

By 1981, Chrysler's losses, though substantial, had begun to diminish, and in 1982 the company broke even. The following year Chrysler turned a profit, enabling it to pay off the federal loans, and in 1984 Chrysler earned record profits, some $2.4 billion. Earnings for the first six months of 1984 alone, $1.5 billion, were more than those for the previous ten years combined.[16] In the end, the Chrysler bailout was simply the first and most dramatic step in the redirection of the goals of government policy toward the auto industry. Shortly thereafter, with the industry as a whole in crisis, industry officials approached the federal government for changes in virtually every aspect of public policy that affected them.

Carter's Plans to Aid the Industry

Chrysler's financial condition spread like a virus to the rest of the automakers in 1979 and 1980. Reluctantly, Jimmy Carter found himself increasingly drawn into the orbit of auto politics. Besides the fact that the nation's largest industry was in dire straits, 1980 was an election year. By the end of 1979 the gravity of the industry's problems was apparent to all of its executives. Thus, Ford and GM separately approached the Carter administration with extensive regulatory "wish lists," requesting substantial changes in regulatory standards. After meeting with industry officials himself, Carter rejected these requests.[17] However, by the spring of 1980, with imports surging, profits falling, and unemployment on the rise, the seriousness of the industry's crisis was undeniable. April unemployment figures indicated that national joblessness had risen to 7 percent – at the time seen as cause for alarm – and auto unemployment hit 21.9 percent, the highest for any single industry in the nation.[18] The Congressional Budget Office estimated that 700,000 people were out of work due to the industry's downturn, costing government $350 million per week in lost revenue and additional outlays.[19] Responding to the industry's requests could no longer be avoided.

Led by Senators Howard Metzenbaum (D-OH) and Donald Riegle (D-MI), twenty senators whose states were directly affected by the auto crisis met in the Capitol in early May with leading industry officials, including GM President Thomas Murphy, Ford Chairman Philip Caldwell, Chrysler President J. Paul Bergmoser, AMC Chairman Gerald Meyers, and UAW President Douglas

[16] "Chrysler's Profit Sets a Record," *New York Times* (July 20, 1984), p. D1.

[17] George Eads and Michael Fix, *Relief or Reform: Reagan's Regulatory Dilemma* (Washington: Urban Institute, 1984), p. 130.

[18] Dale Tate, "Sagging U.S. Auto Industry Pleads for Federal Help," *Congressional Quarterly Weekly Report* (May 10, 1980), p. 1262.

[19] U.S. Congress, House, Committee on the Budget, *Mid Year Perspectives on the Economy. Hearings,* 96th Cong., 2d sess. (July 23–4, 1980), p. 186.

Fraser. Metzenbaum expressed the mood of the meeting. "There is a general feeling that if the auto industry goes down, it will take the rest of the economy with it."[20] Specific pieces of legislation were not discussed but a number of general options were considered, including delays in implementing emissions and fuel economy standards, tax credits for purchases of small U.S.-built cars, loans for car dealers, accelerated depreciation schedules, domestic content legislation, and restrictions on Japanese imports.[21]

Carter met again with industry officials later that month. This time he asked them for "shopping lists" of policy changes that would be of assistance.[22] He promised a response in six weeks and established a task force headed by Transportation Secretary Neil Goldschmidt to develop the plan. A wide variety of government agencies whose policies affected the industry were consulted in formulating the administration's proposals: the Council of Economic Advisors; Treasury Department officials responsible for tax and depreciation policies; regulators at EPA, OSHA, and the Department of Transportation; trade officials from the Office of the U.S. Trade Representative; the Small Business Administration (SBA); Labor Department experts on regional and community dislocation; Justice Department antitrust advisors; and OMB and Domestic Council representatives.[23]

Meanwhile, Congress also moved to redirect automotive policy. In June, a resolution overwhelmingly passed that called for a review of the fiscal, regulatory, and import policies affecting the industry. Acknowledging the industry's importance to the nation and that "new policies" were necessary, the resolution left no doubt that Congress felt that the nation was dependent on a healthy auto industry. Action was required, the resolution stated, because

the massive unemployment resulting from the decline in United States auto production has imposed major costs on Federal, State and local governments across the country in the form of trade adjustment assistance, unemployment benefits, social services, and large losses in tax revenues; and [because] . . . the present difficulty in the American automobile . . . industry results from more than a downturn in the business cycle, is not self-correcting and threatens to inflict lasting structural deterioration and dislocation on the industrial base of the United States. . . .[24]

The resolution called on the administration to take immediate steps to alleviate unemployment in the industry. Two weeks later, Carter traveled to Detroit to present his plan. Although he was greeted by scattered complaints that the plan

---

[20] Tate, p. 1262.   [21] Tate, p. 1262.

[22] Helen Kahn, "Can U.S. Help Industry? Quick Fix Seems Unlikely," *Automotive News* (July, 7, 1980), p. 1.

[23] Kahn, p. 1.

[24] "American Automobile and Truck Industry – Congressional Support," Senate Concurring Resolution 101 (June 24, 1980), 94 STAT. 3669.

would not significantly help the beleaguered automakers, Detroit's executives generally praised Carter for opening a new era of cooperation between government and industry.[25] Republican Party officials accused Carter of deciding to go to Detroit to make his announcement as an attempt to upstage the Republican Party convention scheduled to begin the following week in the city.

Carter's plan was not as extensive as the earlier requests made by Ford and GM. Nevertheless, the plan, announced as a billion-dollar rescue package, included relaxation of federal auto emissions standards, tax relief, and financial aid for affected communities. It also included the creation of a permanent Auto Industry Committee including members of the industry (manufacturers, suppliers, and dealers), labor, and government to deal with the industry's problems on a continuing basis. When Esther Peterson, Carter's consumer affairs advisor, complained that there was no consumer voice in the group, Carter added her to the committee over the objection of Goldschmidt. On the trade front, Carter avoided taking any overt action to restrain imports, deciding instead to request the International Trade Commission to expedite an already filed UAW–Ford petition concerning Japanese imports. (See Chapter 7.) Implementing the Carter plan required actions by an alphabet-soup bowl of agencies including the EPA, NHTSA, OSHA, and SBA, in addition to changes in the tax code. The EPA made three commitments involving emissions standards, with the major savings ($500 million) coming from an interpretation of the Clean Air Act that allowed all 1984 model cars to comply with low-altitude emission standards, even though cars normally emit double the usual amount of HC and CO at higher altitudes.

OSHA announced that it would permit GM and the UAW to develop a less costly way of complying with newly promulgated standards on lead and arsenic exposure, and the agency would consider similar proposals from Ford and Chrysler. NHTSA's principal commitment was to refrain from issuing any new major safety standards during the remainder of 1980. It also promised to "review again" fuel economy standards for light trucks for the period 1983 through 1985 and to "thoroughly consider" post-1985 passenger car standards.[26] The SBA, for its part, loaned $400 million to hard-hit dealers. The Economic Development Administration set aside $50 million for aid to communities affected by auto unemployment. Trade Adjustment Assistance for unemployed auto workers was broadened to include workers in supplier industries.[27] The final element of the plan involved two changes in the tax code: one shortened the allowable depreciation schedules for auto industry equipment and machinery, leading to a savings of approximately $100 million per year; the other accelerated the full depreciation of special hand tools, for a one-time

[25] Edward Lapham et al., "Carter Offers His Plan to Rescue Detroit," *Automotive News* (July 14, 1980), p. 1.

[26] Eads and Fix, p. 130.   [27] Cited in Lapham et al., p. 41.

gain of $100 million.[28] Although the scope of the plan was wide-ranging, the problems of the industry were much larger. Some estimated that the industry needed as much as $60 billion to modernize its plants.[29] Nevertheless, the direction of automotive policy had changed; now the operative word was "relief."

The Transportation Department continued to develop recommendations to aid the industry during the last months of the Carter administration. After the first meeting of the auto advisory committee in September 1980, Transportation Secretary Goldschmidt signaled the new era of automotive public policy when he announced: "Without regard to which administration sits in the White House after the election, this work must be done."[30] In January 1981, days before Jimmy Carter left office, the Transportation Department completed its study of the industry, which included a broad range of policy recommendations. Because of its timing, the recommendations were general in nature. However, the report clearly outlined a new direction for automotive policy, one that the incoming administration largely embraced.

The report drew attention to the industry's dramatic economic downturn by observing that

[i]n 1977 it might have seemed totally unrealistic to project that Chrysler would have shrunk to less than half its world size in two years; that the federal government would be guaranteeing almost $2 billion in various forms of credit to auto companies and dealers; that a nationalized French company would own almost half of American Motors; that Japanese auto production would exceed that of the U.S.; and that Ford and GM would experience record losses and would have drained more than $7 billion of liquid reserves from their international systems within eighteen months.[31]

Noting that the financial problems of the industry extended well beyond the corporate boardroom or the homes of laid-off auto workers, the report concluded that the nation's economic stability was threatened. Blame for the industry's problems was spread across the board. Nothing less than a redefinition of the relations among business, labor, and government was seen as necessary to reassert the industry's preeminence in international competition.[32] Invoking the rhetoric of the industrial policy debate that was going on at the time, the report stressed the need for a "new" socioeconomic compact between

---

[28] Lapham et al., p. 41.

[29] Michael Wines, "Reagan Plan to Relieve Auto Industry of Regulatory Burden Gets Mixed Grades," *National Journal* (July 23, 1983), p. 1536.

[30] Cited in Edward Lapham, "Carter Auto Committee Begins Work," *Automotive News* (September 15, 1980), p. 6. See also Helen Kahn, "President's Auto Committee Chartered as Advisory Group," *Automotive News* (October 6, 1980), p. 2.

[31] U.S. Department of Transportation, *The Auto Industry, 1980* (Washington: GPO, 1981), p. 72. Hereafter referred to as DOT report.

[32] DOT report, p. 1.

industry, labor, and government.[33] "Cooperation," it was argued, had to re-
place the adversarial relations of the past. Eight major recommendations were
made: (1) import quotas should be imposed on Japanese cars; (2) government
should help the industry to obtain capital by altering depreciation schedules
and revising the tax code, perhaps through a reindustrial finance corporation;
(3) labor givebacks were necessary to close wage gaps with competitors; (4) in
return for givebacks, management should give labor profit sharing; (5) rather
than extending the system of mandated fuel economy, there should be a negotiated goal between business and government linking future fuel economy targets with anticipated fuel costs; there should be steady and predictable fuel
price rises, and in general, energy policy should be coordinated with fuel
economy policy; (6) the regulatory approach should be reformed, seeking more
constructive and cooperative relations; (7) antitrust regulations should be relaxed; (8) increased support should be provided for worker retraining and
community redevelopment.[34]

At the same time that this report was sent to Carter, NHTSA, headed by Joan
Claybrook, invited public comment on improvements in fuel economy. The
appointment in 1977 of Claybrook, an associate of Ralph Nader, had dismayed
industrial officials. However, the NHTSA notice illustrates the narrowed options available to even a dedicated advocate of the public interest.

In view of the pivotal position of the automobile industry in this nation's economy, the
NHTSA believes that improving fuel economy should be pursued in a manner consistent with the preservation of a strong domestic automotive industry. A healthy automotive industry is important to the health of the national economy and the well-being of the
many persons working directly or indirectly in the industry and of the communities in
which those persons work. Further, certain levels of sales are necessary for vehicle
manufacturers to be able to generate capital for renewing plant and equipment and for
making further improvements in vehicle quality and fuel efficiency.[35]

Clearly, policy trends were moving according to a new compass heading.

Poletown

While the industry's crisis had widespread repercussions, a local decision directed at a few thousand people in the city of Detroit received national
attention. It was a dramatic contest pitting a small neighborhood against the
combined forces of the municipal government and the nation's largest corporation. In an era of corporate flight and deindustrialization, this case demon-
strates the seemingly limitless lengths to which local officials will go to
preserve jobs and the extraordinary power that large corporations in such
circumstances can wield over communities.

---

[33] For a sample of this debate, see Chalmers Johnson, ed., *The Industrial Policy Debate*
(San Francisco: Institute for Contemporary Studies, 1984).
[34] DOT report, p. 1.   [35] 46 FR 8056 (1981).

In 1980, GM offered the city of Detroit the opportunity to develop a 465-acre site for a new assembly plant it planned to build. GM wanted to acquire the land by May 1981. The new plant, scheduled to open in May 1983, would build GM's large cars: Cadillacs and Oldsmobiles. GM officials made an uncertain promise that the plant would employ 6,000 people. Company representatives indicated that only by annexing property adjoining a closed factory, once the site of a Dodge plant, could their site requirements be met. Sitting in the way, however, was a racially integrated working-class residential neighborhood known as Poletown. For city officials, Poletown, despite its 3,000 residents, was a dying neighborhood of largely abandoned and dilapidated homes. The need for jobs, they reasoned, dictated that the remaining residents would have to go.

The city of Detroit had experienced a long, painful decline during the 1970s, and saw the new plant as a chance to shore up a weakening economic base. The city's condition was indeed bleak. Between 1970 and 1977 Detroit lost 47,000 jobs, more than 9 percent of its workforce. Between 1970 and 1980 the city's population had declined by approximately 20 percent, or by over 300,000 residents, from 1,514,000 to 1,192,000. Property values declined 1.5 percent (property values in the metropolitan area, meanwhile, increased by 116.5 percent).[36] GM had also just announced that it was closing two aging plants in Detroit, threatening the jobs of another 15,000 workers.

A collection of federal, state, and local funds totaling $220 million were used to acquire the area, relocate the residents, demolish the structures, and build the necessary rail and road links to the plant. Besides obtaining the site, GM received a 50 percent property tax abatement over twelve years. With the tax subsidy, the total package reached $350 million. In return, GM paid $8 million.[37] The city of Detroit obtained the land through the use of eminent domain – the power of government to obtain private property for public use. To prepare the site, 3,438 residents were removed, as well as 1,176 houses, 117 commercial and industrial buildings, 12 churches, a 278-bed hospital, and two schools. One thousand people employed in the area would lose their jobs.

Poletown residents struggled to keep their homes and neighborhood intact, challenging the taking in court and demonstrating to arouse public support. They picketed GM headquarters, as well as the home of its chairman, Roger Smith. Their legal challenge argued that the city of Detroit's use of eminent domain was an improper taking of private property. Even as bulldozers reduced

---

[36] These figures are taken from Bryan Jones et al., *The Sustaining Hand: Community Leadership and Corporate Power* (Lawrence: University Press of Kansas, 1986), pp. 23–4.

[37] Ralph Nader and William Taylor, *The Big Boys: Power and Position in American Business* (New York: Pantheon Books, 1986), p. 122. For a detailed breakdown of the costs and sources of revenue for the project, see Jones et al., pp. 89–101.

the area to rubble, their quixotic battle continued, testimony that the neighbor-hood was not a dying community being put out of its misery, as GM and the city claimed.[38] The heart of the legal challenge hinged on the meaning of "public use" in eminent domain law. The basic issue, according to the Michigan Supreme Court, was whether the proposed condemnation was for the primary benefit of the public or the private user, in this case GM. The court ruled (5–2) that the primary benefit from the taking of the neighborhood was for the public and could not be forbidden, regardless of the fact that there was an "incidental" private gain.[39] For the majority, the new use of the property would provide jobs and stimulate the economy; that GM would benefit was largely irrelevant. According to the court's thinking, once a public benefit of the action in question was identified, nothing else mattered. With this reason-ing, there was little else for the majority to explain. The two dissenters on the court, on the other hand, argued that there was much more involved than the majority suggested.

In his dissent, Justice John Fitzgerald argued that the case turned on whether the economic benefits of "the taking of private property with the object of transferring it to another private property" satisfied the public use requirements of eminent domain.[40] To reach this conclusion, one had to determine whether the employment benefits were "incidental" to the private gain of the property transfer. Fitzgerald suggested that a useful way to understand this question was to contrast it to the practice of slum clearance, another taking. Whereas in slum clearance cases it was the clearance that was seen as the primary benefit, and the land resale to private owners that was incidental, the transfer of benefits to GM in the case of Poletown was not incidental. It was only through the transfer that the "public purpose" could be achieved. "Thus," Fitzgerald argued, "it is the economic benefits of the project that are incidental to the private use of the property."[41] Fitzgerald warned that the majority's decision would place "vir-tually no limit to the use of condemnation to aid private businesses . . . [and thus] no homeowner's, merchant's or manufacturer's property, however pro-ductive or valuable to its owner, is immune from condemnation for the benefit of other private interests that will put it to a 'higher use.' "[42] The other dissen-ter, Justice James Ryan, considered one of the most conservative justices on the Michigan court, concurred, writing a separate dissent. He spoke directly to the

[38] See Jeannie Wylie, *Poletown: A Community Betrayed* (Champaign: University of Illinois, 1989).
[39] *Poletown Neighborhood Council v. City of Detroit,* 304 N.W. 2nd 455 (1981), p. 458. Hereafter referred to as Poletown Case.
[40] Poletown Case, p. 460.   [41] Poletown Case, p. 462.
[42] Poletown Case, p. 464, footnotes omitted.

issue of GM's power, arguing that the decision "seriously jeopardizes the security of all private property ownership."[43]

For Ryan, one could not avoid the fact that the city of Detroit had its back to the wall when the "proposal" was made by GM.[44] In reviewing the history of the case, he observed that "government, in all its branches, [was] caught up in the frenzy of a perceived economic crisis."[45] Yet, the genesis of the project did not lie with government. "Behind the frenzy of official activity," he noted, "was the unmistakable guiding and sustaining, indeed controlling, hand of the General Motors Corporation."[46] "The evidence then is that what General Motors wanted General Motors got. The corporation conceived the project, determined the cost, allocated the financial burden, selected the site, established the mode of financing, imposed specific deadlines for clearance of the property and taking title, and even demanded 12 years of tax concessions."[47] Ryan argued that there appeared to be no limits or principles to the majority's use of "public benefit." Virtually anything could now come under this heading. He saw the use of eminent domain on the behalf of large, powerful corporations as raising the question: Who was exercising sovereign political power?

When the private corporation to be aided by eminent domain is as large and influential as General Motors, the power of eminent domain, for all practical purposes, is in the hands of the private corporation. The municipality is merely the conduit. . . . Eminent domain is an attribute of sovereignty. When individual citizens are forced to suffer great social dislocation to permit corporations to construct plants where they deem it most profitable, one is left to wonder who the sovereign is.[48]

One of the often lost details of the Poletown battle, highlighted in the circuit court trial, was that only 70 acres of the 465-acre site were actually to be used for the plant. The rest of the land was allocated for a one-level parking lot and landscaping. Design experts testified that instead of a large open-ground parking lot next to the plant, rooftop parking or a multilevel parking structure would allow the plant to be built on a smaller lot – an area that would sacrifice only about 100 of the least desirable homes.[49] Yet, GM refused to modify its plans. In actuality, then, Poletown residents lost their homes not to create jobs, but because GM refused to alter its plans for a parking lot.

---

[43] Poletown Case, p. 465.

[44] Poletown Case, p. 467, emphasis in original.

[45] Poletown Case, p. 465.   [46] Poletown Case, p. 468.

[47] Poletown Case, p. 470, footnotes omitted.

[48] Poletown Case, p. 481.

[49] See the testimony of Karl Griemel, dean of the Lawrence Institute of Technology School of Architecture, *Poletown Neighborhood Council v. City of Detroit,* No. 80–039–426 CZ (Wayne County Circuit Court, 1980), cited in Emily Lewis, "Corporate Prerogative, 'Public Use' and a People's Plight: *Poletown Neighborhood Council v. City of Detroit,*" *Detroit College of Law Review* (Winter 1982), No.4, p. 907.

The Poletown episode is instructive because it is another example of how corporate officials exercise their privileged power by taking advantage of both the dependence of government on private employers to provide jobs and a faltering economy. This time, however, that power was applied in a local context. The city of Detroit, confronting a declining economic base, could not resist the offer of jobs. In the case of Poletown, this required the destruction of a neighborhood.

Conclusion

By the time Jimmy Carter left office, the direction of public policy toward the auto industry had changed. The political consequences of the nation's largest industry experiencing its first major economic crisis led policymakers to subordinate other policy concerns to the financial needs of the industry. The period of bargaining and compromise was over. Public interest groups observed from the sidelines as Detroit's executives used the industry's economic crisis to their political advantage.

Reagan administration officials would develop these trends even further. Because the administration was so aggressive in supporting this new direction and embraced it across such a wide spectrum of policy issues, many commentators looking back on the 1980s miss the fact that the direction of public policy had changed before Reagan took office. A 1985 *New York Times* article commenting on the Reagan administration's policies toward the auto industry pointed this out: "the Government began easing up on Detroit in the late 1970s – well before Ronald Reagan moved in the Oval Office and advocates of deregulation were appointed to top policy making jobs – when the finances of the big American car makers were nosediving."[50] The direction that the Reagan administration would take toward the auto industry was made explicit before he was elected. Two weeks after the initial Carter plan was released in July 1980, and just days after Reagan secured the Republican presidential nomination, he called for immediate legislation allowing for tax changes in the form of accelerated depreciation schedules and a temporary moratorium on all future regulations. In addition, he called for a careful review of current regulations in order to eliminate or revise those deemed unnecessary. Holmes Tuttle, a Los Angeles Ford dealer and a longtime Reagan confidant, announced there were forty to fifty auto-related regulations that would become likely targets for repeal under a Republican administration.[51]

[50] Reginald Stuart, "Car Makes Are Getting Back in the Driver's Seat," *New York Times* (July 21, 1985), section 4, p. 2.
[51] Edward Lapham, "Repeal of Regulations a Likely Reagan Goal," *Automotive News* (July 21, 1980), p. 2.

6

The Triumph of Corporate Power: Regulatory Policy, 1981–1988

By the time Ronald Reagan took office in January 1981, few questioned that the auto industry was in crisis. In 1980, the industry as a whole had reeled from record losses of $4.2 billion. By contrast, in every year of the previous two decades, the automakers' combined profits were never less than $2 billion (1980 dollars). Meanwhile, GM sustained its first loss since 1921. With the shift in automotive policy under Jimmy Carter and the subsequent election of a stridently probusiness president whose own victory was, in part, a reflection of the business mobilization of the 1970s, the automakers were in a position to obtain wholesale changes in public policy. The industry's economic troubles were turned into a political advantage. In April, 1981, Reagan announced a comprehensive plan to aid the industry that included extensive regulatory rollbacks, discussions leading to import quotas on Japanese cars, and the relaxation of antitrust policy. The industry's reaction, noted one reporter, "bordered on euphoria."[1]

Central to this plan was the rollback of thirty-four safety, emissions, and fuel economy regulations. Standards that had been contested and often delayed but in the end promulgated, were now fair game. What the industry previously had been unable to block it was now able to reverse. To document the Reagan-era policy approach, one policy from each of the three main automotive regulatory areas – safety, emissions, and fuel economy – will be examined. The three examples are the CAA Amendments of 1981 (emissions), the air bag rollback (safety), and the rollback of fuel economy (CAFE) requirements. The attempt to weaken the Clean Air Act is chosen because it is the bedrock of auto pollution control. For safety, the air bag is singled out because it was the subject of the longest-running controversy in automotive regulatory policy

---

[1] Michael Wines, "Regulatory Plan to Relieve Auto Industry of Regulatory Burden Gets Mixed Grades," *National Journal* (July 23, 1983), p. 1535.

history; this safety feature also held the largest potential for preventing injuries and death of any single regulation. Finally, the 1985 NHTSA decision lowering CAFE is chosen because it was the central fuel economy decision of this period.

Policymakers in this period were more responsive to the industry's lobbying than in the previous decade as financial losses mounted and government regulation was widely attacked by a growing chorus of experts financed by the business community. The postwar Keynesian welfare state, which for decades had defined the parameters of American politics, was no longer secure. Corporate officials made it clear that the only way to spur economic growth was to unfetter business from unwanted government regulation. Ronald Reagan came to power offering to cut taxes, reverse the course of the welfare state, and rein in environmental, health, and safety regulation, which were, he argued, strangling the economy. Auto industry officials, and the corporate community in general, realized that they had a historic opportunity to reshape public policy. This is not to suggest, however, that auto industry officials gained all that they wanted. Even though thirty-two of the thirty-four slated rollbacks were accomplished, completely or in part, a closer examination of the three sample regulatory cases indicates that there were political and legal limits to corporate success within this period of triumphant corporate power.[2] Before turning to an examination of these examples, we outline the Reagan administration's plan to aid the industry.

Plans to Aid the Industry

The Transportation Department's January 1981 recommendations, issued less than two weeks before the Reagan inauguration, gave the incoming administration a framework to orient its own deliberations on a plan to aid the industry. At the same time, Congress started its own discussions on the industry's worsening plight. Days before the incoming president's inauguration, the Senate Finance Committee's Subcommittee on International Trade held extensive hearings on the industry's problems. Sen. Robert Dole (R-KS), chairman of the Finance Committee, opened the hearing in dramatic fashion. "It is clear," he said, "to every member of this committee and I am certain to the members of the new administration as well, that this country will not and cannot accept the destruction of this industry."[3] Sen. John Danforth (R-MO), chair of the subcommittee, warned: "The U.S. auto industry is in a state of crisis."[4]

---

[2] For a detailed breakdown of each of the thirty-four rollbacks, see Wines.

[3] U.S. Congress, Senate, Committee on Finance, *Issues Relating to the Domestic Auto Industry. Hearings before the Subcommittee on International Trade*, 97th Cong., 1st sess. (January 14–15, 1981), Part 1, p. 3. Hereafter known as the Finance Committee hearings.

[4] Finance Committee hearings, Part 1, p. 28.

At the hearings, a wide range of groups testified, in addition to representatives of the Big Three. Each offered its own proposals to help the beleaguered automakers. Among the industry-related groups were the UAW; the Automotive Materials Industry Council of the United States (AMICUS), representing 40,000 companies supplying the auto industry; the American International Automobile Dealers Association (AIADA), representing 4,500 small businesses that employed 140,000 individuals selling and servicing imported cars; and the Automotive Importers of America (AIA), an association of auto importers in the United States, excluding Volkswagen and Mercedes-Benz, with combined employment in the United States of 140,000. Suggestions ranged from import quotas, investment tax credits, and accelerated depreciation schedules to reduction of federal regulations. Non–auto industry groups also testified, such as Consumers for World Trade and the Council for a Competitive Economy, arguing against import restrictions.

A few weeks later, the Motor Vehicle Manufacturers Association (MVMA) sent a detailed set of requests to the new president, the same ones, in fact, submitted to Carter a year before, including import restraints, accelerated depreciation rates, extended tax credit carry-forward provisions, less stringent air pollution standards, easing of testing protocols, abolition of fuel economy standards after 1985, a reduction of the 5 mph bumper standard to 2.5 mph, and reevaluation of the air bag standard.[5] Inheriting a set of power relations much to its liking, the Reagan administration quickly set about formalizing a plan to help the industry. To hammer out the details, industry officials met with several key administration representatives and exchanged a series of letters.[6] Unlike the first Carter plan, which had rejected the industry's wish list, the Reagan plan included most of the items. An administration official later wrote that there were three objectives to the plan: aid the troubled industry; demonstrate a successful regulatory relief effort; and avoid congressional pressures for trade restraint.[7]

Stressing the revitalization of the economy as the single most important remedy for the industry, the plan emphasized the importance of the president's Economic Recovery Program. However, because the industry's problems were

[5] See Helen Kahn, "Makers Tell Reagan of Worry, Recommend Actions to Help," *Automotive News* (February 9, 1981), p. 2.

[6] See Ralph Nader and William Taylor, *The Big Boys: Power and Position in American Business* (New York: Pantheon Books, 1986), pp. 100–2; U.S. Congress, House, Committee on Government Operations, *The Administration's Proposals to Help the Auto Industry. Hearings before the Subcommittee on Government Activities and Transportation,* 97th Cong., 1st sess. (May 13–14, 1981), p. 110. Hereafter referred to as The Administration's Proposals to Help the Auto Industry.

[7] Robert Leone, "Regulatory Relief and the Automobile Industry," in George Eads and Michael Fix, *The Reagan Regulatory Strategy: An Assessment* (Washington: Urban Institute, 1984), p. 91.

seen as more than merely a reflection of cyclical fluctuations in the economy, across-the-board policy changes were warranted.[8] Thirty-four regulations were slated for rollback in what the administration described as the "biggest attempt ever to ease federal controls over a single industry." Total savings were estimated at $1.3 billion in capital costs over the following five years and consumer savings of $8 billion.[9] (See Table 1 for a list of regulatory rollbacks.) Most of the rollbacks involved executive branch regulatory decisions; the program also included asking Congress to eliminate requirements that all passenger cars meet 1984 emissions standards for high altitudes. Estimated savings for this one change amounted to $38 million in capital costs and $1.3 billion in consumer costs. On the trade front, the plan reaffirmed a commitment to "free trade." Yet, administration officials were already engaged in discussions with Japan that would lead, a few weeks later, to "voluntary" import quotas. Antitrust enforcement was also slated for relaxation, as was the smog consent decree renewed during the Carter administration. The administration also wanted to accelerate federal procurement of motor vehicles by $100 million for the rest of the fiscal year. Finally, in a gesture in a different direction, the Department of Labor proposed to increase assistance for worker retraining, but there were no specifics attached for this proposal, and these programs were subsequently subject to budget cuts.

There were at least two notable differences between the Reagan plan and the earlier policy outlines developed in the January 1981 Carter report. To begin with, the Carter plan had called for profit-sharing with autoworkers in exchange for wage givebacks. In addition, Carter had established an auto industry advisory committee with consumer, worker, and industry representatives, which Reagan promptly abolished on taking office. In any case, the Reagan proposals subordinated virtually all other policy goals to the financial needs of the automakers. No longer were regulators worried about the environmental or safety consequences of the automobile. Helping the Big Three earn profits was the new order of the day.

To implement these changes, as well as the administration's broader deregulation plans, a controversial alteration in regulatory procedures was used. The discretionary authority of agency decision makers was undercut by the power of White House aides, weakening the procedural guarantees stemming from the Administrative Procedures Act. A task force on regulatory relief, headed by Vice-President George Bush, was also established to provide an

---

[8] White House, Office of the Press Secretary, "Actions to Help the U.S. Automobile Industry," p. 2, reprinted in U.S. Congress, House, Committee on Energy and Commerce, *The Role of OMB in Regulation. Hearings before the Subcommittee on Oversight and Investigations,* 97th Cong.,1st sess. (June 18, 1981), Serial No. 97–70, p. 419. Hereafter referred to as The Role of OMB in Regulation.

[9] Wines, p. 1532.

Table 1. *Summary of Reagan's proposed regulatory rollbacks*

EPA

1 Revise hydrocarbon and carbon monoxide heavy duty truck standards
2 Relax assembly line test procedures
3 Delay assembly line testing for heavy-duty engines
4 Relax nitrogen oxides emissions limits for heavy-duty engines
5 Institute nitrogen oxides averaging for trucks
6 Institute emissions averaging for diesel particulates
7 Eliminate 1984 high-altitude requirements
8 Adopt self-certification for high-altitude vehicles
9 Forgo assembly line testing for high altitudes
10 Consolidate nitrogen oxides waiver proceedings
11 Consolidate carbon monoxide waiver proceedings
12 Adopt equivalent nonmethane hydrocarbon standards
13 No requirement for controls of emissions while fueling
14 Streamline certification program
15 Relax test vehicle exemptions
16 Reduce number of assembly line test orders
17 Explore deferral of paint shop standards

NHTSA

18 Delay passive restraints for large cars
19 Review all passive restraints requirements
20 Modify bumper standards
21 Rescind "field of view" requirements for cars
22 Terminate "field of view" rule making for trucks and buses
23 Withdraw post-1985 CAFE proposals
24 Amend tire grading regulations
25 Amend seat belt comfort regulations
26 Terminate rule making for multipiece tire rims
27 Rescind speedometer/odometer standards
28 Defer theft protection standards
29 Modify brake standards
30 Terminate rule making on low-tire-pressure warning devices
31 Eliminate tire information requirements
32 Terminate rule making on batteries
33 Streamline fuel economy reporting requirements
34 Change vehicle identification requirements

Source: White House Office of the Press Secretary, "Actions to Help the U.S. Auto Industry," April 6, 1981.

additional appeals forum for businesses that felt they were not receiving proper treatment from regulatory agency officials. While White House involvement in regulatory affairs had a long history, the Reagan White House went further than any of its predecessors. As a result, congressional hearings were held to scrutinize the legitimacy of this effort, and legal scholars, among others, generated a voluminous literature on these developments.[10] Environmental, health, and safety regulations were the primary targets of these deregulation efforts. And for George Eads, a participant in Carter's attempt to influence regulatory decisions, the clearest example of this trend was the Reagan plan to help the auto industry. "Regardless of what you think of the individual numbers that are claimed," he testified, "the agencies are being given the signal that results should come out a certain way before the necessary analysis has ever been begun."[11] Joan Claybrook, head of NHTSA during the Carter administration, made a similar point about the Reagan safety rollbacks. "The new proposals marked a major departure in the conception of the federal auto safety program. Safety improvements in cars, the very heart of the NHTSA's safety mission, were now redefined as economic burdens to be avoided. This shift flouted the agency's statutes, scientific evidence, and even the economic realities of auto safety regulation."[12] Clarence Ditlow, head of the Center for Auto Safety, testified that preordained conclusions, instead of reasoned analysis, now determined regulatory decisions.[13] However, rolling back some of the standards proved to be more difficult than it first appeared.

Clean Air Act

Revising the Clean Air Act (CAA) was one of the first major environmental challenges for the Reagan administration. The 1977 amendments were due for reauthorization by September 30, 1981, limiting the time the administration had to seize the initiative to reform the bill.[14] At the time, the law was one of the most detailed environmental laws written, totaling more than 180 pages, three times longer than the original 1970 law. Auto emissions standards were merely one of a number of air pollution issues the legislation covered.

Immediately confronting the administration's effort to revise the CAA was a report from the National Commission on Air Quality, created by the 1977 CAA

---

[10] For an analysis of the presidential role in managing the regulatory process, see Stan Luger, "Administrative Law, Regulatory Policy, and the Presidency," *Presidential Studies Quarterly* vol. XXIII, No. 4 (Fall 1993), pp. 713–26.

[11] The Role of OMB in Regulation, p. 15.

[12] Joan Claybrook, *Retreat from Safety* (New York: Pantheon Books), p. 180.

[13] The Administration's Proposals to Help the U.S. Auto Industry, p. 110.

[14] This summary relies largely on Richard Tobin, "Revising the Clean Air Act: Legislative Failure and Administrative Success," in Norman Vig and Michael Kraft, eds., *Environmental Policy in the 1980s: Reagan's New Agenda* (Washington: Congressional Quarterly Press, 1984).

to prepare a comprehensive assessment of the air pollution control effects of the law. In its March 1981 report, the commission urged the continuation of pollution control as a "national priority . . . requiring substantial investment" throughout the 1980s.[15] No fundamental changes were needed in the law, claimed the commission, only refinements. With this report in place, the prospect of modifying the law decreased. However, administration officials did not give up their plans to make fundamental changes in air pollution regulation. A number of major alternatives were considered, including total elimination of national air quality standards, application of cost–benefit analysis to proposed regulations, elimination of federal sanctions for localities not achieving federal standards, elimination of the requirement that automobile pollution control devices be maintained in proper working order, relaxation of limits on car exhausts, proposals to allow polluted areas to assess their own progress in reducing air pollution, and a proposal to make EPA enforcement discretionary. Drafts of these possible changes were leaked to members of Congress and, given their extreme nature, were used to embarrass the administration and rally opponents. Consequently, even before any formal proposals could be made, the administration was put on the defensive.

In the face of growing opposition, the administration decided to make a strategic withdrawal. Instead of formulating specific proposals for changing the law, it offered "basic principles" to guide reform. Other factors also contributed to this decision. To begin with, administration officials could not agree on concrete proposals for changes. Since the revision process was already underway, with many of the necessary oversight hearings already completed, delay hurt whatever chances existed for changing the law. Part of the reason for the delay was the administration's preoccupation with tax and budget cuts. As Murray Weidenbaum, chairman in 1981 of the Council of Economic Advisors and a leading advocate of deregulation, lamented: "The major reason the administration was so extraordinarily timid in providing leadership [to reform the CAA] was its desire to avoid raising controversial legislative questions that could impede the speedy enactment of its tax and budget initiatives."[16]

With no White House direction, supporters of blunting the law introduced their own bill in the House of Representatives.[17] It contained a number of provisions that would have weakened auto emissions standards and loosened pollution requirements for other industries. Led by Rep. John Dingell (D-MI), chair of the Energy and Commerce Committee and one of Detroit's primary political protectors, supporters of this effort included the Business Roundtable, the NAM, the Chamber of Commerce, the MVMA, and, at least formally, the

[15] Cited in Tobin, p. 232.
[16] Murray Weidenbaum, "Regulatory Reform Under the Reagan Administration," in George Eads and Michael Fix, p. 19.
[17] HR. 5252.

Reagan administration. Environmentalists immediately labeled the proposal a "dirty air" bill, arguing that it would double auto emissions, extend the deadline for meeting national air quality standards by as much as eleven years, and allow for substantial increases in pollution near national parks and wilderness areas. Environmental forces were aided in their effort to stop the bill by the growing scandals surrounding the administration's environmental policies. A number of high-ranking officials including EPA head Ann Gorsuch Burford and a key deputy, Rita Lavelle, were forced to resign. Meanwhile, a series of decisions made by Interior Secretary James Watt added to the belief that the Reagan administration wanted to satisfy business groups regardless of the consequences.

As the administration became embroiled in one environmental controversy after another, membership in environmental groups multiplied. Between 1980 and 1983, for example, membership in the Wilderness Society shot up by 140 percent, the Sierra Club grew by 90 percent, and Defenders of Wildlife and Friends of the Earth expanded 40 percent.[18] Public opinion polls showed that not only was there a large reservoir of support for environmental protection, but that it was growing in response to the administration's attacks on environmental regulation. One poll, for example, showed that from September 1981 to April 1983 the percentage of respondents who agreed with the statement "Protecting the environment is so important that requirements and standards cannot be too high and continuing environmental improvements must be made regardless of cost" increased from 45 to 58 percent.[19]

With stiffening environmental opposition, the bill's prospects plummeted. While John Dingell was able to protect the auto-related provisions in the proposal, other industries found that tougher provisions were being added to the bill as it made its way through the committee. Consequently, the bill languished and was never voted on. Meanwhile, Republican setbacks in the 1982 congressional election and a reenergized environmental movement forced the Reagan administration to focus on derailing legislative efforts to strengthen the law. However, the wide administrative discretion inherent in environmental control allowed the administration to give its business supporters some of what they wanted through interpretations of "compliance," granting of waivers, and lengthening of deadlines. For the rest of Reagan's time in office, clean air politics remained deadlocked. In 1989, President Bush moved to end the legislative logjam when he offered proposals to improve the law. A

---

[18] For an analysis of this trend, see Robert Cameron Mitchell, Angela Mertig, and Riley Dunlap, "Twenty Years of Environmental Mobilization: Trends Among National Environmental Organizations," in Dunlap and Mertig, eds., *American Environmentalism: The U.S. Environmental Movement, 1970–1990* (Philadelphia: Taylor and Francis, 1992), pp. 11–26.

[19] Cited in Weidenbaum, p. 23.

series of other factors had changed by this time as well, and in 1990 Congress finally revised the CAA after a decade of stalemate. (See Chapter 8.)

The lessons from this case indicate that even with the new politics of automotive policy and a willing administration, the industry could not get everything it wanted from Washington. Because tailpipe emissions standards were embedded in legislation, as opposed to administrative regulation, Reagan administration officials could not unilaterally change the standards. With public attention focused on environmental protection, industry lobbyists encountered opposition to changing legislative mandates that was too formidable to defeat. Yet, for their efforts, industry officials were able to delay enactment of tighter emissions standards for almost ten years.

Passive Restraints

Unlike clean air politics, which was primarily fought out in Congress, the effort to repeal the air bag was largely an administrative decision. Because of the way the Reagan administration handled the rollback, however, it ended up before the Supreme Court. The air bag was considered by its advocates as one of the most important public health actions ever taken by the U.S. government. When fully implemented, it was estimated that each year 9,000 lives would be saved and 65,000 serious injuries would be prevented.[20] However, the air bag, one of the longest debated auto safety standards in the history of federal regulation, was a continual source of controversy for two decades until 1991, when Congress finally legislated its inclusion in all cars beginning in 1997. (See Chapter 8.)

Debate over the air bag recapitulated the long-standing question of how much safety should be "imposed" on the public through government regulation. Opponents of mandatory standards argued that individuals, not government, should decide on the safety of products by "voting" in the marketplace through their purchases. Advocates of the air bag, on the other hand, maintained that the social consequences of car crashes outweighed this concern for "consumer sovereignty," and that few car buyers or passengers are equipped, in any event, to evaluate the technical claims made by the industry. In addition, proponents claimed, the way in which cars are sold enables manufacturers and dealers to steer car buyers away from certain options and toward others, presenting what is "on the lot" as the only practical sale.[21]

At the center of the opposition to the air bag stood auto industry executives, who, with few exceptions, consistently opposed the standard, spending more

[20] Claybrook, p. 168.

[21] For evidence, gathered ten years apart, that purchase of air bags was actively discouraged, see Albert Karr, "Saga of the Air Bag, or the Slow Deflation of a Car Safety Idea," *Wall Street Journal* (November 11, 1976), p. 1; Albert Karr and Laurie McGinley, "Auto Shoppers Encounter Stiff Resistance When Seeking Air Bags at Ford Dealers," *Wall Street Journal* (July 31, 1986), p. 27.

energy on it than on any other regulatory proposal. At various times, industry officials argued that this feature was unnecessary, too expensive, and impractical. When the automakers encountered economic hardship in the early 1980s, the arguments marshalled to oppose the standard shifted to its cost.[22] Before examining the attempted rollback, it is first necessary to briefly review the history of rulemaking on the air bag prior to the 1980s to explain how the standard arrived on the Reagan agenda.

In 1969, after it became apparent that manual seat belt usage was low, NHTSA's forerunner announced its intention to issue a passive restraint standard.[23] At that time, a passive restraint requirement could be met only with air bags since no other technology was available.[24] (While the political controversy over the air bag began in the 1970s, industry research began in the 1950s and a number of patents were granted at that time.[25]) In the early 1970s, when NHTSA moved ahead with the standard, industry officials turned to the White House for help. Henry Ford II and Lee Iacocca, then President of Ford, met with President Nixon and convinced him to intervene with agency officials. In a confidential memo, John Ehrlichman, Nixon's chief domestic policy advisor, relayed the president's order, and the air bag was subsequently delayed for two years.[26]

---

[22] David Bollier and Joan Claybrook, *Freedom from Harm: The Civilizing Influence of Health, Safety and Environmental Regulation* (Washington/New York: Public Citizen/ Democracy Project, 1986), p. 81.

[23] For a detailed history of air bag politics from the pluralist perspective, see John Graham, *Auto Safety: Assessing America's Performance* (Dover: Auburn House, 1989).

[24] In 1971 the automatic seat belt was recognized by NHTSA as also meeting the standard, and in 1974 detachable automatic seat belts were approved. At first the detachable belts were coupled with an ignition interlock device, but public opposition led Congress to repeal the use of the ignition interlock. NHTSA continued to allow detachable seat belts as an option for compliance by the automakers. It was this option that became central to the legal battle over the rollback that was decided by the Supreme Court. While the proposed passive restraint standard could be met with passive belts, the debate over the standard was largely framed as if the regulation focused on the air bag alone.

[25] See Mark Green and Norman Waitzman, *Business War on the Law,* rev. 2nd ed. (Washington: Corporate Accountability Research Group, 1981), p. 134; U.S. Congress, Senate, Committee on Commerce, Science, and Transportation, *Motor Vehicle Safety and the Marketplace. Hearings before the Subcommittee on Surface Transportation,* 98th Cong., 2d sess. (February–March 1983), Serial No. 98–16, p. 198.

[26] See U.S. Congress, House, Committee on Interstate and Foreign Commerce, *Federal Regulation and Regulatory Reform. Report by the Subcommittee on Oversight and Investigation,* 94th Cong., 2d sess. (October 1976), p. 188; Greg Mitchell, "Iacocca's Untold Story: Puncturing the Air-Bag Rule," *The Nation* (February 16, 1985), p. 171; Helen Kahn, "Tape Tells of Ford Pitch to Nixon," *Automotive News* (December 6, 1982), p. 6.

Industry officials also turned to the federal courts to stop the air bag, challenging NHTSA's authority to issue a standard that could not be met with existing technology.[27] Ruling against the challenge except on one technical count, the Court of Appeals remanded the standard to NHTSA for further tests. Although the industry won a temporary reprieve, it lost the larger issue of NHTSA's authority to issue technology-forcing regulation. Throughout this period, the battle against the air bag was waged on Capitol Hill as well. Although there were some symbolic victories, industry officials were unsuccessful in achieving a permanent legislative ban on the standard. As a result, NHTSA was about to recommend a new standard in December 1976, but outgoing Ford administration Transportation Secretary William Coleman decided instead to implement a demonstration program.[28] However, Coleman's substitute plan never took effect because the incoming Carter administration issued a final passive restraint standard in July 1977, with compliance slated to begin in 1981.[29]

In late 1980, however, with the industry's economic fortunes plummeting, industry officials made what, at the time, they thought was their last effort to delay the standard when they sought a one-year extension from Congress. President Carter and Transportation Secretary Neil Goldschmidt supported the extension, but a conference committee report that would have granted the extension failed to pass the House.[30] The standard, described by one observer as "one of the most extensively reviewed standards ever promulgated by the federal government," was intact and scheduled for implementation.[31] However, once in office, the Reagan administration moved quickly to stop it. One of the first actions by the new transportation secretary, Drew Lewis, just three weeks after the inauguration, was to grant a one-year delay for compliance and to reopen the entire issue of the standard itself.[32]

By the fall of 1981, Raymond Peck, the newly appointed head of NHTSA, announced its rescission.[33] He argued that his ruling was based on the "uncertainty" of public acceptance of detachable automatic seat belts, which Peck assumed would be the technology that the automakers would choose in complying with the standard. Because of this uncertainty, Peck argued, usage would not increase over that of traditional manual belts. Consequently, they

[27] *Chrysler v. Department of Transportation,* 472 F.2d. 659 (1972).

[28] 42 FR 5,071 (1977).   [29] 42 FR 15,935 (1977).

[30] Judy Sarasohn, "Congress Declines to Let Automakers Off the Hook in Meeting Safety Standards," *Congressional Quarterly Weekly Report* (December 27, 1980), p. 3676; "NHTSA Agreement Is Stalled When Members Bog Down in Air Bag, Bumper Dispute," *Congressional Quarterly Weekly Report* (October 4, 1980), p. 2907.

[31] Carl Nash, "Passive Restraints: A Regulator's View," in Robert Crandall and Lester Lave, eds., *The Scientific Basis of Health and Safety Regulation* (Washington: Brookings Institution, 1981), p. 60.

[32] 46 FR 21,172 (1981).   [33] 46 FR 53,419 (1981).

would be of little or no benefit. In announcing the decision at a press con-ference, paradoxically, Peck added that "It is time to stop the uncertainty about this standard. It is only by rescinding the standard and proceeding with . . . 'a full court press' on technology, that we will be able to make material, substan-tial impact on reducing death on the highway."[34] Peck admitted that his deci-sion was made over the objections of the agency's staff.[35]

The public reaction was swift. Insurance companies took the lead by challenging the rescission in court. A year later, the Federal Court of Appeals rebuffed the administration, ruling that the rollback was arbitrary, capricious, and an abuse of authority. The court found that there was no supporting evi-dence for Peck's contention that detachable automatic seat belts would be of no benefit. Simple logic indicated that many drivers and passengers would leave the detachable belt in place. More important, however, the court rejected the premise that detachable belts were passive restraints in the first place: "Essen-tially, the agency seems to conclude that because some technology will *not* meet the passive restraint standard, it need not mandate compliance by technol-ogy that will. The absurdity of this Orwellian reasoning is obvious."[36]

Industry officials appealed the decision to the Supreme Court, which in turn rebuked the administration and the industry. The Court, following the lead of the Federal Court of Appeals, unanimously ruled that the rollback decision was arbitrary, capricious, and without any rational basis or explanation. The Court argued that if detachable belts did not increase usage, this would only justify amending the requirement to disallow compliance through this particular tech-nology. As for the air bag itself, the Court ruled: "The agency has no basis at this time for changing its earlier conclusions in 1976 and 1977 that basic air bag technology is sound and has been sufficiently demonstrated to be effective in those vehicles in current use. . . ."[37] In overruling NHTSA's action, the Supreme Court also directly criticized the auto industry and its fight against the standard:

The automobile industry has opted for the passive belt over the air bag, but surely it is not enough that the regulated industry has eschewed a given safety device. For nearly a decade, the automobile industry has waged the regulatory equivalent of war against the air bag and lost – the inflatable restraint was proven sufficiently effective. Now the automobile industry has decided to employ a seatbelt system which will not meet the safety objectives of Standard 208. This hardly constitutes cause to revoke the standard itself. Indeed, the Motor Vehicle Safety Act was necessary because the industry was not sufficiently responsive to safety concerns.[38]

---

[34] Cited in Claybrook, p. 169.
[35] Cited in John Graham and Patricia Gorham, "NHTSA and Passive Restraints," *Admin-istrative Law Review* Vol. 35, No. 2 (Spring 1983), p. 222.
[36] *State Farm Mutual v. Department of Transportation,* 680 F.2d. 206, 234.
[37] *Motor Vechicles Manufacturers Association v. State Farm,* 463 U.S. 29, 46.

The passive restraint standard was not reinstated, however. Instead, the Court remanded the decision back to NHTSA, ruling that the agency could change its view of the usefulness of air bags, but the decision would have to be based on a reasoned analysis, thereby inviting another round of rulemaking. In 1984, with a new transportation secretary, Elizabeth Dole, and a new head of NHTSA, Diane Steed, a passive restraint requirement was issued for all cars beginning in 1990, with a phase-in period beginning in 1987. A novel feature was added to the decision that further complicated an already complicated case: if a sufficient number of states legislated mandatory seat belt usage laws by 1987 so that two-thirds of the nation's population was covered, NHTSA would waive the air bag requirement.[39]

This action guaranteed more litigation, as well as an intensive industry lobbying effort directed at the states to pass the necessary legislation. The industry's subsequent lobbying effort illustrates the range of options available to large corporations. In addition to being able to spend more money than any other group involved in the issue, its effort included traditional one-on-one lobbying by high-profile industry executives and the creation of a new lobbying organization, as well as threats over plant location. To carry part of the burden of the industry's state-by-state effort, in 1985 industry officials established Traffic Safety Now, Inc. The *Washington Post* reported that the industry planned to spend $15 million annually for this campaign.[40] Part of this money was spent on grants to already existing state organizations involved in mandatory usage campaigns such as Connecticut's Safety Belt Coalition, which received $137,000.[41]

Other aspects of the campaign involved direct appeals to state officials by some of the industry's most visible personalities. For example, Lee Iacocca, a staunch opponent of the air bag for twenty years before his sudden change in the late 1980s, met with Illinois Governor James Rhodes at Chrysler headquarters in Michigan. Rhodes said that Iacocca made "a very strong pitch" for passage of a usage law and said that "it would forestall the mandatory use of air bags, which he claims are not all they are cracked up to be and which he also claims are virtually useless without using seat belts as well."[42] In addition to sending its own representatives to lobby Illinois legislators, Chrysler and GM hired a former Illinois secretary of state and a former majority leader of the state house to lobby its case. One Illinois legislator said: "the big heaters were all over this one. We had Chrysler, Ford, GM. We had banks they run their financing through. . . . I haven't seen a bill this heavily lobbied in a long

---

[38] *MVMA v. State Farm,* 463 U.S. 29, 47. [39] 49 FR 28,962 (1984).

[40] Warren Brown, "GM to Offer Air Bags," *Washington Post* (February 21, 1985), p. C9.

[41] Irvin Molotsky, "States Debate Laws on Seat Belt Use," *New York Times* (February 28, 1985), p. B5.

[42] Cited in Molotsky.

time."[43] To influence legislators in California, the most valuable state due to its size, the automakers flew several of them to Detroit to tour auto plants. None of these activities was unusual. However, GM also used a far more potent weapon. Opponents charged that GM told a number of state officials that their state would not be considered as a possible site for its new Saturn plant unless they passed a mandatory usage law. Of course, GM denied the charge. Yet, Sen. John Danforth (R-MO) insisted that Missouri legislators told him that they had received this threat.[44]

Twenty-six states passed mandatory usage laws that took effect by 1987, but the population requirement set by NHTSA was never met.[45] Even if this hurdle had been overcome, many of these laws did not meet NHTSA's minimum criteria such as a $25 fine. As a result, in March 1987, NHTSA made its final air bag ruling, but in doing so granted the car makers yet another delay, postponing compliance four years until September 1993.[46] In granting this delay, NHTSA allowed the industry to meet the standard during a phase-in period by using a driver-only air bag, with front seat passengers protected by a standard manual belt.[47] NHTSA believed that allowing for the driver-only provision would accelerate air bag installation. The decision split supporters of the air bag. Insurance groups approved of the decision, despite the limitation, because it seemed to signal an end to the seemingly endless air bag merry-go-round. Several public interest organizations criticized the ruling, including Public Citizen, led by Joan Claybrook.[48]

The effort to roll back the standard, although unsuccessful, was not a complete loss for Detroit. Following the pattern of clean air politics, a decade of delay resulted. With an elaborate process governing the promulgation of regulatory standards subject to judicial review, administration officials, acting on behalf of the auto industry, could not erase the technical findings that were in place supporting the standard. Although the industry's vigorous opposition to the air bag perplexed some observers, a *New York Times* editorial offered a simple explanation: air bags were effective. "American auto makers, always ready to underestimate consumer sophistication and ever resentful of interference by Government, oppose air bags because they would give regulation a good name."[49]

---

[43] Cited in Molotsky.   [44] Molotsky.

[45] See Reginald Stuart, "U.S. Aide Faults Laws on Seat Belts," *New York Times* (January 19, 1986), p. 16; "Auto Makers Granted Extension on Air Bag Rule," *New York Times* (March 26, 1987), p. A18.

[46] 52 FR 10,096 (1987).   [47] 52 FR 10,096 (1987).

[48] See Helen Kahn, "Makers Get 4-Year Delay on Passive Restraints," *Automotive News* (March 30, 1987), p. 58.

[49] "Don't Deflate Auto Safety," *New York Times* (September 23, 1981), p. A30.

Fuel Economy

Fuel economy is the final regulatory area examined. Unlike the two previous examples, the 1985 CAFE rollback was an unmitigated victory for Ford and GM. With large discretion over this policy area, the administration was in a position to satisfy the industry's two largest firms.

Well before the 1985 rollback, the Reagan administration scuttled rulemaking actions already underway for higher future CAFE standards before they could be completed.[50] Rolling back the existing standard was next on the agenda because – reversing themselves – both Ford and GM abruptly claimed that it was impossible to meet the 27.5 mpg requirement. (The 1975 fuel economy legislation allowed NHTSA to establish CAFE standards after 1985 and to roll back the standard to 26.0 mpg if necessary.[51]) In an era when public policy was subordinated to the expressed needs of the automakers, the Reagan administration needed little prodding to act. Since the rollback decision was entangled with trade policy – the import quotas on Japanese cars had the effect of boosting sales of domestic small cars, thereby raising CAFE for Detroit's automakers – it is necessary to describe the connections between these seemingly unrelated policy areas. (See Chapter 7 for a fuller discussion of trade policy during the Reagan administration.)

As a result of the dramatic rise in imports between 1979 and 1980, American automakers secured import protection from Japanese competition. When import quotas were imposed in 1981 through a Voluntary Restraint Agreement (VRA), the supply of small, efficient Japanese cars was limited and car buyers were, in effect, forced to turn to domestic manufacturers for smaller cars. As the sale of domestic small cars increased, the fleet fuel averages of domestic producers rose, allowing Ford and GM to continue selling older, less efficient, larger models. Selling older models was profitable for a variety of reasons, including larger price tags, an established market, and the ability to use already exiting tools and dies. With the end of the quotas in 1985, car buyers had more Japanese vehicles to choose from and many turned away from Detroit's offerings. As sales of domestic small cars decreased, balancing CAFE became a problem for Ford and GM. Neither automaker wasted any time in seeking a political solution to the problem. In fact, immediately after the VRA's an-

---

[50] 46 FR 22,243 (1981).

[51] At the same time that NHTSA considered the petition for a rollback, EPA announced CAFE adjustments to benefit the automakers due to a change in fuel economy testing procedures. The retroactive adjustment might have saved the automakers up to $500 million in potential fines. The Center for Auto Safety filed a suit charging that the EPA had used a back-door approach to relax CAFE. In 1986, the Federal Court of Appeals in the District of Columbia overturned the EPA formula and ordered adjustments in fines that cost the automakers $300 million. See *Center for Auto Safety v. Lee Thomas,* 806 F.2d. 1071 (1986).

nounced end, Ford and GM, on the same day, petitioned NHTSA for a rollback of the standard. Yet, the day before the end of the VRA, Ford only urged NHTSA not to consider higher CAFE standards; it did not ask for a rollback.[52]

The need for a rollback, according to Ford and GM, was due to the unacceptable choice each company faced. They could continue selling larger cars, and pay the inevitable penalty that would accrue for failing to meet the standard, or they could restrict sales of their larger cars to bring their CAFE average within the standard. (The penalty for a firm's fleet not meeting the standard was $5 for each one-tenth of a mile multiplied by the total number of cars sold.) Ford and GM claimed that restricting sales of larger cars was their only real choice, and this would entail plant shutdowns and massive layoffs. To do otherwise would "violate the law," something neither automaker said it would consider. Chrysler, along with others, argued that the talk of plant shutdowns was merely a form of pressure used by the two firms to change the standard. Despite protests to the contrary, Chrysler contended, there was simply too much money to be made selling large cars, even with the fines. Nevertheless, in a replay of the emissions battles of the mid-1970s, the two automakers were able to shift the debate over fuel economy policy to the issue of the economic consequences of layoffs.

Chrysler had opposed the rollback all along, joining forces with public interest and environmental groups. This unusual alliance resulted from the fact that Chrysler could meet the standard. As part of its reorganization after the federal bailout, Chrysler modernized its fleet to sell more efficient vehicles. Because the standard was ten years old, Chrysler felt that a rollback was tantamount to changing the rules in mid-game. For Chrysler, the issue was not whether Ford or GM was capable of meeting the 27.5 mpg standard, but whether these companies did everything possible to comply. And the answer was no. In fact, neither Ford nor GM took corrective action after 1983 when each firm predicted that it would be unable to meet the standard. In fact, each had made product decisions lowering CAFE. Moreover, Chrysler added, threatened plant closings were not part of NHTSA's rule-making responsibility. Indeed, the law prescribed only civil penalties for noncompliance.

GM's potential fine was approximately $400 million, and Ford's was approximately $80 million. Yet, these figures were insignificant in comparison to the profits each company earned on large cars. Although hardly neutral in this debate, Chrysler estimated that GM earned about $8 billion in profits from its large cars, and Ford earned $3 billion. When the fines were viewed as an investment, Chrysler officials suggested, GM's return was approximately

---

[52] Helen Kahn, "More Makers Seek CAFE Relief," *Automotive News* (March 11, 1985), p. 11.

2,000 percent; Ford's return was even higher, 3,800 percent.[53] In any case, the projected economic consequences of layoffs made by the Commerce Department were significant. Analysts estimated that retention of the 27.5 mpg standard, given the expected curtailment of large car sales, would cost 80,000 to 110,000 jobs. Projected sales losses were 750,000 to 1,000,000 units.[54]

Canceling production was not the only economic threat made. Ford, for instance, said it was considering shifting a significant portion of its production – more than 25 percent – of its largest cars to Mexico. (Cars with 25 percent or more foreign content are counted separately for CAFE purposes from domestically produced vehicles.) Consequently, Ford's domestic CAFE average would increase, as these less efficient vehicles would no longer be factored in with its other domestic models.[55] (In 1989 Ford announced its plans to do just this.[56]) It was by no means clear whether CAFE could be blamed for costing domestic jobs, even in light of this effort to take advantage of a loophole in the law. Clarence Ditlow, for example, suggested that CAFE standards helped retain smaller-car production in the United States, and thus jobs, because such vehicles were needed to balance the fuel economy averages of domestically produced larger cars.

By making layoff threats, Ford and GM took advantage of a form of political pressure available only to large corporations. For the Reagan NHTSA, already opposed to CAFE on ideological grounds as an inappropriate interference with the market, the choice was obvious: roll back the standard. To justify the rollback, NHTSA argued that due to the decline in oil prices, market demand for fuel-efficient cars had diminished. Yet, the automakers' inability to meet the standard was not something that resulted from a sudden change in market forces. Given the long lead times that characterize product planning, lower CAFE was fully anticipated by NHTSA for at least two years. In fact, the agency admitted, both Ford and GM had acknowledged two years earlier that they would not be able to meet the standard.[57] However, neither petitioned the agency for a rollback at that time. And two years before that, in 1981, NHTSA had assumed that the automakers would achieve *their* announced goal of 30 mpg by 1985.[58] Ford and GM forced a showdown by petitioning for a rollback

[53]   U.S. Congress, Senate, Committee on Energy and Natural Resources, *Automobile Fuel Economy Standards. Hearings before the Subcommittee on Energy Regulation and Conservation,* 99th Cong., 1st sess. (May 14, 1985), Senate Hearing 99–138, p. 74. Hereafter referred to as Auto Fuel Economy Hearings.

[54]   Auto Fuel Economy Hearings, p. 264.

[55]   Helen Kahn, "Ford Faces Tough Road on CAFE," *Automotive News* (August 19, 1985), p. 2; Richard Johnson, "Big Ford's May Become 'Imports' to Meet CAFE," *Automotive News* (September 2, 1985), p. 1.

[56]   Doron Levin, "Ford to Buy Foreign Parts for Big Cars," *New York Times* (June 20, 1989), p. D1.

[57]   50 FR 40,528 (1985).   [58]   46 FR 8056 (1981).

in March 1985, just months before the beginning of the new model year, when it was impossible to modify product design.

For NHTSA a central question in settling the rollback issue was whether appropriate steps for compliance had been followed. The agency believed Ford and GM intended to comply, but the drop in gasoline prices, which diminished market demand for more efficient cars, prevented implementation of their respective product plans. Consequently, NHTSA accepted the claims made by Ford and GM that the only way they could now meet the standard was by restricting sales. The basic cause of Ford's and GM's failure to meet CAFE standards, the agency reasoned, was product plan changes made between 1980 and 1985.[59,60]

NHTSA was also forced to reinterpret the statutory criterion of "economic practicality" that guides the promulgation of CAFE. Four factors were required to be considered in making CAFE decisions: economic practicality, technological feasibility, the effect of other motor vehicle standards on fuel economy, and the need to conserve energy. In evaluating these factors, NHTSA was obligated to consider the condition of the entire industry, not simply the situation of a single manufacturer that might have the most difficulty. With the agency prevented from basing its decision on the least capable manufacturer, NHTSA claimed that it was basing its decision on the industry's "collective inability" to meet the standards. However, Chrysler had argued all along that it was living proof that the standards were both technically feasible and economically practical. Getting around this hurdle required the agency to define the "industry's capability" as Ford's and GM's ability due to their dominating share of sales – more than 60 percent. This definition had the effect of delegating fuel economy policy to the marketing strategy of these two firms. Chrysler officials pointed this out, noting that in the spring of 1985, while Ford and GM insisted that consumer demand had shifted toward larger cars, both firms were running advertising campaigns announcing reduced financing for their largest cars – Lincoln Continental, Continental Mark VII, Cadillac Eldorado, and

---

[59]   50 FR 40,528 (1985).

[60]   The difference between the 1980 Ford plan and its actual 1985 CAFE was explained by the agency as resulting from Ford's continued sale of large cars and station wagons (which comprised 20 percent of its sales mix) instead of their complete elimination; delay in introducing new front wheel drive models; continued use of significant numbers of V-8 engines instead of their elimination; lower than expected diesel sales; and lower than expected sales of more fuel-efficient cars.

GM's failure was attributed to five factors: a substantial drop in diesel sales; no new introduction of a subcompact economy or electric car; slowdown in the rate of replacing existing cars with lighter-weight front wheel drive models; a sales shift toward larger models and engines; and continuation of several existing lines. Overall, GM's 1985 cars weighed 360 pounds more than anticipated in 1980. As a result of these failures, GM's 1985 CAFE was 25.5 mpg, compared to its 1980 prediction of 30 mpg.

Seville – in order to increase their sales.[61] *Automotive News* also noted the duplicity of corporate officials who contended that the public wanted big cars while offering financial incentives to boost sales.[62]

Subordinating CAFE policy to the marketing plans of Ford and GM stood the law on its head. Mandatory fuel economy standards were established to lead, not to follow, the market in order to lessen the consumption of gasoline. The Reagan administration, however, ignored this intent. It maintained that price alone should be allowed to shape the demand for gasoline. William Silvey, deputy assistant secretary for policy, planning and analysis of the Department of Energy, stressed at the time: "In a free economy, the best way to determine the appropriate price for conserving energy is to allow that choice to be made by individual consumers operating under market price signals." Diane Steed, head of NHTSA, reiterated this point: "It is the administration's position that market forces, rather than CAFE standards, are the most efficient means of achieving appropriate levels of fuel economy in the long run."[63]

The entire debate over the likelihood of plant shutdowns ignored the fact that the law explicitly acknowledged the acceptability of noncompliance, providing for fines in that event. Testifying before a Senate subcommittee, Chrysler officials insisted: "The language and the history of the Act and the administrative practice under it make clear that a manufacturer has the option of paying the penalties and continuing to sell a noncomplying mix of vehicles."[64] In fact, during the 1975 debate over the Environmental Policy and Conservation Act, an amendment permitting the U.S. attorney general to seek a court order barring a manufacturer from selling a noncomplying mix of vehicles was rejected.[65] The only sanction the law provided was the payment of civil fines. Congress declared noncompliance illegal in attempting to reconcile two competing objectives: increasing fuel economy and protecting employment. It wanted to force car makers to increase CAFE, but not at the price of a substantial adverse economic impact. Moreover, in two other instances, according to Chrysler, NHTSA "did not entertain the slightest doubt that a manufacturer would elect to pay the penalties and go on selling a noncomplying mix of vehicles."[66]

In its rollback decision, NHTSA also pointed to the fuel economy improvements made during the past ten years, which it believed rendered higher standards unnecessary. "Overall, the nation is much more energy independent than

---

[61] Auto Fuel Economy Hearings, p. 73.
[62] "Mileage and Marketing," *Automotive News* (July 8, 1985), p. 10.
[63] Auto Fuel Economy Hearings, pp. 21, 23.
[64] Auto Fuel Economy Hearings, p. 93.
[65] U.S. *Congressional Record,* 121 H 5381 (daily edition) (June 12, 1975).
[66] Auto Fuel Economy Hearings, p. 95.

it was a decade ago. . . ."[67] Supporting this claim were the following statistics: from 1975 to 1984 energy efficiency in the economy improved by 21 percent; passenger car petroleum use dropped below 1975 levels, although travel was up 25 percent; domestic oil production increased and total imports dropped 20 percent since 1975; the value of the nation's imported oil bill had decreased 40 percent in the previous five years; the amount of imported oil from Organization of Petroleum Exporting Countries (OPEC) had dropped by 67 percent since its 1977 peak; and as a percentage of the gross nation product, the net oil import bill had decreased from 2.8 percent in 1980 to 1.5 percent in 1984. Yet, NHTSA acknowledged that domestic production was expected to decline from 10 million barrels a day (MMB/D) to 8.5 MMB/D by 1995. At the same time, the agency mentioned that a number of energy analysts predicted that net imports were expected to rise from 4.5–5 MMB/D to 7.5–9 MMB/D by 1995 and approach 50 percent of U.S. petroleum use. Dismissing these estimates, NHTSA asserted that future energy projections were difficult to assess and could be overtaken by new domestic discoveries.

For model years 1986, 1987, and 1988 the Reagan administration rolled back the 27.5 mpg standard to 26.0. For 1989 the standard was rolled back to 26.5 mpg. Yet, despite maintaining that the lower standard was all that the two automakers could reach without product restrictions, Ford and GM exceeded the lowered standard each year and earned credits for future years.[68] The administration's opposition to CAFE did not end with these rollbacks. Legislation was proposed to eliminate CAFE standards altogether. Each time, however, these proposals received limited attention and were never seriously considered.

The rollback of CAFE was a high point of the industry's ability to subordinate regulatory policy to its interests. Detroit had long felt that CAFE standards were onerous because, unlike most safety or emissions standards, which can be met through the addition of particular devices, improving fuel consumption requires the redesign of various aspects of a vehicle.

Assessing the Reagan Plan

The overall contribution of the Reagan plan to the industry's subsequent economic turnaround in the mid-1980s was evaluated by a range of parties. Clarence Ditlow, for example, contended that regulatory changes had virtually no impact on the turnaround.[69] Within the industry, officials wel-

---

[67] 50 FR 40,544 (1985).

[68] U.S. Senate, Committee on Commerce, Science, and Transportation, *Motor Vehicle Fuel Efficiency Act. Report on S.279,* 102d Cong., 1st. sess. Report 102–48, (April 1991), p. 2.

[69] Interview with author, September 26, 1986, Washington, D.C.

comed the new regulatory climate, but could provide little evidence that the plan's savings were significant given the billions of dollars that the automakers needed for modernization, some $60 billion between 1983 and 1988.[70] Robert Leone, a staff member of the Reagan Council of Economic Advisors during the time when the plan to aid the industry was developed, and a Harvard economist when he analyzed the results, also argued that the industry's turnaround could not be attributed to the Reagan plan. "The turnaround," Leone concluded, "resulted mainly from improved productivity and actions by auto industry management to create lower breakeven levels of production in U.S. manufacturing facilities."[71] By March 1983, for example, the U.S. automakers produced the same number of cars as in April 1980 but with 70,000 fewer workers.[72] Nevertheless, Leone argued, the Reagan program did provide some help to the industry. He attributed $1.13 billion of the industry's $7.3 billion increase in income between 1980 and 1983 to the Reagan deregulation effort. Further, Leone suggested that if one assumes that the industry was able to retain 100 percent of the savings the administration claimed would go to consumers, an additional $1.44 billion of industry income could be attributed to the deregulation effort.[73] Yet, Leone's assumptions in calculating the benefits of the rollbacks are, as he himself admitted, "very generous." He assumed, for example, that the industry realized all the savings estimated by the Reagan administration when the plan was announced. "In sum," Leone wrote, "the probusiness sentiments of the Reagan administration have not greatly benefitted the U.S. auto industry."[74]

Leone's speculations concerning the limited economic benefits of the Reagan plan were not surprising. Despite industry claims that its problems stemmed from excessive government regulation, few independent observers agreed. In fact, the ITC ruled in November 1980 that the major cause of the industry's downturn was the recession. Furthermore, changes in regulatory standards affect all car makers, not just domestic producers. If anything, federal regulations may have marginally helped the domestic industry in its battle against imports. Unlike foreign competitors, American automakers can spread the costs of regulation across more vehicles, thereby lowering the unit cost of compliance. Even if these policy changes did help somewhat, they hardly did so as the administration had initially claimed. Neither the sales nor the employment growth forecasted by the administration's analysts came true. In 1983, unemployment among autoworkers was over 300,000 greater than forecast, and sales were 3 million less than predicted.

---

[70] Wines, p. 1532.   [71] Leone, p. 95.
[72] Leone, p. 94.   [73] Leone, pp. 94–5.
[74] Leone, p. 105.

Conclusion

Triumphant industry power characterized regulatory policy during this period. The industry was able to achieve political victories that far exceeded what it had been able to accomplish during the previous period of bargaining and compromise. With its power triumphant, almost no battle previously lost could not be reopened. Once reopened, most were won by the industry. In fact, NHTSA's decisions were so in line with Detroit's interests that Joan Claybrook charged that it "was a wholly owned subsidiary" of the industry.[75] While industry officials were able to obtain almost all the proposed rollbacks, as the examples of the CAA and the air bag show, they were not in a position to obtain all that they wanted. Industry power over regulatory policy was constrained by the structures of bureaucratic policymaking already in place and by the increasing mobilization of environmental forces. Even at the height of its new position of power, its power was not unlimited.

To complete the examination of the politics of this era, a discussion of trade policy follows.

[75] U.S. Congress, House, Committee on Science and Technology, *Small Car Safety Technology. Hearings before the Subcommittee on Transportation, Aviation, and Materials, and the Subcommittee on Investigations and Oversight,* 97th Cong., 2d. sess. (November 30, December 3, 1982), p. 205.

7

The Triumph of Corporate Power: Trade Policy, 1981–1985

During the auto industry's early 1980s financial crisis, industry officials were not content with reversing regulatory standards. They also sought import protection from Japanese cars. Detroit's automakers realized that a new economic environment was taking shape, one that challenged their domination of the American market. At stake was billions of dollars in sales. In 1979, imports had reached a new high at 22.7 percent of the market, up from the previous high of 18.2. In 1980 that figure soared to 28.2 percent. To meet this challenge, Detroit looked to Washington for a political solution in the form of import quotas. As part of its 1981 plan to aid the industry, the Reagan administration granted these requests.

Meanwhile, autoworkers, bearing the brunt of the industry's downturn, sought a political solution to their problems as well. They lobbied for a domestic content law that would have required car manufacturers to proportionally increase the domestic content of cars sold in the United States with increasing sales. The proposal was intended to alter two trends hurting domestic employment: Japanese imports and domestic outsourcing. If Japanese imports were restricted, it was argued, Japanese manufacturers would be encouraged to open auto plants in the United States. At the same time, the law would restrain domestic manufacturers from outsourcing production – opening plants in other countries or buying parts from foreign-based suppliers.

Automotive trade policy during this period reflected the industry's triumphant position. Corporate officials would not have been in a position to obtain import restrictions without the industry's unprecedented downturn. However, import quotas did not result simply from the realization by government officials that the industry was in the midst of a financial crisis and needed help, or from industry lobbying, for that matter, although both factors were important. The unprecedented economic collapse of the automakers, along with rising imports, created a climate of crisis in which policymakers were forced to respond to the industry's demands. Reeling from international competition, mighty domestic firms, which had long dominated markets, were downsizing their operations. In this context, the automakers argued that trade protection would allow them to "catch up" to foreign manufacturers who, according to the Big Three, had suddenly transformed the car market – a replay of claims previously used by other industries such as steel.[1] For many policymakers, import quotas were a way to shore up America's declining manufacturing base. Even the concept of a declining manufacturing base was something that just a few years earlier had been unthinkable.

Import Quotas

International Trade Commission's Decision

To set the stage for the Reagan-negotiated import quotas, it is necessary to first examine the International Trade Commission's (ITC) December 1980 decision on the impact of Japanese imports on the industry's financial crisis. (The ITC, established in 1975 as the successor to the U.S. Tariff Commission, is a U.S. regulatory agency responsible for various aspects of U.S. trade law.) As industry economic losses mounted throughout 1980, imports were increasingly blamed for Detroit's troubles. In June, the UAW petitioned the ITC for trade relief as a domestic industry injured by imports. Ford quickly joined the petition. At issue was whether Japanese imports were the "substantial cause of serious harm to the industry," the prerequisite for pursuing trade relief of this type. If the ITC found this to be the case, it could issue recommendations for trade relief to the president, who could then decide whether or not to follow these recommendations.

Before the commission could measure the impact of imports on the domestic automakers, it first had to decide which domestic market segment should be compared with Japanese cars. Although seemingly innocuous, the outcome of the commission's decision would hinge on this issue. The UAW–Ford petition argued that large and small cars should be separated into two separate "markets." If the commission had accepted this definition, it would have had the effect of magnifying the impact of Japanese imports on the American car market because of the overwhelming preponderance of small cars produced by Japanese manufacturers. Writing for the commission's majority (3–2), ITC Chairman Bill Alberger rejected this suggestion, asserting that there was no legitimate reason to segment passenger automobiles into different markets; for commercial purposes, he argued, they were roughly equivalent. Even domestic producers, he noted, had claimed that there was a consumer shift from large to

---

[1] For an analysis of the steel industry, see William Scheuerman, *The Steel Crisis: The Economics and Politics of a Declining Industry* (New York: Praeger Publishers, 1986).

small cars, an indication of the fluidity within the car market. Accordingly, Alberger concluded that the passenger car market might be heterogeneous but it was still a single market, allowing for an overall comparison of imports and domestics, despite the difference in the average size of each.

Once this issue was settled, the commission had to determine if the industry was suffering serious financial injury. U.S. trade law required the commission to take into account all economic factors that it considered relevant to this question, including "the significant idling of productive facilities in the industry, the inability of a significant number of firms to operate at a reasonable level of profit, and significant unemployment or underemployment within the industry."[2] To this list the commission added declining domestic sales and increasing inventories. Unquestionably, according to the ITC, the American passenger car industry was suffering serious losses. However, the decline in sales among domestic manufacturers was almost entirely due to the drop in large-car sales. Because domestic producers concentrated on producing large cars, this decline was devastating and rather sudden.[3] Despite the industry's distress, the ITC ruled that increased imports were not the substantial cause of such injury, when "substantial cause" is defined as "a cause which is important and not less than any other cause."[4] A far greater cause of the industry's plight, the commission argued, was the general recession of the economy. The rapid shift to smaller cars was still another but less important factor.

Central to the ITC's reasoning was the apparent lack of correlation between the growth in import volume and the losses suffered by domestic producers. From 1976 to 1978, domestic sales were strong and the industry earned record profits. (In 1976 domestic producers sold 8.6 million cars; in 1977, 9.1 million; and in 1978, 9.3 million.) Yet, during this time, imports increased, from 2 million units in 1975 to 2.9 million in 1978, or by 43 percent. In 1979, on the other hand, imports actually declined by 4 percent. However, between January

---

[2] Cited in U.S. International Trade Commission, "Certain Motor Vehicles and Certain Chassis and Bodies Thereof," Report to the President on Investigation TA-201–44 Under Section 201 of the Trade Act of 1974, USITC Publication 1110, (December 3, 1980), p. 16. Hereafter referred to as ITC Decision.

[3] The sudden nature of the industry's decline, the commission pointed out, could be seen in the drop in a number of indicators: utilization of domestic capacity, net operating profits, cash flow, and employment. Utilization of domestic capacity had peaked in 1978 at 86.2 percent but declined to 79.5 percent by 1979. During January–June 1980 it fell to 66.5 percent. Net operating profits from domestic operations from 1978 to 1979 fell by 76 percent, from $5.6 billion to $1.3 billion, and continued to fall; net losses in January–June 1980 were $2.9 billion. Cash flow substantially dropped for the domestic automakers, declining from $8.9 billion in 1978 to $5.1 billion in 1979 to a negative $356 million in January–June 1980. Employment also dropped, from 1,003,430 in 1978 to 971,929 in 1979. The first six months of 1980 saw another 22 percent drop.

[4] P. L. 93–618, Trade Act of 1974, Section 201(b)(4).

and June 1980, Japanese imports increased by 200,000 units over the same period from the previous year, although imports from other countries declined. Considering the robust domestic sales before 1979 at the same time that imports increased, the industry's problems could not be pinned on imports. They were explained by an overall drop in sales: between 1978 and 1979 sales slipped by 1 million units and continued to decline during the first half of 1980 by 1.1 million units compared to the same period in 1979, a drop of 18.5 percent. Alberger pointed out that the market share of imports had grown by maintaining a constant or slightly increasing volume in the face of falling overall demand. Accordingly, the downturn in overall demand was an independent factor that had to be analyzed separately to account for its effects on the decline in demand of domestically produced cars.

To assess separately the impact of general recessionary conditions and the increasing market share of imports, the ITC compared the actual decline in domestic sales to the decline that would have occurred if imports had not increased their market share in 1979–80 – in other words, if imports and domestic vehicles had equally shared the overall decline in sales. The ITC concluded that declining demand accounted for over 80 percent of the net decline in U.S. producers' sales, while less than 20 percent of the decline was due to increasing imports. Meanwhile, between January and June 1979 and January and June 1980, about two-thirds of the decline in domestic producers' sales was attributable to declining demand and only one-third to the increased share of imports.

In ruling against the petition, the ITC found only that imports were increasing and were competing directly with domestic products. Therefore, the commission rejected the claim that imports were the substantial cause of serious harm and did not recommend import restrictions on Japanese cars. The commission's minority disagreed and based their dissent on a different method of comparing the effects of imports to the other causes of the industry's problems. They subscribed to the UAW–Ford position that it was necessary to separate the various economic factors causing declining demand. The ITC, the dissenters argued, should not have compared the impact of import sales to the effects of the general economic recession. Instead it should have compared the effect of imports on the domestic industry to each of the component parts of recession: unemployment, high interest rates, and higher energy costs, for example. When compared to the consequences of each of these factors separately, imports were the most significant cause of harm. For the majority, however, these individual factors were all interrelated elements of general recessionary conditions; with an economic recovery, they would all dissipate.

With a negative ITC ruling, President Carter assumed there were no legal grounds to pursue import relief. And without an affirmative ruling, the Justice Department contended that implementing import restrictions would violate antitrust law.[5] The forces of protectionism had to look elsewhere. Attention shifted to Congress and the incoming Reagan administration.

Congressional Responses

Prior to the ITC decision, members of Congress sensitive to the industry's financial slide introduced resolutions in both the House and Senate authorizing the president to negotiate a limit on Japanese cars and to immunize agreeing parties from antitrust liability.[6] At first, these resolutions received little attention. After the ITC's ruling, the House moved quickly and passed (317–57) a resolution calling for a limit on imports. After a threatened filibuster prevented the Senate from voting on the resolution, the 96th Congress adjourned, sinking the effort for the time being.

Concern over auto trade escalated as the 97th Congress convened in January 1981. Industry supporters in both houses introduced a number of new resolutions. However, these were almost immediately overshadowed by efforts to legislate quotas. Sen. John Danforth (R-MO), chairman of the Subcommittee on International Trade of the Senate Finance Committee, introduced a bill to limit annual Japanese imports to 1.6 million cars. Danforth, a leading advocate of trade protection for the industry, explained his support for import restrictions in terms that were to become a repeated refrain: "As much as I believe in free trade, I also believe automobile import restrictions are necessary for the health of this basic American industry."[7] Danforth's interest in the auto industry was easily explained: Missouri was the second leading car-producing state in the nation at the time.

Meanwhile, the economic condition of the industry appeared perilous. In mid-February, Ford announced its 1980 loss of $1.54 billion, the largest loss for a single corporation in American history. A few days later, this record was surpassed when Chrysler announced its $1.71 billion loss. Support for restricting Japanese imports grew quickly and included Chrysler, Ford, and the UAW, as well as the domestic parts industry. GM was less firm in endorsing these proposals, largely because nearly 85 percent of its sales involved large cars and therefore would be less affected by restricting Japanese imports.

---

[5] George Schwartz, "Auto Import Quotas: A Case Study in Protectionism," *Business and Society Review* no. 39 (Fall 1981), p. 65.

[6] Michael Lochman, "The Japanese Voluntary Restraint on Automobile Exports: An Abandonment of Free Trade Principles of the GATT and the Free Market Principles of the United States Antitrust Laws," *Harvard International Law Journal* vol. 27, no. 1 (Winter 1986), p. 103.

[7] U.S. Congress, Senate, Committee on Finance, *Issues Relating to the Domestic Auto Industry. Hearings before the Subcommittee on International Trade,* 97th Cong., 1st sess. (March 9, 1981), Part 2, p. 5. Hereafter referred to as Finance Committee hearings.

Some members of Congress saw the Danforth bill as necessary to send a clear signal to the Japanese and the Reagan administration that something had to be done about car imports. Sen. Lloyd Bensten (D-TX), a cosponsor of the bill, was one of them.

Without the hammer of [this bill] I am convinced there would be the real danger that the problem of automobiles would be treated as just another item on the platter of United States–Japanese trade issues. We would voice our concern and the Japanese would acknowledge there might be a problem. Then they would negotiate for as long as possible and give up as little as possible. By the time we had a joint communique the most important industry to our economy and our national security might be battered beyond repair, sacrificed on the altar of free trade.[8]

That the ITC had already ruled that imports were not the cause of the industry's problems was largely ignored. This misperception was nurtured by a sophisticated lobbying effort.

One notable aspect of this effort was the work of the Automotive Materials Industry Council of the United States (AMICUS), which represents 40,000 companies supplying the auto industry. The lobbying effort of AMICUS, developed by a Washington legal firm, involved the following components:

-prepare point of view articles signed by representatives of supplier industries for *Business Week, New York Times, Nations Business,* plus letters to the editor by supporting members of Congress;
-lobby members of Congress who have automotive supplier plants in their district and members of the Senate Finance Committee and House Ways and Means Committee;
-have AMICUS representatives seek to be interviewed by network newscasts – 60 Minutes, Good Morning America, Today Show;
-arrange discussions on the floor of the House and Senate where each supporting member gives a short speech;
-write speeches favoring the imposition of import curbs for inclusion in the Congressional Record by friendly members;
-secure meetings with syndicated columnists and editorial writers of leading papers and give information;
-ask supplier companies' political action committees to support candidates sympathetic to problems of domestic industry.[9]

These activities were coordinated with the appropriate unions.

One of the groups with the most to lose from import restrictions, the American International Automobile Dealers Association (AIADA), fought against restricting imports. AIADA's objections, made before the VRA's announcement, prefigured much of the debate that followed. They stressed several points: quotas would cost more jobs in the import industry than would be saved

---

[8] Finance Committee hearings, Part 2, p. 7.   [9] Schwartz, p. 68.

in the domestic industry; each job saved would cost $245,000 in higher prices
to consumers; the ITC's authority would be undermined, as would the credibility of its procedures; Congress would be subject to increased political pressure
from other industries for trade protection; efforts to seek more open foreign
markets would be hurt; and provisions of the General Agreement on Tariffs and
Trade (GATT) would probably be violated. In addition, AIADA emphasized
that the actual threat to the domestic industry was not that foreign manufacturers would displace American producers, but that American-based multinationals would produce cars abroad for sale in the United States.[10]

The Reagan Administration Responds

The import issue presented the newly elected Reagan administration
with a dilemma. Ostensibly dedicated to free trade, it faced a Congress that was
threatening to become protectionist and an industry clamoring for help. And
after the ITC ruling against import restraints, it appeared that Congress might
take matters into its own hands. However, the free trade agreements embodied
in GATT (a post–World War II centerpiece of international trade relations,
whose goal has been to reduce trade barriers), and American trade law, as well
as U.S. antitrust prohibitions, constrained the available options. The Reagan
administration looked for a way out of this thicket, one that would do several
things simultaneously: satisfy the industry, appease protectionist sentiment in
Congress, and yet appear to support free trade while steering clear of potential
legal entanglements. They turned to the Japanese to solve this problem by
having the Japanese themselves voluntarily limit exports to the United States.
Still, this solution did not avoid all of the legal obstacles confronting the
administration. Because of the negative ITC ruling, negotiating with the Japanese to restrain imports potentially violated antitrust law. To avoid this hazard,
the administration claimed that it never "negotiated" with Japan regarding
import restraints, labeling its contacts with the Japanese as "talks, briefings, or
discussions."[11] In any case, the United States made an offer the Japanese could
not refuse. Either the Japanese could impose import quotas and collect the
"scarcity rent" that inevitably results when prices rise due to limits in supply, or
they would face the possibility of congressionally mandated quotas, whereby
the United States would be in a position to sell import licenses to Japanese
firms.

Orchestrating the limits on Japanese imports while avoiding the appearance
of violating GATT and American antitrust law required a series of meetings
between American and Japanese officials, held during March and April in
Washington and Tokyo.[12] In May the Japanese announced a VRA limiting

---

[10] Finance Committee hearings, Part 1, p. 186.
[11] Lochman, p. 104. (footnotes omitted).
[12] For a brief summary of these discussions, see Lochman, pp. 104–5.

annual imports to 1.68 million cars. At the same time as it circumvented treaty obligations under GATT and American antitrust law, the VRA gave the industry what it wanted and avoided the precedent of congressionally mandated trade sanctions. It also allowed for "foreign sovereign act of state" claims to be used to protect Japanese manufacturers legally (discussed later).

The Japanese Ministry of International Trade and Industry (MITI) issued written directives to each automaker stating the maximum number of units it could export to the United States. The quotas were based on a percentage allocation of the respective market share averaged over the previous two years. To monitor compliance, each firm reported its exports to MITI. Initially lasting for three years, the VRA was extended for a fourth year in 1984, an election year in both the United States and Japan. Prudence dictated keeping it out of the headlines with a quiet renewal. However, the number of cars permitted under the quota was increased to 1.85 million. The unusual nature of this "voluntary" agreement was lampooned in a *New York Times* editorial, which observed that since the Reagan administration had volunteered to inform the Japanese of the poor condition of the U.S. auto industry and the Japanese had voluntarily agreed to restrict imports to the United States, "all that remains is for the American consumer to volunteer to pay a billion dollars more for all the cars they buy this year."[13]

Legal scholars debated the implications of the VRA, with three major areas of controversy: its relationship to GATT, the Trade Act of 1974, and American antitrust law. Donald deKieffer, general counsel to the United States trade representative, a participant in the meetings between U.S. and Japanese trade negotiators, later described the efforts that were made to ensure that the quotas would be safe from a legal challenge:

These meetings could best be characterized as technical consultations concerning the subtleties of antitrust law, and the vagaries of Japanese commercial statutes. Experts in both disciplines attempted to reconcile the two systems to provide for Japanese action which would constitute adequate "compulsion" to conclusively permit the foreign defense to be raised by the Japanese companies.[14]

The experts referred to were not staff attorneys of the federal government. They were lawyers representing the UAW and various Japanese and American auto industry trade groups, including manufacturers, dealers, and parts makers.[15]

Nevertheless, the legal status of the VRA remained in doubt. Some maintained that the VRA was a violation of GATT because it circumvented the Most

---

[13] "Mr. Reagan's Gift to Big Auto," *New York Times* (May 2, 1981), p. A22.

[14] Donald deKieffer, "Antitrust and the Japanese Auto Quotas," *Brooklyn Journal of International Law* vol. VIII, no. 1 (Winter 1982), p. 67.

[15] deKieffer, p. 65, fn.36.

Favored Nation principle, by which all trade benefits have to be granted to all nations that are parties to the agreement. Because the VRA restricted only Japanese cars to the United States, it gave other nations a relative advantage. Potentially, these other nations could import an unlimited number of Japanese cars and could export an unlimited number of cars to the United States. In essence, both Japan and the United States were excluded from an advantage or privilege given to other contracting parties.[16] Yet, the Japanese had no grounds to object under GATT because they had imposed the quotas on themselves, nor would other nations be in a position to object since they would lack the standing to bring a suit. Technically the United States could retaliate against Japan for violating GATT, but would not since it had requested the restraints in the first place.[17] The VRA also sidestepped provisions of GATT that allow for import restrictions when imports are a direct threat to a domestic industry, the so-called escape clause mechanism. The ITC had already ruled that the industry was not eligible for this kind of relief. Domestic procedures for complying with the escape clause were also circumvented. Congress had established these mechanisms, as part of the 1974 trade act, to end voluntary agreements that were not the result of independent fact finding – a role given to the ITC.

The final legal issue raised concerned American antitrust law. Because Japanese producers were limiting exports, it appeared that they had, in effect, conspired to restrain trade. Opponents of this view contended that the "act of state" doctrine and the "foreign sovereign compulsion defense" insulated the VRA from antitrust investigation. According to these doctrines, each sovereign state is bound to respect the independence of every other sovereign state. This bars the American courts from questioning the validity of acts by a recognized foreign state within its own territory, even if such acts violate international law or the foreign sovereign's own law.[18] Thus, the VRA, negotiated and implemented by MITI, protected Japanese car makers from antitrust prosecution since the Japanese car makers were compelled by an act of state.[19] At the same time, presumably the Reagan administration was protected from antitrust prosecution because it did not impose the quotas and insisted throughout that it did not negotiate with the Japanese.[20]

The complicated political maneuvering necessary to deliver trade protection to Detroit represented only one part of the VRA's significance for the politics

---

[16] Lochman, p. 117. [17] Lochman, p. 130.

[18] Richard Yao, "Japanese Car Quotas and Antitrust – A Reexamination," *New York University Journal of International Law and Politics* vol. 15, no. 3 (Summer 1983), p. 699.

[19] Lochman; Barbara Ann Sousa, "Regulating Japanese Automobile Imports: Some Implications of the Voluntary Quota System," *Boston College International and Comparative Law Review* vol. V, no. 2 (Summer 1982), p. 453.

[20] Yao.

of this period. The other part involved the economic consequences of the import quotas.

Economic Evaluations

Those who supported the quotas argued that they would give American car makers the opportunity to catch up with the Japanese; with less import competition, they would be better able to modernize their operations. Quotas were seen as a temporary measure facilitating the transition to a more competitive and modern domestic industry. With the profits that would accompany the VRA due to the inevitable increase in domestic sales, increased investment in plant and equipment was expected. However, the industry's investment decisions did not fulfill these expectations. In the years immediately following the initiation of the VRA, investment actually decreased. In fact, investment declined by a full 30 percent between 1981 and 1983. In contrast, between 1975–6 and 1979–80, real investment outlays increased by 88 percent. Meanwhile, investment in plant, equipment, and special tooling rose by more than 87 percent.[21] With the politically engineered abatement of competition, however, the domestic industry had less need to modernize its plants or product. Only after 1984 did investment exceed pre-VRA levels, when industry profits had rebounded to all-time record levels for two years running.

While investment did not increase, prices certainly did. Domestic producers, as well as importers, were quick to take advantage of the opportunity to raise prices. Virtually all independent analysts agreed that the American car buyer paid a steep "tax" to the auto industry as a result. One Wall Street auto analyst put it bluntly: "The American consumer is paying through the nose and getting rooked by the wise people in Detroit and Washington. Quotas don't hurt importers and they've driven up prices. Everyone is benefiting except the American consumer."[22] Estimates of the aggregate cost in higher prices resulting from the VRA varied widely, depending on the particular methodological assumptions used. One study suggested that by 1986 overall import restraints cost consumers $26 billion;[23] another study of four years of quotas put the figure at $15.7 billion[24]; yet another study, covering the first three years, put the figure at $2.5 billion.[25] A study that focused on 1984 alone saw the cost to

[21] Robert Crandall, "Import Quotas and the Automobile Industry: The Costs of Protectionism," *Brookings Review* vol. 2, no. 3 (Summer 1984), p. 12.
[22] David Healy, cited in Leslie Wayne, "The Irony and Impact of Auto Quotas," *New York Times* (April 8, 1984), Section 3, p. 1.
[23] Cited in Geoff Sundstrom, "Import Demand Seen Falling; Quotas Called Irrelevant," *Automotive News* (March 24, 1986), p. 6.
[24] U.S. International Trade Commission, cited in "Auto Quota Costs Weighed," *New York Times* (February 15, 1985), p. D3.
[25] Cited in Geoff Sundstrom, "Study Eyes First 3 Years of VRA," *Automotive News* (October 15, 1984), p. 41.

consumers as $13 billion,[26] while another put the 1984 figure at $5 billion.[27] These estimates translated into an extra cost of between $650 and $2,500 per car. Just as estimates varied for the total cost of the VRA, so did estimates of the number of jobs that were retained by the VRA, as well as the cost to consumers for each job saved. Four studies that tried to put a dollar figure on the cost of each job saved came up with widely different results: $90,000,[28] $160,000,[29] $240,000,[30]; and $520,000,[31] The magnitude of these costs was not totally unexpected. Before the VRA was formally announced, AIADA predicted that the cost of each job saved by the VRA would be $245,000.[32]

Needless to say, auto industry officials rejected the suggestion that they had taken advantage of import restrictions and inflated prices. They explained the rise in prices as the result of the "improved quality" of new cars. What they did not want to acknowledge was that it was easier to upgrade vehicles, and in so doing raise prices, while competition was artificially restrained. A comparison of the consumer price index (CPI) and the auto price index (API) suggests that the VRA did affect Detroit's ability to raise prices. Prior to the VRA (1976–80), the two stayed together, with the API slightly above the CPI, except for 1980, when U.S. car makers were exposed to accelerated Japanese competition. However, after 1981, the API annually exceeded the CPI at an increasing rate. See Table 2.

After four years of import quotas, the Reagan administration decided to allow the VRA to lapse. By this time, Detroit was earning record profits and the dismal days of its economic crisis seemed long gone. Yet, the Japanese decided against completely unrestrained exports to the United States. Instead, they allowed exports to rise to 2.3 million cars, a 24 percent increase. Even though demand for Japanese cars was high, Japanese officials were afraid that unrestrained increases in exports to the United States would aggravate trade relations and fuel protectionist pressures. As a result, the Japanese chose to proceed with moderation. At the same time, Japanese car manufacturers moved to open assembly plants in the United States to mitigate potential conflicts over imports that might arise in the future.

---

[26] U.S. Congress, House, Committee on Banking, Finance, and Urban Affairs, *Competitiveness of the U.S. Automobile Industry. Hearings before the Subcommittee on Economic Stabilization,* 99th Cong., 1st sess. (February 19, 1985), Serial No. 99–2, p. 28.

[27] Wharton Econometrics, cited in Wayne, p. 12.

[28] Cited in "The Auto Quota: We Asked for It . . . ," *New York Times* editorial (March 6, 1985), p. 22.

[29] Crandall, p. 16.

[30] Cited in Geoff Sundstrom, "Fate of VRA Still Up in the Air," *Automotive News* (February 25, 1985), p. 70.

[31] *Competitiveness of the U.S. Auto Industry,* p. 35.

[32] Finance Committee hearings, Part 1, p. 185.

Table 2. *CPI, API, and price of new cars ($), 1976–83*

	1976	1977	1978	1979	1980	1981	1982	1983
CPI	100	106	114	121	144	159	169	175
API	100	112	118	127	137	162	181	196
Average price	$5,470	$6,120	$6,470	$6,950	$7,530	$8,850	$9,910	$10,700

Source: U.S. Congress, House, Committee on Banking, Finance, and Urban Affairs, *Competitiveness of the U.S. Automobile Industry. Hearing before the Subcommittee on Economic Stabilization,* 99th Cong., 1st sess. (February 19, 1985), p. 31.

Conclusion

The import quotas on Japanese cars were formulated outside the normal boundaries of American trade policy to circumvent the legal guidelines of trade law and yet defuse protectionist sentiment in Congress. This move was spurred by the industry's financial collapse and the unprecedented situation of significant import competition. The American automobile makers, some of the largest corporations in the world, sought to be insulated from market forces. Because of the way policy changes were crafted, there were no guarantees that the industry would reinvest the profits resulting from import protection. There were expectations, of course, that this would occur, but they went unfulfilled.

Domestic Content Legislation

The temporary nature of the import quotas did not resolve the problem of outsourcing by the Big Three. Arguments invoking the same goal that the industry invoked in support of its agenda – a healthy domestic industry providing jobs – were employed by the UAW to attract widespread support of its proposal for a domestic content law. For the autoworkers, a healthy domestic industry was one that employed American workers. For the automakers, on the other hand, a healthy industry was one that earned profits. Whether American workers were employed or not was largely irrelevant, except when it came to public relations efforts or lobbying rhetoric.

Autoworkers saw this proposal as an essential weapon to prevent the outsourcing of jobs and to force high-volume Japanese exporters to open plants in the United States. GM and Ford, as well as several large business lobbies, fought against the bill. Although it passed in the House of Representatives in two Congresses, the Senate withheld its approval and the Reagan administration remained adamant in its opposition. For an industry in which the union and companies frequently were united in Washington policy battles during this period, this was one of the unusual instances in which the cleavage over an automotive policy issue seemed to fall along class lines. Temporarily, the union jettisoned its junior-partner stance toward the industry and locked horns with its corporate masters. But the alignment surrounding domestic content legislation was more complex than a simple model of class conflict can convey. Chrysler, the weakest of the Big Three and the company with the fewest foreign affiliates, supported the bill because it felt more vulnerable than its brethren to foreign competition.

Much of the controversy over domestic content legislation stemmed from the fact that it represented, in embryonic form, the social control of investment, restricting the prerogative of corporate officials to control where to invest their capital. A group of fifty progressive economists praised this attribute of the bill in a letter included in the *Congressional Record* during the final House debate. They argued, in part, that the bill

would regulate, to some extent, the investment activities of giant multinational auto companies, domestic and foreign. This may be seen as a first step toward democratic control over the investment activities of giant multinationals, which, if unhindered seek to play off country against country and community against community in the search for maximum profits.

In conclusion, we support this domestic content law as a step to preserve a domestic auto sector, as a step toward planned international trade and investment that is preferable to tariffs and quotas, and as a step toward making multinational corporations . . . more accountable to the citizens of the countries in which they operate.[33,34]

Although the domestic content bill never became law, an examination of the congressional dynamics of the bill is warranted because its twists and turns suggest that despite triumphant industry power during this period, a strong undertow in a very different direction was also apparent. Formally known as the "Fair Practices in Automotive Products Act," the domestic content bill was originally introduced in 1982. The bill appeared to be fairly straightforward. For every 100,000 cars a manufacturer sold in the United States, 10 percent of the value of each car would have to be American content. Manufacturers could choose how to comply, selecting any aspect of auto production, as long as the percentage of domestic value-added content corresponded to the proportional requirements.

At the time, only the two largest Japanese car exporters would have been significantly affected by the law, assuming 1981 import-sales volume. Other exporters, selling fewer than 250,000 cars annually, would have had little

---

[33] *Congressional Record,* House of Representatives (November 2, 1983), p. H9057.
[34] The economists included Gar Alperovitz, Barry Bluestone, Martin Carnoy, Jeff Faux, David Gordon, Michael Harrington, Bennett Harrison, Robert Heilbroner, David Kotz, Robert Lekachman, Ann Markusen, David Moberg, Michael Piore, Michael Reich, Derek Shearer, and Tom Weisskopf.

difficulty in reaching 25 percent domestic content.[35] The Congressional Budget Office (CBO) estimated that a minimum of 15 percent of the wholesale value of an imported car already qualified as domestic content if expenditures in the United States for advertising, transportation, raw materials, and accessories were counted. Domestic content could be increased by another 10 percent relatively easily if foreign car makers purchased additional American-built components. Thus, only the three Japanese auto makers with annual sales over 250,000 (Toyota, Nissan, and Honda) would have to alter their business plans significantly if there were a domestic content law. Otherwise, they would be limited to selling 250,000 cars a year. Since the smallest of the three, Honda, already had an American facility, the company would not have to change its investment strategy fundamentally to comply with the law. Whether Toyota or Nissan would shift the necessary investment to the United States was debatable at the time. Although the CBO believed that neither Toyota nor Nissan would shift its production facilities, the UAW argued that the U.S. market was too important to not take advantage of; Toyota's annual American sales were 714,000, and Nissan's were 580,000.

Introduced in early 1982, the bill was not voted on by the House until December, when it was approved just as the 97th Congress prepared to adjourn. Never making it out of committee in the Senate, the bill died. Reintroduced at the start of the new session, the bill was the object of a concerted union lobbying effort. For a second time the House approved the bill, but again the Senate failed report it out of committee, this time for good. Throughout this unsuccessful course, President Reagan threatened a veto.

Prospects for passage initially seemed dim, but the bill quickly gained wide support in the House, so much so that a Commerce Department official was stunned: "We never thought the bill would get out of subcommittee. Now all of a sudden, it has over 200 co-sponsors."[36] Support was due to several factors. Not only was 1982 an election year, and the nation in the deepest recession since the 1930s, but the auto industry was at a historic low. Advertised as a measure to increase jobs, the bill offered legislators a way to respond to concerns over job losses. UAW leaders, calling the initiative their highest legislative priority, relentlessly lobbied for the bill, and its relative success was due in part to these efforts.[37] Several other unions also lent their support,

---

[35] U.S. Congress, House, Committee on Ways and Means, *Fair Practices in Automotive Products Act. Hearings before the Subcommittee on Trade,* 97th Cong., 2d sess. (September–October 1982), Serial No. 97–30, p. 247.

[36] Gordon Lee, "Detroit's Advocates in Congress Want To Stamp Cars with 'Made in America'," *National Journal* (July 10, 1982), p. 1221.

[37] Alan Murray, "House Passes Auto Domestic Content Bill," *Congressional Quarterly Weekly Report* (December 18, 1982), p. 3072.

including the Amalgamated Clothing and Textile Workers, the International Union of Electrical, Radio and Machine Workers, the United Rubber Workers, and the AFL–CIO. Yet, the initiative was not simply being propelled by interest group pressures or broader concerns for jobs. There was also an undercurrent of racism and resentment toward the Japanese that was apparent. Known as "Japan bashing," blame for America's economic problems was placed on the shoulders of the Japanese and on what many described as unfair methods of competition, instead of the more complicated task of analyzing the failures of American corporations or the inevitable dynamics of international capitalist competition.

Rep. Richard Ottinger (D-NY), the original sponsor of the bill, saw it as part of the larger game of international trade relations. "This bill," he declared, "is a shot across the bow to alert the administration and foreign countries that there is some concern about the decline of the American auto industry. The U.S. has been a sucker in this trade business and has generously given away free access."[38] Ottinger hoped that the ultimate consequence of a domestic content law would be to open markets for U.S. exports.

Debate over the bill was histrionic, with overheated claims hurled back and forth. Some supporters contended that it was the only thing standing between economic and military decline. For Ottinger, the auto industry's decline threatened the nation's entire industrial base and, correspondingly, its security: "From a national security standpoint it would be suicidal to lose our industrial base so critical to sustaining any prolonged military effort. From an economic standpoint, we cannot hope to be competitive in the spectrum of world markets if we lose our industrial base. . . ."[39] Other supporters, such as Rep. John Dingell (D-MI), chairman of the House Energy and Commerce Committee, typically one of the industry's chief allies in Congress, painted the bill as a jobs saver. "This legislation," he said, " . . . is one of the most important jobs protection and economic revitalization bills that [we] . . . will consider this year."[40]

Opponents argued that it was the beginning of protectionist policies that would destroy the international trading system. William Brock, the United States trade representative, called the bill "the worst threat to the international trading system and our own prosperity to be put before the Congress in a decade."[41] The Department of Commerce called it "blatantly protectionist"

---

[38] Cited in Lee, p. 1221.
[39] U.S. Congress, House, Committee on Energy and Commerce, *U.S. Auto Trade Problems. Hearings before the Subcommittee on Commerce, Transportation and Tourism,* 98th Cong., 1st sess. (April 12,28 and May 6, 1983), Serial No. 98–47, p. 18.
[40] *U.S. Auto Trade Problems,* p. 36.
[41] Cited in Lee, p. 1221.

and a "legal and administrative nightmare."[42,43] Rep. Sam Gibbons (D-FL), chairman of the Subcommittee on Trade of the Ways and Means Committee, opened hearings on the bill declaring: "This is the worst piece of economic legislation that this Congress has seriously entertained in 50 years."[44] One trade expert, writing during the summer of 1983 after the first House passage, suggested that the House had "adopted the strongest piece of protectionist legislation since the Smoot-Hawley Tariff in 1930."[45]

House opponents armed themselves with dozens of amendments to weaken or kill the bill. What they hoped would do the trick was the passage (195–194) of an amendment offered by Millicent Fenwick (R-NJ) that stipulated that the bill could not supersede any treaty. Amendment supporters believed this would enable the courts to invalidate the measure for violating GATT. In fact, Rep. Phil Gramm, (D-TX), a fervent opponent of the bill, gloated after the amendment passed: "We just gutted the bill."[46]

John Dingell pledged to union lobbyists that in the next session the amendment would be deleted. And when the bill was reintroduced in February 1983, it was not included. However, the amendment was added as the bill made its way through the labyrinthine committee system. After it was approved without amendments by the Subcommittee on Commerce, Transportation, and Tourism, the full Energy and Commerce Committee added the Fenwick amendment. Meanwhile, the Subcommittee on Trade of the Ways and Means Committee, holding its own hearings, came out in opposition to the entire bill, and the full Ways and Means Committee reported the bill unfavorably. Despite being presented with conflicting committee reports, the House passed the bill for the second time. Yet supporters were frustrated since the bill's final version

---

[42] *U.S. Auto Trade Problems,* pp. 67, 71.

[43] Part of the complication that would arise with the law involved U.S.–Canadian auto trade. In 1965 both nations entered the Canada–U.S. Automotive Products Trade Agreement, known as the Auto Pact. It allowed for duty-free new cars and parts to pass between both countries for qualifying companies. Canada dropped its 25 percent duty, but in return, manufacturers were required to make one vehicle in Canada for each one sold there. The pact allowed for the integration of the North American market and led to billions of dollars of investment in Canadian plants by the American auto makers.

The agreement would have to be renegotiated, or Canada given an exemption, if the domestic content law became law. Exempting Canada from the law would have created a loophole for Japanese car makers and others to avoid a domestic content law. Since the agreement stated that a vehicle must not have more than 50 percent foreign content in order to qualify for duty-free status, an exemption would allow foreign firms to use Canada as a springboard, to use the 50 percent limit regardless of the total volume of exports.

[44] *Fair Practices in Automotive Products Act,* p. 2.

[45] Thomas Brilleck, "The Growing Shadow of Trade Protectionism," *Journal of Legislation* vol. 10, no. 2 (Summer 1983), p. 391.

[46] Cited in Murray, p. 3072.

contained the Fenwick amendment, leaving the bill with an ambiguous standing even if it became law.

At issue was whether the bill violated the free trade principle of GATT. The Ways and Means Committee believed the bill violated GATT and pointed to a study done by the Congressional Research Service that argued that local content requirements were generally in violation of GATT.[47] The Energy and Commerce Committee rejected this view, also citing a report from the Congressional Research Service, but from a different division. This report questioned the legal nature of GATT itself because it had come into effect by an executive agreement, not through congressional action. To support this interpretation, this report pointed to the conference report of the Trade Act of 1974, which contained a provision that stipulated: "The authorization of appropriations for payment by the United States for its share of the expenses to GATT does not imply approval or disapproval by the Congress of all articles of the GATT."[48]

As a result of these conflicting interpretations, the legal status of both GATT and the domestic content bill was by no means clear. In addition, it was not clear whether the Japanese would retaliate against the United States if the bill became law. After meeting with MITI officials during the winter of 1983, members of a delegation from the House Energy and Commerce Committee had varied opinions. Rep. Norman Lent (R-NY), for instance, believed the Japanese would retaliate, hitting agriculture first. John Dingell, who led the group, thought the Japanese would accept a domestic content law.[49] He pointed out that Japan had never protested against GATT or retaliated against other nations with domestic content laws.[50]

In addition to these controversies, there was substantial disagreement over the bill's net impact on employment. Again, the House Energy and Commerce Committee and the Ways and Means Committee came to opposite conclusions.

---

[47] U.S. Congress, House, Committee on Ways and Means, *Domestic Content Legislation and the U.S. Automobile Industry: Analyses of HR. 5133, The Fair Practices in Automotive Trade Act,* Committee print prepared at the request of the Subcommittee on Trade by the Congressional Budget Office, Congressional Research Service and the United States Trade Representative, 97th Cong., 2d sess. (August 16, 1982), Committee Print WMCP 97–33, pp. 82–3. See also U.S. Congress, House, Committee on Ways and Means, *Fair Practices and Procedures in Automotive Products Act of 1983. HR. 1234, Report* (June 30, 1983), House Report 98–287, Part 2.

[48] Cited in U.S. Congress, House, Committee on Energy and Commerce, *Fair Practices and Procedures in Automotive Products Act of 1983. HR. 1234, Report* (June 30, 1983), House Report 98–287, Part 1, p. 24.

[49] *U.S. Auto Trade Problems,* pp. 16–17.

[50] *U.S. Auto Trade Problems,* p. 100. For a detailed sketch of foreign domestic content laws, see pp. 117–67, summarized on pp. 128–35.

Those who supported the proposal argued that there would be a net gain in domestic employment, while opponents contended that either there would not be a net gain or the gain would be minimal, with car prices rising dramatically. The most optimistic projections came from the UAW and Richard Ottinger, estimating a net gain of 1 million jobs with no increase in prices.[51] On the other side, the CBO estimated a net loss of 104,000 jobs because increases in auto and related employment would be offset by losses in other sectors of the economy, such as agriculture, ports, aerospace, and transportation. The CBO based its projection on several assumptions challenged by supporters: American auto firms would not outsource production, the Japanese would not open production facilities in the United States, and the Japanese would retaliate against other industries. Still another estimate by the Commerce Department predicted that the net job gain would be minimal, 6,500, but at a cost of substantially higher prices, the equivalent of $740,000 per job added.[52] The Congressional Research Service saw short-term employment gains but long-term ruin.[53]

Not surprisingly, much of the opposition to the bill came from those involved in importing or exporting. In general, importers and exporters feared that the restriction of auto trade would threaten trading activity in other industries. Lining up against the bill was the International Longshoremen's Association and the American Association of Port Authorities, each with a direct stake in unrestricted trade, as well as a number of farm groups, including the National Farmers Union and the National Grange, which feared losing their export markets.[54] According to the National Grange, annual exports of agricultural products exceeded $40 billion at the time and were "extremely vulnerable to retaliatory action by our trading partners." Three of the most powerful corporate lobby groups – the Business Roundtable, the NAM, and the U.S. Chamber of Commerce – also opposed the bill. They saw it as tampering with corporate autonomy over investment decisions. However, not all members of the business community opposed the bill. Both *Business Week* and *Automotive News* believed that domestic content legislation was a sound way to handle increasing imports and cope with declining employment in the industry.[55] Nevertheless, as Detroit rebounded and general unemployment diminished, support for a domestic content law dissipated. Despite its failure, the bill's reception suggested that the power relations of this period were unstable.

---

[51] *U.S. Auto Trade Problems,* p. 180, 45.   [52] *U.S. Auto Trade Problems,* p. 84.

[53] *Domestic Content Legislation and the U.S. Automobile Industry,* pp. 78–80.

[54] See *U.S. Auto Trade Problems,* p. 630. For a list of groups against the bill, see pp. 602–3.

[55] See "A Better Way to Handle Auto Imports," *Business Week* (April 13, 1981), p. 178; "Now Is the Time," *Automotive News* (February 11, 1980), p. 24.

Conclusion

The industry's ability to shape trade policy was evident in its success in securing import restraints and in stopping the domestic content bill. Initially thwarted by a negative ruling by the ITC, the industry exploited its political influence – based on its overall structural position, enhanced by plummeting sales and the fact that imports were making unprecedented inroads into the U.S. economy – to limit competition. Although the domestic content bill never became law, its limited success, given the array of forces against the bill, was noteworthy.

By the end of the Reagan administration, the industry had enjoyed almost a decade of triumphant power initiated during the Carter administration. It had achieved policy victories across a wide range of issues: regulatory rollbacks, antitrust relaxation, import quotas, and the defeat of domestic content legislation. Although not every battle went its way, virtually no major decision ran directly counter to its interests. Government policy was guided by the principle of assisting the automakers in terms of what the industry itself demanded. Environmental, safety, and trade policies were subordinated to the interests of the corporate bottom line. This pattern continued even after the industry rebounded financially. But when the Reagan administration left office, a new set of relations emerged. After the election of George Bush, the automakers were not able to count automatically on policymakers to put their interests first.

8

Interregnum: 1989–1996

With the Reagan administration's departure from office, the ten-year period of triumphant auto industry power came to a close. As president, George Bush brought with him an administration that was not automatically resistant to using mild governmental mandates to protect public health and the environment. As a result, the industry's relations with government entered a new phase that continued with the Clinton administration. During this period, the automakers lost some of their ability to influence public policy compared to the previous decade, yet their influence was greater than during the earlier period of bargaining and compromise. By the end of Bush's first year in office, the ensuing shift in the dynamics of policymaking led *Automotive News* to select this new set of relations as its 1989 Story of the Year.[1]

The Clinton administration's approach to the industry was much the same. Despite Clinton's 1992 campaign promise that he would become the real "environmental president," the Democratic president did not push for any major environmental standards during his first term – where this analysis ends – and postponed consideration of any new policies that would have imposed stricter mandates on the automobile. Thus, *Automotive News* described the first Clinton term as having "no major regulatory or legislative initiatives that ran counter to industry interests."[2] The central automotive policy issues for the Bush years were the 1990 Clean Air Act (CAA), a government-supported battery research project, the failed congressional effort to increase fuel economy standards, the safety provisions of the 1991 Intermodal Surface Transportation Act Efficiency, and a trade agreement with Japan to reduce the auto trade deficit between the two nations. For the first term of Clinton's presidency, the main auto-related policies were a cooperative re-

---

[1] John K. Teahen, Jr., "Story of the Year," *Automotive News* (December 25, 1989), p. E2.

[2] Phil Frame, "Industry Is Among Election Winners," *Automotive News* (November 18, 1996), p. 1.

search and development agreement between the federal government and the Big Three (the super-car project); a new regulatory standard for head injuries; and a 1995 trade agreement with Japan, which aimed at correcting the same lingering auto trade deficit as the earlier Bush agreement.

Given the overall pattern of Republican and Democratic support for the industry, weeks before the 1996 election the industry press concluded that, whatever the outcome, Detroit could not lose. While Bob Dole had a "consistent pro-industry stance," Clinton had opened doors for the Big Three, and the two sides had been "uncommonly close" ever since.[3] After the reelection of Clinton, along with a Republican Congress, Elliott Hall, head of Ford's Washington office, said: "We thought it was the best thing to happen."[4] Indeed, what could be better than having a president willing to use government programs to help the industry, with a Republican Congress in place to protect the industry against new regulatory burdens?

Together, the Bush and Clinton administrations mildly prodded the auto companies on pollution and safety but protected them from efforts to raise fuel economy standards. At the same time, Detroit was actively supported by Washington on trade issues. This support took two forms. Each administration negotiated trade agreements with the Japanese to open up the Japanese market to American producers. In addition, increasing concerns over the international competitiveness of the United States led to the development of the most noteworthy features of this period: the advanced battery consortium and the super car project, both joint industry–government research projects in which the federal government provided matching dollars for technology development. These projects represented the embrace of neoliberal bureaucratic arrangements. "Neoliberal" is used here to describe government policies based on business–government cooperation in which government actively and consciously supports business. (For many, the model for this institutional arrangement is the Japanese MITI.) Unlike the policies of the previous era that were geared to helping the industry meet crises already upon them – for example, the Chrysler bailout and import quotas – these new initiatives were designed to promote long-term international competitiveness.

A concern for the international competitiveness of the domestic industry led the U.S. automakers to transform their trade association into a more explicitly nationalist lobbying arm representing only the Big Three. In late 1992, the Motor Vehicle Manufacturers Association changed its name to the American Automobile Manufacturers Association and kicked out of its organization Honda, Volvo, and heavy-truck makers, all of which had previously met the criteria for membership. (This political structure was turned upside down by

---

[3] Phil Frame, "Clinton or Dole? Detroit a Winner," *Automotive News* (August 19, 1996), p. 1.

[4] Cited in Frame, November 18, 1996.

the 1998 Daimler–Chrysler merger, which necessitated another reorganization of the industry's collective voice.)

During this period, the economic condition of the industry fluctuated wildly. Detroit earned billions in profits in the late 1980s, only to lose more money in the early 1990s than it had lost during the downturn of 1980. By the mid-1990s the industry was once again earning record profits. The effects of the industry's losses in the early 1990s on the policymaking environment were muted in comparison to the previous decade's billion-dollar losses. There were a number reasons for this. Following years of record profits and coming only a short time after the industry's previous crisis, these losses appeared as either cyclical, a problem that would take care of itself, or due to the industry's own poor business decisions, a situation less conducive to mobilizing political support. However, these losses still had an impact on the debate over CAFE and trade policy to the benefit of the industry's political influence. Yet, the record profits of the mid-1990s did little to undercut the image of the industry as under siege from import competition and needing government assistance. For many observers, the future of Detroit was embedded in the larger issues of globalization and international competitiveness. Regardless of its momentary financial health, this broader context provided Detroit with political ammunition to fight its battles.

What emerges from this ensemble of policies is a pattern of neoliberal cooperation and support tinged with a few moderate new mandates. However, since the policy contours of this period are still evolving, it is described as an "interregnum," a period between two regimes.

The Bush Administration

Riding a growing wave of environmental concern in 1988, George Bush announced that he wanted to be known as the environmental president. This new eco-sensitivity was also spurred by the diminishing resonance of rhetoric that blamed government red tape for economic stagnation, a claim made increasingly implausible after eight years of Reagan-appointed regulators. Besides, the economy, at least according to the Reagan administration, was reaching unparalleled levels of prosperity.[5]

The Clean Air Act

Environmentalists looked to the incoming Bush administration with hopes that the CAA, among other things, would be revised. George Bush made it clear during the 1988 campaign that he wanted a kinder, gentler nation where the environment would be protected. He soon recommended legislation that

---

[5] For an analysis of growing economic inequality during the Reagan years, see Thomas Edsall, "The Reagan Legacy," in Sidney Blumenthal and Thomas Edsall, eds., *The Reagan Legacy* (New York: Pantheon Books, 1988), pp. 3–49.

launched an eighteen-month struggle culminating in the passage of the CAA of 1990. One of the major aspects of this legislation involved the automobile industry because of the centrality of auto emissions to urban air pollution. Before outlining of the law's provisions and examining the political battles that shaped the law, it is appropriate to reiterate the contribution of auto emissions to air pollution and the air pollution problems facing the nation at the time.

Motor vehicle emissions remain the main source of urban air pollution. For their part, passenger cars produce approximately half of the nation's CO emissions; 45 percent of volatile organic emissions compounds (VOC), the main component of smog; and about one-third of NO pollution. They also produce half of the nation's cancers linked to toxic emissions. In 1988, more than 110 million Americans lived in areas that exceeded federal ozone standards. Urban smog reached record levels due to record heat, with ozone levels 5 percent higher than those of the previous record year. Smog levels exceeded federal standards in each of the twenty-four largest metropolitan areas.

Four major air pollution problems were targeted by the 1990 CCA: urban smog, air toxics, acid rain, and stratospheric ozone depletion. (Only those parts of the act directly related to the automobile will be discussed here.[6]) The standards for motor vehicles and fuels included more than ninety provisions covering conventional vehicles, requirements for cleaner-burning fuel, a new mandate for clean fuel vehicles, and a first-time requirement to control emissions from nonroad vehicles including trains, ships, lawn mowers, and farm and construction equipment.[7]

New emissions standards for cars and light-duty trucks were scheduled to be phased in beginning in 1994 and to be fully implemented for all new vehicles in 1996, requiring a 35 percent reduction in HC and a 60 reduction in NO. A second round of emissions reductions (tier II), scheduled to go into effect in 2003, required an additional 50 percent reduction unless the EPA finds that this standard is unnecessary, technically unfeasible, or not cost effective. Starting in 1998, the durability requirements for emission controls were doubled from five years or 50,000 miles to 10 years or 100,000 miles. "On board" diagnostics indicating the malfunctioning of emission controls are also required. The clean fuel requirements set a host of standards for gasoline. In addition, in areas with

---

[6] Full-scale examinations of the law are available elsewhere. See, for example, Gary Bryner, *Blue Skies, Green Politics: The Clean Air Act of 1990 and Its Implementation,* 2nd. ed. (Washington: Congressional Quarterly Press, 1995); Richard Cohen, *Washington at Work: Back Rooms and Clean Air,* 2nd. ed. (Boston: Allyn and Bacon, 1995); Henry Waxman, "An Overview of the Clean Air Act Amendments of 1990," *Environmental Law* vol. 21 (1991), pp. 1721–1816.

[7] For a detailed analysis, see Henry Waxman, Gregory Wetstone, and Philip Barnett, "Cars, Fuels, and Clean Air: A Review of Title II of the Clean Air Act Amendments of 1990," *Environmental Law* vol. 21 (1991), pp. 1947–2019.

serious ozone pollution – the twenty-four smoggiest cities in the nation – fleets of more than ten cars refueled at a central location, such as school buses, taxicabs, and delivery vans, were required to use alternative fuels such as ethanol, methanol, and natural gas. When fully phased in, this requirement was expected to cover 250,000 new vehicles per year. In California, the state with five of the seven worst ozone-polluted areas, car makers were required to sell 150,000 clean-fuel vehicles in 1996 and 300,000 in 2001.

California was singled out for tougher standards because of its long-standing status as the state with the most polluted air. While other states have been prevented from setting their own emissions standards since 1970, California has been allowed to set stricter rules than those established by the federal government. The 1990 CAA preserved this exemption. As part of its efforts to improve air quality, California's Air Resources Board (CARB) set stricter emissions standards than those in the pending federal bill just before the final clean air vote was taken in Washington. Another part of the 1990 federal law allowed other states to adopt California's standard at their discretion, which a number of northeastern states subsequently did.

Part of California's clean air package mandated that by 1998, 2 percent of the vehicles sold by large sellers must be zero-emission vehicles (ZEV), which meant, in practice, electric cars. (The ZEV mandate had been spurred, in part, by GM's announcement earlier that year of a prototype electric vehicle.) By 2003, the ZEV mandate would increase to 10 percent. However, in 1996, CARB ruled that the 1998 mandate would be rescinded because battery technology was not yet commercially viable. The 2003 mandate, however, remained intact. As part of the compromise that led to this recision, automakers agreed to sell tier II vehicles nationwide beginning in 2001, three years earlier than the federal mandate required.

The dynamics of the 1990 clean air fight were rooted in the 1980s stalemate over reauthorizing the 1977 clean air amendments. In 1981, as the law's expiration approached, it was apparent that neither side – those who sought its repeal and those who wanted to make the law tougher on polluters – had the support necessary to make any headway. For the rest of the 1980s there were no advances in either direction. When Reagan left office, however, a major impediment to improving the law was gone.

By the late 1980s, a number of other factors had also changed, each contributing to the emergence of a new clean air bill. The 1986 election had returned control of the Senate to the Democrats, who, overall, were more likely to support environmental legislation. At the same time, public opinion polls indicated that environmental concern was growing. In fact, during the 1988 presidential campaign, George Bush found surprising success with the issue of environmental protection, putting Democratic presidential nominee Michael Dukakis on the defensive for the pollution of Boston's harbor. Most observers simply overlooked Bush's role while vice-president as chair of the White House task force on regulatory relief, which had acted as a back channel for corporate lobbyists frustrated with regulatory agency officials; a main target of the task force was environmental regulation.[8] While Bush's shift from protector of polluters to environmental president was, in part, an effort to emerge from Reagan's shadow, it was also a calculated tactical move, born during the campaign, to ride the rising tide of environmental concern. According to Vince Breglio, a director of polling for the campaign, it became apparent during the summer of 1988 that the public was not showing interest in "Reagan's issues" (jobs, inflation, the economy). Thus, campaign advisors began looking for wedge issues further down their agenda list.[9] Bush's pollsters found that among the "second-tier" issues was the environment, an issue growing in importance after a disastrous summer of beach closings caused by medical waste washing up onshore; record temperatures, which stoked fears about global warming; and record smog, which choked the nation's cities.

Other environmental problems were also becoming widely known. The first "toxic inventory" of chemicals released into the atmosphere, issued by the EPA in 1988, showed that approximately 2.7 billion pounds of air toxics were emitted in 1987. Environmentalists suggested that this tabulation did not measure the full extent of the problem because it was based on self-reporting by corporate officials and there was nothing to ensure that companies had reported their emissions. But perhaps the most dramatic event that spurred environmental concern was the March 1989 Exxon Valdez disaster, which dumped 11 million gallons of oil into Alaskan waterways.

A change in Senate leadership was also important. In 1989, Robert Byrd (D-W VA) stepped down as majority leader and was replaced by George Mitchell (D-ME). Byrd, a defender of his state's high-sulfur coal industry (a large contributor to acid rain), had blocked clean air efforts for years. Mitchell, representing a state suffering from the effects of acid rain, was one of the Senate's leading environmental advocates, having chaired the Environmental Protection Subcommittee of the Committee on Environment and Public Works.

Despite these changes in the executive and in the Senate, the main battle over auto emissions standards was fought in the House of Representatives, where two longtime combatants over clean air legislation remained at center stage. Both Democrats, both were also members of the Energy and Commerce Committee. In one corner was John Dingell (D-MI), chair of the Energy and Commerce committee and long Detroit's main protector in Washington. In the

---

[8] For an analysis of this development, see Stan Luger, "Administrative Law, Regulatory Policy, and the Presidency," *Presidential Studies Quarterly* vol. xxiii, no. 4 (Fall 1993), pp. 713–26.

[9] George Hager, "The 'White House Effect' Opens a Long-Locked Political Door," *Congressional Quarterly Weekly Report* (January 20, 1990), p. 139.

other corner was Henry Waxman (D-CA), chair of the Subcommittee on Health and the Environment, representing one of the most heavily auto-polluted districts in the nation. Waxman was a tireless proponent of cleaner air and tighter auto emissions standards. Throughout the 1980s, the two had fought each other to a standstill. After Bush presented his clean air recommendations – seen as simply setting the floor for the debate that followed – observers on all sides expected a bruising battle between the two. Members of the House dreaded having to choose between Dingell, one of the most powerful – and vindictive – legislators, and Waxman, a leading environmentalist, who had the power of public opinion on his side.

Complicating the overall picture was one of the central ingredients of American politics today: money. Because of the economic ramifications of new clean air legislation, lobbying efforts and campaign giving by interested parties took off. Corporate campaign contributions and lobbying efforts dwarfed those of environmentalists. Yet, drawing conclusions about the influence of money on the final bill is extremely difficult because so much was spent by so many conflicting industry groups. Nevertheless, one partial account of campaign giving in 1989 – a nonelection year – is worth reviewing. Members of the House Energy and Commerce Committee received $612,000 from industry sources directly affected by the CAA, an average of $15,000 each, from a total of 154 political action committees (PACs).[10] Among the seventeen largest contributors, campaign giving increased by 55 percent over 1987, the previous nonelection year. Auto industry PACs were the top three contributors in 1989. Auto industry expenditures to influence clean air legislation did not end there. From 1981 to 1988, for example, GM noted on congressional disclosure forms that it had paid lawyers and lobbyists $1.8 million to work against clean air legislation. During the same period, according to the U.S. Public Research Interest Group, the PACs of GM, Chrysler, and Ford gave $700,000, $630,000, and $470,000, respectively, to congressional candidates, while 150 industry PACs opposed to clean air legislation gave $23 million.[11]

The expected battle between Dingell and Waxman never materialized. A series of early skirmishes between the two led each side to question its strength for a final showdown on the House floor. In October 1989, a year before the final vote was taken, Dingell and Waxman agreed to put aside their differences and reach a compromise on auto emissions. The magnitude of the agreement between the two longtime adversaries was captured when Rep. Michael Bilirakis (R-FL), a member of the Energy and Commerce Committee, ex-

---

[10] Chuck Alston, "As Clean-Air Bill Took Off, So Did PAC Donations," *Congressional Quarterly Weekly Report* (March 17, 1990), pp. 811–17.

[11] Cited in Alexandra Allen, "The Auto's Assault on the Atmosphere," *Multinational Monitor* (January–February 1990), p. 25.

claimed: "When I saw [Waxman] and [Dingell] in the same room . . . I knew that the earth had moved. . . ."[12]

Waxman won tighter emissions standards than those embodied in the Bush proposal and the likelihood of a second round of tougher standards (tier II). Dingell stretched out compliance dates and obtained EPA discretion to waive tier II. Dingell also was able to obtain Waxman's pledge not to push for increasing fuel economy standards as part of the CAA, postponing the issue for a separate legislative initiative. (Meanwhile, in the Senate, Donald Riegle [R-MI] led a parallel effort that succeeded in severing fuel economy standards from the CCA. Helping his efforts was President Bush's threat to veto the entire bill if it contained new fuel economy standards.) Both sides pledged to support the compromise throughout the inevitable twists and turns in both the House and Senate. While the automakers grumbled about the agreement, Dingell convinced them that his power to forge the best possible deal would be strongest early in the debate, before the bill wound its way through the legislative process.[13] Waxman, on the other hand, was able to point to the standards embodied in the agreement as the first improvement in emissions regulations in almost fifteen years. The Waxman–Dingell compromise represented a small portion of the jockeying that went on in Washington for over a year. Before a legislative effort of this magnitude was completed, a seemingly endless round of negotiations took place on myriad other issues. Dingell's decision to compromise reflected the awareness by one of the House's shrewdest tacticians that the tide had turned.[14] Environmental forces were simply too strong to defeat. After nine years of delay, it was time to make a deal; reluctantly, industry officials went along.

Conclusion: The ability of the auto industry officials to influence the outcome of clean air legislation represented the low point of their power during this period. While the final clean air bill represented a setback for the auto industry, considering the ten-year delay in its passage, it still cannot be thought of as a major defeat. Industry officials were able to delay tighter mandates on vehicle emissions even though their products are the major source of urban air pollution, with significant morbidity and mortality consequences. And even though cars would now have to meet stricter pollution requirements, the new federal standards were not as strict as the standards set by California. The final costs of

[12] Cited in George Hager, "Energy Panel Seals Pact on Vehicle Pollution," *Congressional Quarterly Weekly Report* (October 7, 1989), p. 2623.

[13] Cohen, p. 83.

[14] For an account of Dingell's role in looking out for the auto industry, see Jayne O'Donnell, "Dingell – Intimidator, Import Foe, Hill Giant," *Automotive News* (October 24, 1988), p. 3; see also Nathaniel Nash, "How a Huntsman Stalks His Legislative Prey," *New York Times* (June 4, 1986), p. A24.

meeting the new federal tailpipe standards were estimated to be between $170 and $600 per car.

The tighter emissions standards required by the law were not fundamentally different from earlier efforts to mitigate auto-related pollution. Each version of the CAA – 1970, 1977, and 1990 – attempted to solve the problem of air pollution by mandating emissions standards. None questioned the centrality of the automobile to American society. As a result, the air in the nation's cities was still polluted. There are simply too many cars on the road driving too many miles. Until this situation is confronted, remedial efforts such as the CAA will continue to fail.

United States Advanced Battery Consortium

One outgrowth of the battle over clean air legislation was the creation of an industry–government research project on battery technology. The California mandate for a ZEV made it imperative that battery technology be dramatically improved. Michael Davis, an assistant secretary of energy, realized that the Energy Department was spending approximately $20 million a year on battery research of all kinds, with no clear focus or goal. He initiated discussions that led the Bush administration and the U.S. automakers to agree to form a jointly funded cooperative research project that would direct its efforts to improve battery technology.[15] As part of the agreement, all patent rights were left to the companies, and they retained complete control over the direction of research.

While developing new battery technology was the immediate goal of the project, improving the international competitiveness of the U.S. auto industry was also intended. In officially announcing the project at a 1991 White House ceremony, Bush highlighted the role that government can play in aiding American business as it responds to the global economy: "The group gathered here points to a new way of doing business, combining industry and Government's intellectual and productive assets to sustain our competitiveness in the whole international arena."[16] He added that alternatives such as electric vehicles were the answer to foreign dependence on oil and air pollution. This stood in contrast to government regulation that mandated increased fuel economy, which he described as "senseless overregulation [that] is always a one-way dead end." The federal government's contribution to the project for 1992 was $130 million. However, despite Bush's opposition to raising fuel economy standards, the issue would not go away.

---

[15] Michael Shnayerson, *The Car That Could: The Inside Story of GM's Revolutionary Electric Vehicle* (New York: Random House, 1996), pp. 82–3.

[16] Public Papers of the Presidents of the United States: George Bush, 1991, Book II (Washington: Government Printing Office, 1992), p. 1327.

Global Warming, the Gulf War, and CAFE

Because consideration of higher fuel economy standards were severed from the CAA, supporters of higher standards had to fight this issue separately. Normally, Corporate Average Fuel Economy (CAFE) standards are the administrative responsibility of NHTSA. The 1975 legislation establishing CAFE standards delegated to the agency the authority to set the standards after 1985, mandating the 1985 passenger car standard at 27.5 mpg. The Bush administration's opposition to raising CAFE forced advocates of higher standards to shift their efforts to Congress. From 1989 to 1991, numerous bills were introduced; hearings and debates were held, but in the end the standard was untouched.

The increased sense of urgency over CAFE in the late 1980s was spurred by two factors, one old, one new. To begin with, oil imports continued to increase. Between 1985 and 1988 domestic oil production declined from 9 million barrels a day (MBD) to 8.1 MBD, while oil imports reached 7.2 MBD. And, of concern to many, OPEC accounted for 3.4 MBD of this total, up from 1.8 MBD in 1985. The trends clearly pointed in the wrong direction: decreasing domestic production and increasing imports, with a large share coming from one of the world's most politically volatile regions. If this was not enough to demonstrate the need to lessen fuel consumption, surely the 1990 Iraqi invasion of Kuwait and the resulting Gulf War would.

Added to these old concerns over oil consumption was a new one: global warming. Since the debate over the relationship between global warming and CAFE preceded the Gulf War, it is examined first. Global warming received prominent attention during the late 1980s for a simple reason: these years were hot. By the end of the decade, Americans had experienced the seven warmest years since 1880 and the three most serious drought reductions in the U.S. grain harvest since 1950. For many Americans, discussion of global warming is associated with the destruction of the tropical rain forests, whose loss deprives the earth of vegetation that absorbs CO_2 and produces oxygen. The subsequent buildup of CO_2 traps the daily heat from the sun, which leads to rising global temperatures. Yet, a far larger source of the problem is the burning of fossil fuels, particularly the gasoline used in cars. In fact, these sources of global warming dwarf the impact of deforestation.

In any case, according to many within the U.S. business community and their agents in the think tanks of Washington, the talk of global warming amounted to nothing more than pseudoscientific speculation. The evidence is strong, however, that global warming is already occurring. And most independent scientists agree that climatological warming trends will affect population distributions, crop yields, hydroelectric power, rainfall, and ocean currents and may melt polar ice caps, causing a rise in ocean levels. Increasing temperatures will also worsen smog, and lead to more skin cancers and the onset of cataracts.

To better understand the relationship between gasoline usage and global warming, it is useful to put into perspective the U.S. contribution to worldwide greenhouse emissions. Overall, carbon emissions account for 50 percent of global warming gases, three-quarters of which results from the burning of fossil fuels. Transportation usages account for approximately two-thirds of all oil used, and passenger cars account for about 60 percent of usage within the transport sector. As a result, cars consume about one-third of all U.S. energy and emit about two-thirds of U.S. CO_2 emissions. With only 5 percent of the world's population, the United States contributes more greenhouse gas emissions than any other nation and is responsible for 20 percent of CO_2 emissions worldwide. This imbalance was pointed out in 1989 by Sen. Richard Bryan (D-NV), the Senate's leading advocate of higher CAFE, when he noted that U.S. CO_2 emissions from gasoline alone were greater than global warming emissions from all sources in each of the following regions of the world: Latin America, Japan, the Middle East, West Germany, Southeast Asia, the United Kingdom, Africa, and France.[17] Because of the significant role transportation plays in contributing to global warming, it is an obvious target for improvement, one in which small changes in the fuel economy of the nation's fleet can have a large impact on total carbon emissions. Testifying before a Senate subcommittee in 1989, Richard Morgenstern, director of the EPA's Office of Policy Analysis, pointed out that if 1985 were used as a base year, a 1 mpg improvement in the nation's fleet fuel economy would reduce carbon emissions by 9 million metric tons. Globally, a 1 mpg improvement in CAFE would reduce carbon emissions by 40–50 million metric tons per year.[18]

Yet, the nation's automakers remained steadfast in their opposition to improving CAFE to alleviate global warming or for any other reason, for that matter. They argued that singling out the nation's automakers to help mitigate global warming was unfair because CAFE improvements in the United States would have almost no effect globally. Ford officials, for example, claimed that doubling the fuel economy of the entire domestic fleet would reduce global warming gases by only one-half of 1 percent. Environmentalists, however, offered a different view. They claimed that past improvements in CAFE had already made a significant contribution to the lessening of global warming gases, and future reductions were feasible and important. Marc Ledbetter, of the American Council for an Energy-Efficient Economy, noted in 1989 that had the improvement in CAFE between 1976 and 1988 not occurred, total

---

[17] U.S. Congress, Senate, Committee on Commerce, Science and Transportation, *Motor Vehicle Fuel Efficiency Act of 1989. Hearings before the Subcommittee on the Consumer,* 101st Cong., 1st sess. (September. 7, 1989), p. 2.

[18] U.S. Congress, Senate, Committee on Commerce, Science, and Transportation, *Global Warming and CAFE Standards. Hearings before the Subcommittee on the Consumer,* 101st. Cong., 1st sess. (May 2, 1989), p. 101.

carbon emissions would be 107 million metric tons higher, about 7 percent of total U.S. carbon emissions. At the time, cars and light trucks emitted 200 million metric tons of carbon per year. Cars and light trucks, he added, were the single largest source of carbon emissions. Accordingly, while improving CAFE was not the only remedial measure necessary to lessen global warming emissions, it was clearly "one of the most important."[19]

In many ways, the Bush-era battle over raising CAFE standards was a replay of the initial arguments used against CAFE in the 1970s. Supporters of the standards stressed the negative consequences of gasoline usage, while the industry and its allies suggested that, left alone, market forces were sufficient to solve any of these problems. There are several weaknesses in the view that market signals can be relied on to stimulate demand for fuel-efficient cars. First of all, this argument assumes the existence of a competitive market fully capable of registering consumer demand. Given the oligopolistic concentration of the auto industry and the ability of car dealers to sell what is on the lot, the auto industry is not a good candidate for substantiating such claims. Further, the long lead time involved in product design and manufacturing, measured in years, creates a considerable lag between market signals and corporate responses. Moreover, expecting individual consumers to alter their purchasing patterns to alleviate environmental damage ignores the free rider problems associated with collective action. Because each individual knows that changing his or her own behavior will have little overall effect on a problem, there is a disincentive to do so voluntarily.

In addition, relying on future gasoline price increases to encourage the sale of more efficient cars misses the fact that since the original law went into effect, cars have become significantly more efficient. As a result, the operating costs of driving have relatively diminished, along with dollar savings that can be gained from further efficiency improvements. Thus, Michael Renner of the Worldwatch Institute noted in 1988, "At current U.S. fuel prices, for someone driving 10,000 miles a year, an improvement from 10 to 20 MPG will save $500 annually; but doubling that to 40 MPG promises 'only' an additional savings of $250, and doubling again, a comparatively meager $125." Overall, the percentage of operating costs per mile for gas and oil was 15 percent in 1986, down from 26 percent in 1975. Accordingly, whatever pressure market forces previously exerted to improve fuel economy had reached the point of diminishing returns.[20]

In 1989 at least six different bills were introduced in Congress to increase CAFE standards. Most of these new proposals would have changed the law from its existing mandate – a flat corporate average for all car makers – to one

---

[19] *Global Warming and CAFE Standards,* pp. 240–41.

[20] Michael Renner, *Rethinking the Role of the Automobile,* Worldwatch Paper 84 (Washington: Worldwatch Institute, 1988), pp. 33–4.

in which each producer would be required to meet a percentage increase from its 1988 fleet average. This method would have set a higher standard for Japanese producers than for the Big Three because the Japanese sold more efficient cars than their American counterparts. None of the sponsors of this approach were willing to state openly that this new formula was intended to have this effect, but in off-the-record conversations it was readily admitted.[21] Regardless of this new twist, Detroit remained opposed to raising CAFE.

Many environmentalists had hoped that the successful revision of the CAA would provide the momentum needed to push CAFE levels up. When Iraq invaded Kuwait, exposing once again the vulnerability of oil supplies for the U.S. market and leading to a sharp hike in gasoline prices, CAFE supporters believed that the stage was set for a legislative victory. This belief was shared by many industry insiders, who also worried that the war was exactly the sort of national crisis that would undercut its lobbying clout. Tim McCarthy, a lobbyist for the Motor Vehicle Manufacturers Association, worried that "This Persian Gulf crisis will hit us with both barrels. . . ."[22] The main legislative effort centered on the Bryan bill, named for Senator Richard Bryan (D-NV), which, using 1988 as a baseline, would have increased CAFE by 40 percent by 2001. Soon after he introduced the bill, it received bipartisan support and had thirty-three cosponsors.

Auto industry supporters dug their heels in and were able to take advantage of the Senate's antimajoritarian rules to stop the Bryan bill. On an initial vote in August 1990, the Senate had voted 68–28 to limit debate on the bill, seemingly ending a filibuster led by Sen. Donald Riegle and setting the stage for later approval. However, during the next few weeks, industry lobbyists mounted a coordinated campaign to reverse this decision in order to prevent a vote on the merits of the bill. Their efforts paid off when, in a second vote to limit debate, eleven senators (eight Republicans and three Democrats) switched sides and the motion failed. The frustration felt by CAFE supporters was evident when Bryan rhetorically asked for an auto industry "answer to every parent in America whose son or daughter is in the Middle East because of our oil dependence."[23]

Even if the Senate had approved the bill, there was little hope that it would soon become law. To begin with, President Bush continued to threaten a veto. Despite the Bush administration's initial rhetoric generally supporting remedial efforts to lessen global warming emissions, it downplayed the need to respond immediately. Within the administration, conflicts quickly emerged

[21] Margaret Kriz, "Going the Extra Mile," *National Journal* (May 11, 1991), p. 1096.

[22] Cited in Diana Kurylko, "Odds Tilt to CAFE Bill as Senate Faces Gulf Crises," *Automotive News* (September 3, 1990), p. 1.

[23] Cited in Richard Berke, "Bill to Raise Cars' Fuel Efficiency Dies with Senate Vote on Debate," *New York Times* (September 26, 1990), p. A1.

over global warming and environmental policy in general, with White House Chief of Staff John Sununu and OMB Director Richard Darman outflanking EPA chief William Reilly. However, in 1989 the administration did raise CAFE back to 27.5 mpg, the standard before the Reagan rollback. Meanwhile, in the House of Representatives, events in the Gulf were upsetting power relations and John Dingell's control over CAFE.

Just days before the second Senate vote, the Energy and Power Subcommittee of the House Energy and Commerce Committee, chaired by a Dingell ally, Philip Sharp (D-IN), held its first CAFE hearings in years. Reflecting the politically unstable mood, the hearing was heated and acrimonious. The *Detroit Free Press* reported that it produced "plenty of fierce debate and old-fashioned, red-faced table pounding."[24] John Dingell crossed swords with Rep. Barbara Boxer (D-CA), the House sponsor of the Bryan bill, and with Rep. George Miller (D-CA). Repeatedly interrupting each other, they quarreled over their knowledge of fuel economy technology, the Gulf War, and which cars their families drove. However, even if CAFE supporters had somehow managed to circumvent Dingell's committee, there was little chance that the House would be able to vote on the bill before the session adjourned.

Efforts to defeat the Bryan bill ran the gamut of tactics used today. In 1990, the industry's trade association alone spent more than $1.3 million for official lobbying. This sum was dwarfed the following year. To ensure that its voice was heard, the Big Three, with more than fifty people in their Washington offices, not counting those employed by the automakers' trade association, still felt the need to hire additional outside lobbyists. The companies also enlisted help from the UAW and car dealers. Employees of the car makers were given form letters to send to their representatives, and car dealers were asked to pressure members of Congress directly. In addition, the industry's trade association spent $500,000 to hire a Washington public relations firm to establish a front organization to aid its lobbying efforts: the Coalition for Vehicle Choice (CVC). Harkening back to the industry's early days, when the companies fought initiation of safety legislation by setting up organizations to carry their message, the CVC gave the appearance of a grass-roots group concerned that higher CAFE standards would force the automakers to curtail the sale of large vehicles used to haul heavy loads. The coalition brought together diverse groups such as the American Farm Bureau Federation, the Livestock Marketing Association, the National Roofing Association, and the International Professional Rodeo Association, as well as a group of boat owners. Yet, the membership roster failed to mention the Big Three, the main sponsor of the coalition. A Washington political consulting firm was also hired to create local pressure on both Senator Bryan and Sen. John Rockefeller (D-W VA). Called

---

[24] David Everett, "Lawmakers Get Mileage Out of Auto Debate," *Detroit Free Press* (September 20, 1990), p. A1.

Nevadans (or West Virginians) for Fair Fuel Economy, these shell organizations initiated local letter-writing campaigns but neglected, once again, to note their connection to the automakers.[25] When Bryan discovered this ploy, he complained directly to the chief executives of the Big Three, but industry officials insisted that there was nothing inappropriate about these activities.

The industry's lobbying efforts were preceded by large-scale campaign contributions geared to creating a more receptive Congress. Between 1984 (when CAFE returned as a serious issue) and 1991, the *Wall Street Journal* reported that the industry and its related trade associations invested more than $20 million in campaign contributions to members of Congress.[26] It is always difficult, of course, to prove the precise impact of campaign contributions, in part because they may reward already existing positions instead of changing a vote. Choosing which votes to measure presents another set of problems because of the large number of bills that never get voted on or are amended at early stages of the legislative process. Another problem is that some bills exempt specific, but unnamed, companies from the ostensible mandates of the legislation. Thus, what appears to be a law that a firm might be unhappy with may in fact provide exemptions and benefits hidden from view.[27] Putting aside these limitations, one study of senators who voted on the second motion to cut off the 1990 CAFE debate showed a strong correlation between the amount of money received from the auto industry and the votes cast. Of those who received more than $20,000 between 1985 and 1990, 64 percent voted for the industry position; of those who received between $12,000 and $20,000, 42 percent voted with the industry; of those who received less than $12,000 (including those who received nothing), only 15 percent voted with the industry.[28]

When Congress convened in January 1991, CAFE supporters reintroduced their proposals. And once again, the industry opened its wallets to defeat them. The CVC received a $10 million infusion from the Big Three and hired Diane Steed, the head of NHTSA during the Reagan administration, to lead the group. In February, while fighting was underway in the Gulf War, Bryan held hearings on his reintroduced bill. Anticipating that critics on behalf of the automakers would predict dire consequences, including depriving consumers of full-sized family vehicles if the bill were passed, he added, "We will hear that these

[25] Jeffrey Denny, "King of the Road," *Common Cause Magazine* (May–June 1991), p. 22.

[26] Jill Abramson, "Car Firms Kick Lobbying Effort Into High Gear in Bitter Fight Over Fuel-Economy Legislation," *Wall Street Journal* (September 20, 1991), p. 14.

[27] For a discussion of these issues, see Dan Clawson et al., *Money Talks: Corporate PACs and Political Influence* (New York: Basic Books, 1992).

[28] Philip Stern, *Still The Best Congress Money Can Buy* (Washington: Regnery Gateway, 1992), p. 174.

standards will single-handedly cause economic disruption in the auto industry and a loss of jobs for American workers."[29] Bryan rejected each of these claims in turn, arguing that CAFE did not cause the industry's problems; the recession did. In fact, he argued, CAFE had forced Detroit to modernize its products, thus making the industry more, not less, competitive. He also called attention to the fact that industry officials were adamant in their opposition to CAFE through good economic times and bad. Nevertheless, he felt compelled to stress, "I am not unmindful, and I am certainly concerned, about the health of the industry as well as the United States economy." Clearly, the Senate's leading advocate of higher CAFE standards understood that the battle he was fighting required him to demonstrate his sensitivity to the economic condition of the nation's automakers. Because the industry was losing money, Bryan knew that many members of Congress would be reluctant to go against the industry. However, for Bryan, more was at stake than the automakers' bottom line. Consequently, he added, "While I am concerned about the industry and the economy, I am also concerned about the nation's longterm energy security and our global environment."[30]

In March, the automakers took their message directly to the Bush administration when the chairmen of the Big Three met with key cabinet members, leading Republican senators, and Federal Reserve Board Chairman Alan Greenspan. Elliott Hall, Ford's vice-president of Washington affairs, remarked that although Detroit's top executives visit the White House about once a year, this visit was timed to influence pending CAFE legislation, as well as trade issues with the Japanese. Two weeks later, the top executives of the Big Three made their case directly to President Bush.

Throughout this effort, Detroit stressed a new argument against CAFE: higher standards would harm occupant safety. To meet higher standards, industry officials claimed, they would have to sell only small cars (the same argument made in the 1970s), and because small cars were less safe, raising CAFE standards would result in more deaths on the road. Bush administration officials liked what they heard and started calling the Bryan bill the "Highway Fatality Act" or the "National Highway Death Act."

The claim that smaller cars were inherently less safe than larger ones set off a furious debate among public interest groups, government agencies, and safety experts. Those arguing that higher CAFE would inevitable lead to less safe vehicles included the auto industry, the Bush administration and its Department of Transportation, and the Insurance Institute for Highway Safety (IIHS), an insurance industry alliance that does research on safety. Opposed to

---

[29] U.S. Congress, Senate, Committee on Commerce, Science, and Transportation, *Motor Vehicle Fuel Efficiency Act. Hearings before the Subcommittee on the Consumer,* 102nd Cong., 1st sess. (February 21, 1991), p. 2.

[30] *Motor Vehicle Fuel Efficiency Act,* 1991, p. 3.

them were consumer advocates such as the Center for Auto Safety, Public Citizen, and the Institute for Injury Reduction, which claimed that design, not size alone, determined safety. They cited evidence showing that certain small cars had better crash ratings than larger cars. In addition, traffic fatalities had been dropping over the previous fifteen years as cars became lighter in order to meet CAFE standards. Supporting this side of the debate in varying degrees were reports produced by the General Accounting Office, the Congressional Office of Technology Assessment, and the National Academy of Sciences.[31]

Many members of Congress were puzzled by the technical complexity of the debate, as well as the split within the safety community. Clarence Ditlow, head of the Center for Auto Safety, tried to cut through the confusion when he pointed out that if the automakers simply sold the same mix of vehicles by weight as they did in 1990, but achieved the fuel economy of the best vehicle already on the market for each particular class (calculations were made for ten different weight classes), fuel economy would increase from 27.8 to 34.4 mpg.[32] However, this simple insight was drowned out by the industry's massive lobbying efforts.

Not content to rely on this issue alone to firm up support in Congress, the automakers hosted forty-one members of Congress for a two-day trip to Detroit to present the industry's case. The congressional delegation met with top executives and union leaders and toured factories. At these meetings, industry officials estimated that the Bryan bill would cost them $62.5 billion over five years and would lead to massive layoffs. In addition, Jackie Stewart, the former race-car driver, was on hand at Ford's proving grounds to drive members on high-speed circuits of the test track. (The schedule was set up by Debbie Dingell, the wife of John Dingell and a Washington lobbyist for GM.) Afterward, delegation members reported gaining a new appreciation for the industry's problems.

Appearing to have matters under control, the automakers soon found themselves on the defensive when NHTSA issued its annual fuel economy report. For the third straight year, fuel efficiency had decreased. In fact, the average fuel economy of cars sold in the United States was at the lowest level since 1985 as both imports and domestic cars became bigger, loaded with more options, and therefore less efficient. As a result, Detroit's protest that higher CAFE was not practical seemed hollow to those inclined to question the industry's claims. However, when industry officials announced that their 1991

---

[31] See John Cushman, Jr., "Gas Mileage and Safety, Or Statistics in Collision," *New York Times* (October 31, 1991), p. A13; Max Gates, "Science Academy Fuels CAFE Fire," *Automotive News* (April 13, 1992), p. 8.

[32] Center for Auto Safety, *The Safe Road to Fuel Economy* (Washington: Center for Auto Safety, April 1991).

first quarter losses had reached almost $2.7 billion, the prospects for new CAFE standards sank.

Almost forgotten in the wrangling in Washington was the fuel savings that the Bryan bill promised. By 2005, 2.8 million barrels of oil a day would be saved. This figure was four times the pre–Gulf War imports from Kuwait and Iraq combined. It was more than the entire amount of Persian Gulf imports from all nations, which were 1.87 million barrels a day. In addition, by 2005 the higher standards would reduce CO_2 emissions by 500 million tons per year. The total savings of the Bryan bill by 2020 would amount to 15 billion barrels, more than three times the amount of undiscovered, economically recoverable oil off the Atlantic, Pacific, and eastern Gulf of Mexico coasts.[33]

Conclusion: The industry's defeat of higher CAFE standards was its biggest victory during this period. Marshalling its tremendous resources to lobby against the bill, the industry was able to overwhelm advocates of higher standards. Once proposals for higher standards were severed from the CAA, the industry was in a better position to define the parameters of the debate. Industry officials deflected attention away from concerns over oil imports, and focused the debate over CAFE standards on the issues of safety and jobs, at a time when the automakers were experiencing substantial losses. Without the momentum of clean air politics on their side, supporters of higher CAFE standards simply were no match for the industry. Supporters of increasing CAFE standards hoped that their day would come again. Senator Bryan put it simply: "We will be back to deal with improving fuel economy because the automobile is where the oil is consumed."[34]

Safety and the Intermodal Surface Transportation Act

Progress on vehicle safety standards was stifled during the Reagan and Bush years as NHTSA remained largely in Detroit's grip. As a result, bills were introduced in each session of Congress between 1985 and 1990 to improve occupant safety. Each time, they passed the Senate but failed in the House of Representatives, where John Dingell bottled up the bills in his committee. Now, in a repeat of the dynamics of the 1990 CAA, improvements in safety were made part of a much larger piece of legislation that had its own momentum, the mammoth 1991 transportation financing bill: "The Intermodal Surface Transportation Efficiency Act."[35] Although the House version of the bill did not contain any auto safety provisions, once the conference committee

[33] U.S. Congress, House, Committee on Interior and Insular Affairs, *Strategies for Energy Independence. Oversight Hearings before the Subcommittee on Water, Power and Offshore Energy Resources,* 101st Cong., 2nd sess. (September 11, 1990), p. 24.

[34] Cited in Diana Kurylko, "Lobbying Efforts by Industry, Labor Help Strangle Senate CAFE Bill," *Automotive News* (October 1, 1991), p. 4.

[35] P. L. 102–240.

met, Senate conferees were able to include them in the final version of the bill.[36]

The bill required air bags on both the driver and passenger sides of all cars by 1997. Another provision of the bill required NHTSA to promulgate a head injury protection standard. Each action was necessary, supporters argued, because of NHTSA's failure to carry forward its administrative responsibilities. Rule making on the air bag had stretched on for twenty years because of agency foot dragging and the opposition of the Nixon and Reagan administrations, spurred by auto industry animus. NHTSA's 1987 passive restraint standard allowed for passive seat belts, and during a phase-in period it allowed air bags to be installed on the driver's side only. Passive seat belts are inadequate for several reasons. The first, and most obvious, reason is that even passive belts require the active buckling of the lap portion. If the lap portion is not buckled, the passenger can slide out from under the shoulder portion during the impact from a crash. Most important, though, is that even with a lap and shoulder belt, crashes at speeds exceeding 25 mph may provoke a rapid forward and backward rotation of the head on impact, resulting in permanent brain injury. Air bags, in contrast, allow for a more controlled deceleration of the head and reduce the likelihood of brain damage.

The need for a congressionally mandated head injury standard was due to the agency's failure to take corrective action for brain injuries. The rule-making action for such a standard begun in 1970 was terminated by the agency in 1979. The agency took no further action until the mid-1980s, when it resumed research efforts. However, nothing concrete resulted from NHTSA's preliminary efforts. And in NHTSA's 1990 revision of the side impact standard, when the agency acknowledged that brain injuries were the most prevalent cause of fatalities resulting from side impacts, the problem was not addressed. Instead the revision focused on preventing thoracic and pelvic injuries. Meanwhile, about 8,000 deaths, or half of all the deaths that occur each year from all side crash impacts, are caused by brain injury.[37]

Industry officials would have preferred not to have Congress order additional safety features on cars. However, air bags were already being installed in many cars in response to NHTSA's 1987 standard and growing consumer demand. In addition, the necessary rule making for a head injury standard would take years and then would not go into effect for several more years. (This effort was completed in 1995 and is examined later.)

---

[36] For some unique aspects of the lobbying effort for this bill, see John Cushman, Jr., "Transit Bill Becomes a Private Debate," *New York Times* (November 25, 1991), p. A11.

[37] Diane Lestina, Peter Gloyns, and Stephen Rattenbury, *Fatally Injured Occupants in Side Impact Crashes* (Arlington: Insurance Institute of Highway Safety, 1990).

Trade

As Detroit's losses mounted in 1990 and 1991, industry officials looked back to the 1980s' quotas on Japanese imports as an idea whose time had come again. Consequently, when the top executives of the Big Three met with President Bush in March 1991 to discuss CAFE, they also stressed that trade with Japan was one of their top concerns. Lee Iacocca, the head of Chrysler, made the most pointed pitch for reinstituting quotas on Japanese cars and trucks. Ford and the UAW also wanted the trade restrictions. The timing of this plea was important: Detroit was hemorrhaging red ink as sales sunk to their worst level in eight years. In the final quarter of 1990 the Big Three had lost $2.1 billion, and first quarter losses in 1991 were $2.7 billion.

Yet, for a number of reasons, the Bush administration was wary of instituting trade restrictions. While the VRA with Japan in the 1980s had contributed to the U.S. auto industry's record profits, these profits were paid for by car buyers in the form of higher prices. Asking car buyers to pay billions in higher prices again, and so soon, was not something officials in Washington wanted to experiment with. Industry losses this time appeared to be nothing more than the result of the normal cycle of auto sales combined with poor business decisions. However, given the ongoing trade deficits with Japan, if the administration did nothing, it would appear that Bush was oblivious to the recession plaguing the nation. Sharpening the feeling of crisis was GM's announced downsizing of 74,000 workers in December 1991. Surveying this heightened concern and the changing mood in Washington toward the automakers, *Automotive News* reported in January 1992 that Congress was now looking for ways to help the industry.[38]

When Bush made his ill-fated trip to Japan in January 1992, he brought along top executives of the Big Three to demonstrate his attentiveness to the problems facing the nation's largest industry. The United States was running a $30 billion auto deficit with Japan. While Japanese producers sold over 20 percent of all vehicles in the United States – and approximately 30 percent of all passenger cars – American car exports accounted for less than 1 percent of the Japanese market. However, the trip almost immediately turned into a disaster and then became a metaphor for Bush's plummeting standing in public opinion. Instead of standing up for American interests, the leader of the only remaining superpower in the world, it seemed, was acting like a car salesman; he was complaining, moreover, to the competition that his vehicles were not selling. And when Bush vomited on the Japanese prime minister during a state dinner, many saw the mishap as emblematic of the entire trip and of Bush's declining reelection prospects.

[38] Max Gates, "Mood Has Switched: Congress Now Seeks to Aid Auto Industry," *Automotive News* (January 27, 1992), p. 1.

The trip also hurt the image of America's auto executives. They appeared as whiners, blaming Japan for their own self-inflicted wounds caused by decades of sloppiness and arrogance. Sen. John Danforth (R-MO) remarked: "The crying of the auto executives was demeaning and embarrassing to the auto companies and to the entire country."[39] Adding to this public relations debacle were prominent stories in the media, including the *New York Times,* the *Wall Street Journal,* and *Time,* pointing out the multi-million-dollar salaries these auto officials earned as their companies were losing billions.[40] Their counterparts in Japan, meanwhile, earned a small fraction of that amount.

For their part, Japanese officials saw the auto trade deficit simply as a result of consumer choice based on the quality of the cars sold by each nation's automotive companies. They attributed Detroit's lack of success in selling cars in Japan to the failure to understand the Japanese market. United States automakers tried to sell the same product in Japan as they did in the United States, without making changes to fit Japanese tastes and styles. Detroit tried to sell large American cars that were unsuitable for Japan's narrower roads, and companies such as GM did not sell cars with the option of placing the steering wheel on the right side, the common practice in Japan. For the Americans, on the other hand, the trade imbalance was due to the closed nature of the Japanese market, whose regulations and norms kept out foreign-made goods.

Despite the public relations problems generated by the trip, Bush did win some concessions, although many observers questioned how meaningful they were. To begin with, Japanese automakers agreed to increase their annual purchase of American-made auto parts from $9 billion to $19 billion by 1994. They also promised to increase the American content of their transplant vehicles from 50 to 70 percent. Finally, the Japanese pledged to eliminate fourteen certification requirements for imported vehicles that U.S. producers contended were a barrier to selling their cars in Japan. Critics still insisted that the trip gained little but embarrassment for the United States. The promises made by Japanese car makers were already planned, and the pledge to purchase U.S.-made parts was so vague as to allow Japanese car makers to buy parts from the approximately 300 Japanese suppliers with factories in the United States instead of from U.S.-owned parts makers.

This case is a reminder of the importance of giving careful attention to the specific historical context within which policy contests occur. Although the industry's losses in 1991 and 1992 were larger than those in 1980, Detroit

---

[39] Cited in Max Gates, "Senate Split on Success of Bush Trip," *Automotive News* (January 27, 1992), p. 34.

[40] See Anthony Lewis, "Metaphor for Failure," *New York Times* (January 5, 1992), p. A13; Jill Abramson and Christopher Chipello, "High Pay of CEOs Traveling with Bush Touches a Nerve in Asia," *Wall Street Journal* (December 30, 1991), p. 1; Thomas McCarroll, "Motown's Fat Cats," *Time* (January 20, 1992), pp. 34–5.

could not obtain the same favorable policy responses from Washington. A simple model of political change that focused only on falling or rising profits would suggest that policy makers would always intervene or respond to industry requests at such times. However, the impact of these trends is significantly affected by other factors, such as when they occur. Because Detroit's losses in this period followed the cycle of losses and profits in the 1980s, they did not have the same dramatic impact that those earlier losses had. Yet, in light of Detroit's central economic position, policymakers could not simply turn their backs on the industry either.

With Bush's 1992 loss to Bill Clinton, the players in the administrative branch changed, but the overall direction of policy remained remarkably the same.

The Clinton Administration

The environmental community greeted Bill Clinton's election with elation. After twelve years of Republican administrations often hostile to their agenda, environmentalists felt that they would now be welcomed into the corridors of power. Vice-President Al Gore had a respectable record on environmental issues as a member of Congress and had just written a book about environmental protection.[41] In it Gore called for raising fuel economy standards to 40 mph and argued for phasing out the internal combustion engine within twenty-five years. However, if those who thought Clinton's election would begin a new cycle of environmental protection had examined his record as governor of Arkansas and had listened closely during the 1992 campaign, they would have noticed that Clinton was not likely to go after polluters.

Clinton's environmental moderation was apparent in the evolution of his position on CAFE standards before he took office. At the start of the 1992 campaign, Clinton had called for raising CAFE to 40 mpg by the year 2000. As the campaign progressed, he softened his position. By August, in a meeting with the top executives of the automakers, he said that his earlier suggestion had only been a "goal," which could best be met by using incentives rather than mandates.[42] This increasingly friendly approach to Detroit continued after the election. As president, Clinton proposed no significant initiatives that the U.S. automakers were unhappy with and instead forged what inside observers described as a "close working relationship" with the Big Three. This relationship extended to all levels of the executive branch. Ford's Elliot Hall proclaimed: "We have unprecedented access to all the Cabinet positions that relate to the auto industry. . . ."[43] One consequence of that access was apparent when it came time to appoint a new administrator for NHTSA. The industry ex-

---

[41] Al Gore, *Defending the Earth* (New York: Penguin Books, 1993).

[42] Peter Stone, "Detroit's Smooth Ride," *National Journal* (May 21, 1994), p. 1176.

[43] Stone, p. 1177.

ercised an effective veto over fourteen potential nominees who they said were too close to the consumer movement, delaying the final selection for a year.[44]

The most prominent policy action of the Clinton administration was not a new regulatory standard or the relaxation of an existing one. Instead, a joint industry–government research project was implemented, modeled after the United States Advanced Battery Consortium.

Partnership for a New Generation of Vehicles

The Partnership for a New Generation of Vehicles (PNGV) initiated in the early months of Clinton's presidency, was formally announced at the White House in September 1993. The agreement established a joint ten-year industry–government research project with three targets: the advancement of manufacturing techniques in order to lower production costs; the development of technologies for near-term improvements in fuel economy, safety, and emissions; and, most prominent, the development of production prototypes of cars capable of tripling the fuel economy of the average car.

At the September ceremony, Clinton first reminisced about his father's Buick dealership and the 1967 Mustang he had restored before he underscored the importance of the auto industry. "Since the auto industry is responsible for one out of every seven jobs in the United States, it is clearly incumbent upon all of us to support this effort and to make sure it succeeds."[45] Clinton saw the agreement as an example of the kind of public–private partnership his administration wanted to develop to keep America competitive in the global marketplace. It was also part of his administration's commitment to "reinvent" government – to get rid of wasteful and costly regulation" [and] "to break the wasteful gridlock in Washington over auto issues."[46] He closed his remarks by stressing that the agreement was a "clear signal to America that the core of the American industrial economy, the auto industry, is looking to the future with confidence and that the United States Government is going to be their partner in that successful march."[47]

To establish the agreement, Clinton officials had to overcome Detroit's skepticism about entering into the partnership. Industry officials were wary of Clinton's offer of research money because they were afraid that by accepting federal money and agreeing to a particular fuel economy goal, they would be giving environmental critics something to use against them. To assuage this apprehension, Clinton agreed to a moratorium on fuel economy increases.

---

[44] Mark Dowie, *Losing Ground: American Environmentalism at the Close of the Twentieth Century* (Cambridge: MIT Press, 1995), p. 182; see also Insurance Institute for Highway Safety, "What Gives? Nobody Tapped for NHTSA Post," *Status Report* vol. 28, no. 10 (August 21, 1993), p. 3.

[45] Public Papers of the Presidents of the United States: William Clinton, 1993, Book II (Washington: Government Printing Office, 1994), p. 1627.

[46] Clinton Papers, pp. 1627–8.   [47] Clinton Papers, pp. 1628–9.

(When the Republicans gained control of Congress in 1995, they guaranteed that CAFE would not be raised by prohibiting NHTSA from doing so.) Despite this gesture, solidifying the relationship between Detroit and the new administration was not easy. Susan Tierney, an assistant secretary at the Energy Department, said of the process, "There was suspicion from Day One. We spent a lot of time nursing what our agenda was. They weren't courting us, we were courting them."[48] The project soon had an annual budget of $300 million.

Notwithstanding all the hoopla at the White House, the PNGV agreement received mixed responses, some of which broke predictably along ideological lines. Conservative free-market advocates thought it was wrong for government to be involved in shaping research agendas, particularly applied research, which was best market driven. Others feared that the program represented a step toward corporate statism. Yet the Chamber of Commerce and the NAM, hardly liberal entities, praised the agreement. For the liberal advocates of industrial policy, the PNGV was just the kind of partnership that other countries, such as Japan, had embraced to aid their own industries. Among environmentalists, opinion was divided. Joan Claybrook, head of Public Citizen, ventured that it was good to have long-term projects on the future of automobiles, but she was concerned because the industry had used the agreement to block increases in fuel economy standards. Other environmentalists noted that the subsidies were extremely generous in light of Detroit's consistent opposition to government regulation. Because the Big Three could veto research proposals, these critics felt that the agreement was nothing more than a giveaway.

This project was a significant development of the pattern begun by the Bush administration to harness the resources of the federal government to promote the long-term competitiveness of the domestic auto industry. The growing awareness of globalization forced policymakers to realize that clinging to the verities of the past – that the government that rules least rules best – was a handicap in a world where other nations thrived because of business–government partnerships, industrial policy, and administrative guidance of economic development.[49]

Safety

If members of the environmental community were disappointed with Clinton's stand on CAFE, advocates of improved safety standards were downright distraught over the actions of Clinton's NHTSA. Writing in September 1996, on the occasion of the thirtieth anniversary of the federal auto safety act, Ralph Nader called for the resignation of Transportation Secretary Frederico Peña, NHTSA Administrator Ricardo Martinez, and Federal Highway

---

[48] Cited in Stone, p. 1179.

[49] For a brief survey of these patterns, see Graham Wilson, *Business and Politics: A Comparative Introduction,* 2nd ed. (Chatham: Chatham House, 1990).

Administration Administrator Rodney Slater (who subsequently became transportation secretary in Clinton's second term) for failing to carry out the safety mission of their offices. Pena and Slater were criticized for, among other things, doing nothing to stop the repeal of the national speed limit, and for failing to inject safety considerations into both administrative and legislative initiatives that affected truck safety. Martinez was chastised for emphasizing driver behavior programs (e.g., safety belt usage and campaigns against drunk driving) at the expense of vehicle standards to lessen injuries in a crash. In calling for their resignations, Nader rebuked the administration and charged that the three federal officials

prostrated themselves in ignominious kowtows before a resurgently reactionary megaindustry lobby that itself is oblivious to shame, guilt or disgrace. Instead of applying the laws to the application of known technologies and law enforcement mechanisms that efficiently prevent casualties and reduce further this epidemic of violence on the highways . . . [they] drove these programs backwards . . . beyond what the Reagan and Bush appointees would have dared to do.[50]

Industry officials, on the other hand, gave Martinez positive reviews.[51]

An exception to NHTSA's general lack of action on occupant safety was a head injury standard, begun during the Bush years pursuant to a congressional mandate. The standard, completed in 1995, required the automakers to meet new performance standards for side impacts by 2002, with a phase-in of the standard scheduled to begin in 1998. NHTSA estimated that fatalities due to head injuries in passenger cars would be reduced by 873 to 1,192 per year, and 675 to 975 moderate to critical injuries would be reduced each year. Because those involved in rollover crashes would also benefit from the new standard, an additional 244 to 334 fatalities and 189 to 273 moderate to critical injuries would be prevented.[52] The total per-vehicle average cost for passenger cars was $33, and the cost for larger vehicles (trucks, buses, and multipurpose, passenger vehicles that weigh 10,000 pounds or less) was $51.[53] While this standard advanced occupant safety, an examination of the agency's own estimates reveals that one vehicle sold at the time already met the entire new standard, and varying percentages of other vehicles tested contained components that met certain aspects of the new standard. In the end, the agency's action did little more than ratify existing industry practice, and was hardly a technology-forcing strategy, one of the original goals of federal safety regulation.

[50] Ralph Nader, *Driving in Reverse: The Crash of the Successful Federal Traffic Safety Program* (Washington: Center for the Study of Responsive Law, 1996), p. 17

[51] See, for example, Phil Frame, "Has Martinez Dropped the Ball at NHTSA?" *Automotive News* (July 24, 1996), p. 1.

[52] 60 FR 43048 (1995).   [53] 60 FR 43047 (1995).

Trade

Because the 1992 Bush agreement did not resolve the trade imbalance between the United States and Japan, the Clinton administration could not avoid confronting the issue. The U.S. automakers continued to press Washington to try to open the Japanese market, particularly for auto parts. As in an obligatory rematch between two opponents, the United States and Japan returned to the negotiating table to mitigate the long-standing source of friction. Although the Japanese met the target for increasing their purchases of auto parts made in the United States, the trade deficit between the two nations, and especially between their respective automotive sectors, remained. In 1994, for example, the U.S. trade deficit with Japan was $66 billion; automotive goods accounted for 55 percent of the total. Japanese companies continued to have a large stake in the American market, with automotive exports to the United States reaching $36 billion in 1993. Of this total, motor vehicles accounted for almost $24 billion; parts accounted for the rest.

Clinton's trade negotiators complained to their Japanese counterparts about the trade imbalance and called for the opening of the Japanese market to American businesses, much as their predecessors did. Little had actually changed since President Bush's visit. The Big Three accounted for less than 1 percent of the cars in Japan, whereas Japanese automakers continued to sell over 20 percent of all vehicles and 30 percent of passenger cars in the United States, one-third of which were assembled in the United States. And once again, American auto executives and trade negotiators blamed the imbalance on the closed nature of the Japanese market. Before the main round of the negotiations began, a series of meetings was held in Detroit between representatives of the industry and the administration's trade negotiators to map a strategy.

Soon after the talks began, they foundered. In response to the impasse in the negotiations, Clinton administration officials, led by United States Trade Representative Mickey Kantor, recommended that tariffs be imposed on Japanese-made auto parts, the primary target of the negotiations. Detroit objected to this strategy because they bought a large number of Japanese-made parts for their vehicles.[54] The Clinton administration chose instead a 100 percent tariff on thirteen Japanese luxury cars. To help spur an agreement, President Clinton endorsed the sanctions as negotiators continued their efforts. Most of the affected cars' prices would have increased between $20,000 and $30,000, some even more. In Japan, one estimate suggested that the cumulative ripple effects of the sanctions would cost the Japanese economy $16.5 billion.[55]

---

[54] William Greider, *One World, Ready or Not: The Manic Logic of Global Capitalism* (New York: Simon and Schuster, 1997), p. 213.

[55] Edith Terry, "Sanctions Will Hurt Japanese a Lot," *Automotive News* (June 26, 1995), p. 1.

American dealers of the affected cars argued that their businesses, with \$7 billion in assets, would be threatened with bankruptcy. The total dollar value of the cars subject to the tariff came to \$5.9 billion. In all likelihood, the sanctions would have meant the collapse of Japanese luxury car sales in the United States. Only a last-minute deal, signed just hours before the sanctions were to go into effect, settled the dispute. Journalist William Greider argues that the Clinton administration backed off on some of its demands as part of a secret deal with the Japanese to manage currency exchange rates and Japan's banking crisis, each of which threatened world financial markets.[56]

Japanese officials agreed to increase purchases of U.S.-made auto parts in a pattern similar to that of the 1992 Bush agreement. The Japanese Big Five (Toyota, Honda, Mazda, Mitsubishi, and Nissan) agreed to buy an additional \$6.75 billion in parts from foreign suppliers, \$2 billion of which were to come from the United States. They also agreed to increase transplant production in the United States from 2.1 to 2.65 million units in 1998. The number of dealers in Japan selling U.S.-made cars was to be increased by 1,000 in order to increase imports from 45,000 to 160,000 by 1998. The Japanese also agreed to open their market to foreign-made parts. This was to be accomplished by the Japanese government's agreement to loosen regulations on authorized repair garages, allowing smaller independent shops to make repairs, thereby increasing the likelihood that foreign-made parts would be purchased. Opening the repair market to U.S. suppliers was viewed by many as the main goal of U.S. negotiators because of the large market for replacement parts resulting from the periodic inspections that all Japanese cars must undergo.

However, few independent observers thought that the agreement would significantly reduce the \$36 billion deficit. Again critics said that it merely formalized plans that the Japanese already had in place. Others complained that there was no mechanism to enforce the agreed-to terms. In fact, the Japanese were quick to point out that any agreements on purchasing numbers were not formal binding commitments. Mickey Kantor assured critics that although the agreement was vague in a number of places, "This is more than moral suasion, this is two Governments saying what we expect the companies to do. It is not something the firms can ignore."[57]

While the Bush trade agreement had been a response to the auto industry's financial slide, the Clinton-negotiated agreement came at a time when the industry was earning record profits. Yet, the trade imbalance between the United States and Japan continued, and thus policymakers confronted a similar problem: responding to conflicts generated by the trade deficit and improving the long-term competitiveness of the U.S. automakers.

[56] Greider, p. 254.
[57] Cited in David Sanger, "U.S. Settles Trade Dispute, Averting Billions in Tariffs on Japanese Luxury Autos," *New York Times* (June 29, 1995), p. A1, C4.

Conclusion

The political power of the auto industry during the Bush-Clinton years was uneven. Industry officials could not stop Congress from tightening emissions standards after almost a decade of delay. However, while the new standards were an improvement, they did not threaten the centrality of the automobile to American society. Instead, the 1990 law continued the remedial efforts in place for twenty years, which have left the nation's cities with dirty air.

Fuel economy policy was the area where the industry was most successful. Both Presidents Bush and Clinton supported the industry and protected it from new mandates. During the Bush administration, CAFE supporters turned to Congress to raise standards, and for a time of their goal seemed to be within reach. Industry officials responded with a concerted expenditure of time, energy, and money to defeat these efforts. By contrast, during the Reagan years, no such effort was required. Safety policy was another area in which industry officials could not simply count on winning, and in fact they sustained a minor loss. But the safety policy issues at stake were small.

The novel feature of this period – joint industry–government research projects – was an indication that global competition had enhanced the industry's political influence by bringing policymakers to focus on the industry's long-term competitiveness. A similar pattern was evident in trade policy as both administrations, under widely different economic conditions, sought to shore up the industry's competitive position. These two policy areas suggest an evolving relationship between Washington and Detroit that will likely continue. Cooperation may be the order of the day when it is in Detroit's interest, but the automakers have not become more receptive to new regulatory standards to mitigate the environmental damage of auto usage or to improve vehicle safety.

Conclusion: Corporate Power and American Democracy

> The problem of modern democracy is much less the fencing of political power
> than its rational utilization and provision for effective mass participation in its
> exercise.
>
> Franz Neumann[1]

It is difficult to fully grasp the impact of the automobile on American society.
Appearing wholly natural, the entire man-made landscape has been reshaped
for the use of motor vehicles. Cars are one of the characteristic commodities of
our time, offering a blend of modern technology and individualism. They have
been linked to the deepest elements of the psyche, merging power and violence, freedom and sexuality. Billions of dollars have been spent on advertising
to define freedom as equivalent to individual mobility, to equate a new car with
success, and to imbue particular models with different social identities. Indispensable in selling cars, these cultural values have also provided the automakers with a reservoir of latent public support. Understanding a broad range
of social phenomena such as family life or dating patterns, traffic congestion or
suburban development, air and noise pollution, or accidental deaths requires an
analysis of an automobile-oriented culture and the power of its producers.

The endless highways of our metropolitan landscapes, often choked with
traffic, evoke many of the contradictions of modern society. While individual
cars offer convenience and mobility, they become increasingly less practical
with each additional car they have to compete with. When cities are built or
rebuilt for cars, the city – the sense of place so integral to civilized living –
deteriorates. If the environment built for automobiles (drive-in restaurants,
strip malls, and parking lagoons) is so aesthetically barren that it is aptly

---

[1] Franz Neumann, *The Democratic and Authoritarian State* (New York: Free Press,
1957), p. 128.

described as a "geography of nowhere,"[2] it is a geography that nevertheless came from somewhere. This study has attempted to show that many of the roots of such an environment lie in the pervasive power of the auto industry.

Always formidable, the auto industry and its officials have never been far from the centers of power in Washington. With lobbying power second to none, the automakers' influence on public policy is apparent throughout each period examined. They have shaped the way safety and environmental issues associated with cars are defined, and they have ensured that their interests are never ignored by policymakers even during those times when industry influence has been constrained. Rarely can a voice be heard in the corridors of power in Washington that questions the automobile itself. Loud complaints from industry officials about a particular regulatory proposal or legislative mandate do not mean that these policies are actually a threat to the industry. To do that would confuse political rhetoric with reality.

To influence the political system, the industry deploys its resources in a number of ways.[3] Each of the automakers has its own lobbyists and public relations staffs in Washington and can call on the resources of its firms as needed. Top managers are sometimes used to contact high-level government officials. Outside lobbyists and public relations firms are hired for help on specific issues, and often different firms are responsible for different policy issues. At the same time, collectively the automakers are represented by trade associations and are connected to the broader U.S. business community through the U.S. Chamber of Commerce and the NAM; their chief executive officers belong to the Business Roundtable. In addition, the U.S. auto companies regularly organize coalitions with groups representing many kinds of business that are linked to the industry to take on specific industrywide battles, and they join still other corporatewide coalitions whose purpose is to influence nonindustry specific policy issues. The economic power of the industry is thus readily translated into the capacity to bring together wide networks of economic and political groups to shape public policy.

The full extent of industry spending to influence government cannot be measured precisely. Many elements of such efforts fall outside the official definition of lobbying on congressional disclosure forms. Two such examples are technical research to support its political positions and advertising to shape public opinion. As a result, Andrew Card, head of the industry's trade association until the Daimler-Chrysler merger, (and former U.S. transportation secretary) admitted that the industry's trade assocaition's declared lobbying expen-

---

[2] James Howard Kunstler, *The Geography of Nowhere,* (New York: Simon and Schuster, 1993).

[3] For a summary of industry efforts, including a breakdown of major industry lobby groups and their expenditures, see Harry Stoffer, "Auto Lobby: $100 Million Voice," *Automotive News* (December 29, 1997), p. 1.

ditures underestimated the amount of money actually spent.[4] The same gap is evident if one looks at the size of the budgets and staffs of the Washington offices of the automakers compared to the amount that is officially designated as lobbying activity. Taking these considerations into account, in 1997 *Automotive News* estimated that the industry spent over $100 million a year to influence government, a figure far in excess of the amount officially declared as lobbying.[5] In contrast, the entire 1996 budget of the main public interest group devoted to auto safety, the Center for Auto Safety, was approximately $600,000.

Industry groups also make substantial campaign contributions and hire top-level former government officials to ensure access to policymakers. In the 1995–6 election cycle, for example, industry interests made over $5 million in PAC contributions and an additional $2.5 million in soft money donations.[6] With auto production spread across forty-eight states, legislators throughout the nation are easily made aware of the local impacts of an industry downturn. And to make its case most effectively, in recent years the industry has hired individuals who have previously served in high-level political positions such as transportation secretary, head of NHTSA, and assistant secretary of state, as well as long-time top NHTSA civil servants involved in regulatory affairs. In past years, a number of industry officials have served in positions such as secretary of commerce, secretary of defense, secretary of housing and urban development, as well as in important bureaucratic posts at the FTC and the White House, including White House counsel. In their product liability suits, individual firms have hired highly visible, politically connected lawyers to represent their interests, such as Kenneth Starr.

In each of these ways, the automobile industry is strategically positioned to have its corporate voice heard. Public interest and environmental forces simply cannot match this array of instrumental resources. Thus, there is nothing fair about the group politics that pluralists have long celebrated. The dice are loaded; the playing field is uneven.

Yet, this summary of how the auto industry organizes its political activities does not exhaust the sources of its influence, although this is where mainstream accounts of power typically end. Added to this extensive array of instrumental resources is the industry's privileged economic position. The direct and indirect economic impact of the industry combined is virtually unrivaled. Not only do whole communities depend on the auto industry for jobs but, given their size, the economic fortunes of the automakers have national repercussions. As a result, policymakers often do not have to be pressured to respond to industry requests because economic growth and political stability can hinge on a

[4] Stoffer, p. 30.   [5] Stoffer, p. 1.

[6] Harry Stoffer, "PACs Press Forward with Fund-Raising Bids," *Automotive News* (June 23, 1997), p. 3.

healthy auto industry. Policymakers are thus subject to overwhelming pressures, both internal and external, on auto industry matters. Enhancing this privileged position is the absence of effective political counterweights.[7] The United States lacks a social democratic party that might challenge the industry's political power or contest the ideological dominance of corporate America. Similarly, the labor movement has historically downplayed direct political engagement, choosing instead a business unionism in the post–World War II era that has focused primarily on wages and benefits.

Nevertheless, as the history of government regulation of the automobile shows, corporate influence over public policy has not been monolithic. The industry's success at avoiding public examination broke down in 1966, at which time Detroit could no longer prevent government scrutiny of vehicle design. Public interest forces have had other successes, most notably the extension of regulation to pollution emissions and fuel economy. However, the dominance of the automobile itself goes largely unchallenged. Government regulation remains within a narrow range of reforms that does not seriously challenge the preeminence of the automobile in American society and hence does not challenge the industry's central economic position. And when the industry has experienced economic downturns, policymakers have further narrowed the options considered and have typically subordinated public policy to the needs of financial recovery.

As a result, when corporate officials mobilize their political resources in the context of economic decline and invoke these conditions in order to influence policy outcomes, they are able to maximize their influence. In this way they take advantage of their structural position. Notable examples are the Carter and Reagan plans to aid the industry and the defeat of proposals to raise fuel economy standards during the Bush administration. But the success of such efforts is historically contingent. The impact that economic losses or downturns have on the policy process varies with the particular historical moment in which they occur. Different policy responses followed the industry's downturns in the early 1980s and early 1990s. In the earlier period, public policy across the board was subordinated to the industry's economic interests. More recently, when losses were greater, the industry's influence was uneven and Washington's response was smaller. Clearly, there is a no direct correlation between changes in the economy and policy responses.

While there is structure of power that the industry dominates, public interest forces can shape public policy under circumstances that appear to favor the industry (e.g., the 1975 fuel economy law and the 1990 clean air legislation). However, the successes of public interest forces are more noteworthy for the

---

[7] Colin Gordon, *New Deals: Business, Labor, and Politics in America, 1920–1935* (New York: Cambridge University Press, 1994), pp. 12–13.

hurdles that had to be overcome and the delays that were experienced than for the setbacks the automakers have encountered. The success of public interest forces depends more on the broader social pressures generated by new norms, values, protest, and social turmoil than simply by lobbying activities, however persistent and well informed.

Despite the industry's hold over much of public policy, government regulation has improved the vehicles we drive. Cars are safer, cleaner, and more efficient today than they would have been if there were no federal safety or environmental standards. If examples are needed of government policies that can be effective – notwithstanding their narrow goals – automobile regulation should be high on the list. Yet, after decades of safety and environmental regulation, the death toll and environmental damage due to cars are still significant. Tallying up the human and environmental costs of the car culture may be the simplest indication of the enduring power of the auto industry. Cars would be considerably safer, more efficient, and cleaner than they are today if industry officials had not consistently and strenuously fought virtually every effort to achieve these goals. Why has there been such fierce resistance, particularly considering the narrow goals of policy reform? Ideological opposition to any constraint on business autonomy, coupled with a concern for short-term profits, has animated each conflict over public policy. The protracted fight against the air bag is the most obvious example. Even when standards have been set by the federal government, industry officials have continued to fight them. Accordingly, Leon Robertson, a leading public health scholar of automobile safety, concluded that "The sad fact seems to be that for the motor vehicle manufacturers, federal safety standards are like the tax code: rules to be gotten around in any and every way possible."[8]

Meanwhile, safety advocates have been disappointed with NHTSA. Under continual industry pressure, the agency has suffered from bureaucratic inertia. Ralph Nader, on the twenty-fifth anniversary of the publication of *Unsafe at Any Speed,* observed that NHTSA has had to battle "the White House, the Office of Management and Budget, cliques in Congress . . . and, above all, . . . an intransigent, bullying automobile industry. . . ." Because of all of this, Nader added, the agency has only been able to turn "the rising tide of traffic deaths and injuries into a declining epidemic of trauma."[9] Yet, government safety standards have saved countless injuries and, according to the Center for Auto Safety, over 1.2 million lives over the past thirty years.[10]

---

[8] Leon Robertson, "Motor Vehicle Injuries: The Law and the Profits," *Law, Medicine & Health Care* vol. 17, no. 1 (Spring 1989), pp. 70–1.

[9] Ralph Nader, *Unsafe at Any Speed,* updated ed. (New York: Knightsbridge Publishing, 1991), pp. ix–x.

[10] Clarence Ditlow, "3 Million Lives Lost, 1.2 Million Saved," *Lemon Times* vol. 15, no. 4 (1996), p. 1.

For most of its history, NHTSA has adopted the industry's definition of traffic safety problems and downplayed improvement of vehicle design. It is disheartening that much of the improvement in vehicle safety resulted from an initial flurry of standards in the early years of federal regulation.[11] The agency has avoided pushing the industry to improve vehicle safety much beyond its existing practices. As a result, the bulk of the agency's regulatory standards have simply codified already existing options. The 1995 head injury standard is a recent example of this direction. Instead of implementing a technology-forcing strategy, NHTSA's energies have been directed at driver behavior and at recalling vehicles with safety defects. The problem with focusing on recalls is that only 13 percent of motor vehicle crashes result from mechanical failure, and most of these failures are due to inadequate maintenance rather than defects. Meanwhile, only half of all owners respond to recall notices.[12]

The most recent example of NHTSA's focus on driver behavior is evident in its emphasis on "road rage," a new psychological disorder created to fit the already existing model of the "nut behind the wheel" view of traffic safety. Noting a 37 percent increase in traffic between 1987 and 1997, while construction of new roads increased by 1 percent, NHTSA head Ricardo Martinez suggested before a House subcommittee that a police car in the rear view mirror was the best method to calm such drivers. Members of the subcommittee, Republicans and Democrats alike, shared the view that the solution to driver frustration was more roads, ignoring the history of traffic escalation, with its inexorable law that more roads generate more traffic and simply increase congestion rather than alleviating it. One member of the committee, however, Earl Blumenauer (D-OR), understood this paradox, pointing out that building more roads was "the equivalent of giving a wife beater more room to swing."[13]

Recommendations for Future Policy Changes
Studies of public policy often conclude with a series of recommendations offered to rectify the problems previously identified. And this work does offer a few proposals. However, the goal of this study has not been to diagnose flaws in policy formation or implementation. Instead it has attempted to unravel the dynamics of corporate power to explain its impact on American democracy. Whether meaningful improvements in auto regulations occur in the future does not depend on a list of recommendations developed by this author or any other author, for that matter.

[11] Jeffrey Mashaw and David Harfst, *The Struggle for Auto Safety* (Cambridge: Harvard University Press, 1990).

[12] Mashaw and Harfst, p. 13.

[13] For a report on this hearing, see Matthew Wald, "Temper Cited as Cause of 28,000 Road Deaths a Year," *New York Times* (July 18, 1997), p. A14.

Future improvements in auto regulation will depend on political muscle: the organization and pressure generated by public interest forces. Currently, public interest activists are preoccupied with holding on to yesterday's gains, now under attack by an emboldened business community. Yet, one of the lessons of this study is that power, while structurally rooted, is historically contingent. A reborn and reinvigorated environmental movement could realign power relations in many areas of society and thereby constrain the power of business. This is by no means an easy task or one that can be achieved in short order. To revive such a movement, traditional lobbying will not do. If public interest forces are to be resurgent in the future, they will have to focus their efforts on changing the nation's political and ideological climate. This requires attention to old-fashioned electoral politics, new forms of political education, and broad-based political agitation. Indeed, the task before public interest groups is to see themselves, and to act, as a movement, rather than simply as Washington-based interest group advocates.[14] Otherwise, policy battles will be fought on terrain that favors the superior resources of the business community, including its strong influence within both the Republican and Democratic parties.

While the policy recommendations offered are unlikely to be implemented in the short run, they are worthy of consideration because in the long run a different political climate could make them possible. There are certain less than sweeping changes to auto regulatory standards that would improve public health and safety. Cars that do not protect passengers from serious and fatal injuries caused by collisions at reasonable speeds should not be sold. Crash ratings should be required on all new car labels, just as fuel economy ratings currently are. Pollution emissions and fuel economy policies need to be expanded to mitigate the fouling of the environment, with its attendant health consequences and waste of natural resources. The smog that continues to plague our cities, despite decades of emission controls, is a daily reminder of the inadequacy of the current direction of policy.

Simply focusing on passenger cars would ignore the growing number of sport utility vehicles (SUV) on the road. These vehicles exacerbate each of the environmental and safety problems associated with cars. To begin with, SUVs – which now account for almost half of the family vehicles sold and a tremendous portion of the profits for Detroit – are subject to lower pollution, efficiency, and safety standards than passenger cars. As a result, they pollute more, use significantly more fuel, and pose a number of safety risks to their drivers, as well as to those in passenger cars that collide with them.[15] Since the

---

[14] For an elaboration of this argument, see Frances Fox Piven and Richard Cloward, *Poor People's Movements: Why They Succeed, How They Fail* (New York: Vintage Books, 1977); see also Mark Dowie, *Losing Ground: American Environmentalism at the Close of the Twentieth Century* (Cambridge: MIT Press, 1995).

[15] See Keith Bradsher, "A Deadly Highway Mismatch Ignored," *New York Times* (Sep-

overwhelming majority of these vehicles never perform tasks for which they were initially designed – off-road driving or hauling heavy loads – they need to be subject to standards similar to those of passenger cars. The safety problems associated with SUVs led the Insurance Institute for Highway Safety to call on the automakers to redesign these vehicles, the first time it called for a redesign of an entire class of vehicles.[16]

Although improving the safety, efficiency, and emissions of cars is vitally important, advancing public health and protecting the environment requires that alternatives to the automobile be substantially expanded. Relying on cars, regardless of how efficient they are, will do nothing to relieve traffic congestion, enhance the livability of our cities, or provide transportation for those who do not have access to a vehicle: the young, the elderly, the disabled, and the poor. And given the overreliance on cars for ground transportation, even very efficient and clean cars will still foul the air and deplete natural resources. Thus, public transportation systems that combine and expand light rail, heavy rail, and buses should be among our nation's top priorities. Unfortunately, federal government transportation subsidies have been moving in the opposite direction. From 1980 to 1990, for example, federal highway spending increased from $8.6 billion to $12.5 billion, while funding for public transit was cut from $4 billion to $3.2 billion. And the Newt Gingrich–led 104th Congress cut public transit spending for 1996 by an additional 30 percent.[17] Zoning regulations will also have to be returned to pre–World War II patterns, which integrated multiple uses into neighborhoods, so that "walking to the store" becomes common once again.

For the communities dependent on auto production, there needs to be greater control over the flow of capital to prevent them from being devastated by capital flight. All one has to do is visit Flint, Michigan, to see the brutal effects of corporate flight. In the twenty years since 1978, GM's Flint workforce has plummeted from 78,000 to about 30,000. Government policies that influence capital flows already exist, of course. A host of local and state economic development policies provide tax breaks and other benefits to attract and keep corporations in their jurisdictions. The fierce jockeying by political leaders to obtain or retain auto-related plants continues to escalate.[18] Even under the best scenarios, these policies create a dynamic of legally sanctioned bribery be-

tember 24, 1997), p. 1; Keith Bradsher, "Trucks, Darlings of Drivers, Are Favored by the Law, Too," *New York Times* (September 30, 1997), p. 1; Keith Bradsher, "Further Problems of Safety Found for Light Trucks," *New York Times* (December 12, 1997), p. 1.

[16] Keith Bradsher, "Insurers Saying Sport Utilities Need Redesign," *New York Times* (January 10, 1998), p. 1.

[17] Linda Baker, "End of the Line," *In These Times* (November 25, 1996), p. 23.

[18] For an account of this trend, see Allen Myerson, "O Governor, Won't You Buy Me a Mercedes Plant," *New York Times* (September 1, 1996), Section 3, p. 1.

tween public officials and corporate executives. And when corporate executives seeking public benefits merely have to mention to local officials that they are considering leaving the community, this dynamic approaches extortion. For any particular community to forego the competition to attract or maintain jobs would be tantamount to unilateral disarmament. As long as current practice continues, local agreements that extend public benefits to private corporations should attach provisions stipulating the conditions under which monies would have to be returned to the community if the company leaves or otherwise does not provide the jobs it promised. On a national level, domestic content legislation is needed to link corporations explicitly to the nation in which they sell their products.

Conclusion

Twenty years ago, Charles Lindblom wrote that democratic political thought had not faced up to the peculiar nature of the large corporation or the disproportionate resources that enabled business to make demands on government that must be met.[19] He then concluded with a very simple point. The large corporation does not fit within democratic theory or vision; the market imprisons democracy.[20] While Lindblom's conclusions were hardly original, they received significant attention, coming as they did from one of American political science's leading pluralists. However, long before Lindblom's discovery, scholars working from a critical perspective realized that democracy and large corporate entities were incompatible bedfellows. Almost twenty years before Lindblom's work, a study of the oil industry, as one example, concluded that its central lesson was "the incompatibility of a socially irresponsible system of power with the goal of a truly democratic society."[21] Nevertheless, since the time Lindblom wrote, it appears that what should have been learned has been ignored or forgotten. For most social scientists today, the corporation is seen exclusively as an economic institution that may or may not get involved in trying to influence political decisions. Power is defined solely in terms of influencing government decisions.[22] However, attempting to influence government decisions is only one aspect of politics. As this study has attempted to show, the modern corporation's decisions shape, if not define, the context and the problems that government responds to. And these decisions distribute

---

[19] Charles Lindblom, *Politics and Markets* (New York: Basic Books, 1977), p. 356.

[20] Charles Lindblom, "The Market as Prison," *Journal of Politics* vol. 44, no. 2 (May 1982), pp. 324–36.

[21] Robert Engler, *The Politics of Oil: Private Power and Democratic Directions* (Chicago: University of Chicago Press, 1961), p. 465.

[22] For a recent example of mainstream political science's narrowed definition of politics from one of its leading scholars, see James Q. Wilson, "The Corporation as a Political Actor," in Carl Kaysen, ed., *The American Corporation Today* (New York: Oxford University Press, 1996), pp. 413–35.

tremendous social costs to others. Transportation networks, air pollution problems, the traffic death toll, and oil consumption, not to mention international trade deficits, a shrinking manufacturing base, and how work is experienced by a large number of Americans, can each be traced, in part, to decisions made by auto industry officials. Indeed, the impact of the automobile industry on American society confirms sociologist Robert Lynd's point that "power is no less 'political' for being labeled 'economic'; for politics is but the science of 'who gets what, when and how.' "[23]

The structural form of today's large corporation – a vertically integrated, horizontally concentrated, conglomerate – was developed by business officials not only to gain control over markets but to insulate themselves from external forces. Vertically integrated firms explicitly organize their operations to reduce market transactions. Horizontally concentrated firms have the ability to control the development of technology, to shape demand through advertising, and to maintain pricing policies in the face of downturns in the business cycle. Conglomerates are able to shift resources among their units to take advantage of tax law and trade policies and to stay ahead of market forces. Each of these arrangements shows that with its internal planning mechanisms, the modern corporation is far removed from Adam Smith's view of economic producers as autonomous, competitive actors.

Many economists have argued that those who worry about the size and scope of large corporations can put their concerns to rest. The vertically integrated firm, they maintain, is an economic improvement over smaller firms that must rely on endless market transactions to carry out their business activity; and the hierarchical relations that develop from vertical integration are the result of nothing more than operating efficiencies. This perspective resembles the claim made by the advocates of "scientific management" or Taylorism: removing power from workers to control the labor process was simply a means of using scientific methods to increase production efficiency. Left out of this formulation, as critics now point out, is the issue of power and control within organizations, as well as the question of efficiency for whom and at what social cost.[24]

Those who view the growth of the large firm as merely a consequence of operating efficiencies reduce the motivations of corporate officials to the single element of economic calculation, ignoring all other factors that shape decision making. Yet, as one recent commentator has emphasized, within the corporation is a class structure among various constituencies shaping what is pro-

---

[23] Robert Lynd, Forward to Robert Brady, *Business as a System of Power* (New York: Columbia University Press, 1943), p. viii.

[24] See, for example, Harry Braverman, *Labor and Monopoly Capitalism: The Degradation of Work in the Twentieth Century* (New York: Monthly Review Press, 1974); Richard Edwards, *Contested Terrain: The Transformation of the Workplace in the Twentieth Century* (New York: Basic Books, 1979).

duced, how it is produced, and by whom.[25] In reviewing these issues, the organizational sociologist Charles Perrow suggests that, in fact, the operating efficiencies gained from hierarchical control are relatively minor because of a range of inefficiencies that are inherent in large bureaucratic organizations. The growth of the large corporation, he emphasizes, is motivated by a much less neutral concern than efficiency. "Profits," he writes, "come from control of markets and competition, control of labor, and the ability to externalize many other costs that are largely social in nature, that is, to force communities and workers to bear them and not have them reflected in the price of goods and services."[26] Indeed, K. William Kapp, in a similar vein, wrote almost fifty years ago that "capitalism must be regarded as an economy of unpaid costs, 'unpaid' in so far as a substantial proportion of the actual costs of production remain unaccounted for in entrepreneurial outlays; instead they are shifted to, and ultimately borne by, third persons or by the community as a whole."[27] A recent and admittedly rough attempt to estimate the social costs that corporations shift to others puts this figure at $2,622 billion per year (1994 dollars), a figure almost double the entire federal budget and equal to almost half of the nation's 1993 gross domestic product.[28] To reach this figure a number of factors were aggregated, including the cost of pollution, unsafe products, worker injuries, and corporate fraud.

At present, nations, regions, cities, and communities are beholden to the decisions of a small number of corporate planners who now control the economic destiny of much of the globe. Approximately 25 percent of the world's productive assets are controlled by 300 corporations.[29] Thus, corporate planning is now truly global in scale. A significant portion of world trade is the exchange among different units of the same corporation, and is as much a reflection of the corporation's financial schemes as a manifestation of "international" competition. As the large corporation has become increasingly global in reach, American corporate officials see themselves existing in a space beyond the nation-state. Thus, GM Chairman Charles Wilson's 1953 statement made during his confirmation hearing as defense secretary, now popularized as "What's good for GM is good for the country," which was once seen as the

---

[25] For an elaboration of this argument, see John McDermott, *Corporate Society: Class, Property and Contemporary Capitalism* (Boulder: Westview Press, 1991).

[26] Charles Perrow, "Markets, Hierarchies and Hegemony," in Andrew Van De Ven and William Joyce, eds., *Perspectives on Organization Design and Behavior* (New York: John Wiley & Sons, 1981), p. 372.

[27] K. William Kapp, *The Social Costs of Private Enterprise* (New York: Schocken Books, 1971, [1950]), p. 231.

[28] Ralph Estes, "The Public Cost of Private Corporations," *Advances in Public Interest Accounting* vol. 6 (1995), pp. 329–51.

[29] Richard Barnet and John Cavanagh, *Global Dreams: Imperial Corporations and the New World Order* (New York: Simon and Schuster, 1994), p. 15.

height of hubris, today seems quaintly parochial.[30] Yet, just as Wilson's equation was hardly correct at the time it was made, what's good for GM today – corporate flight, layoffs, foreign investment, extorting local communities for tax breaks, lobbying against environmental protection – is surely not what's good for America.

Currently, corporations enjoy extensive political rights. In the late nineteenth century, corporations were afforded the constitutional rights of a person and were able to fight early state and national efforts to regulate corporate behavior as an intrusion on their rights. While the debate over the boundaries of government regulation of commerce was seemingly settled during the New Deal, more recently corporations have successfully invoked various elements of the Bill of Rights to fend off unwanted government actions. Corporations, entities created by the state, now regularly invoke constitutional rights once the sole preserve of individuals. Indeed, one legal scholar surveying this trend concluded that it "symbolizes the transformation of our constitutional system from one of individual freedoms to one of organizational prerogatives."[31]

The growth of these organizational prerogatives raises the issue that connected the populist era to the New Deal: to what extent is concentrated economic power incompatible with meaningful democratic possibilities? One achievement of the populists was the passage of the antitrust laws, whose purpose was to prevent oligopolistic concentration. Enforcement of the antitrust laws, something never really tried, would slow the merger activities that consume so much of the resources of American corporations. However, antitrust is basically a backward-looking movement, trying to recapture a mythical free market as the solution to the problem of accountable power. As long as economic investment decisions and internal corporate operations remain solely in private hands, democratic accountability for key aspects of American society will be inhibited. The raison d'etre of the corporation is profit. Expecting corporations to be concerned with anything else, particularly as international economic competition accelerates, is unrealistic.

The problem of corporate power in American society is to make economic decisions accountable by injecting democratic rights into currently private corporate prerogatives. An old refrain for some, it remains as important as ever. Although democracy is not a panacea for the problems confronting American society, it must be part of any advance on current arrangements based on largely unfettered corporate power. Some will contend that the government

---

[30] The actual statement made by Wilson was: "for years I thought what was good for our country was good for General Motors, and vice versa. The difference did not exist. Our company is too big. It goes with the welfare of the country. Our contribution to the nation is quite considerable."

[31] Carl Meyer, "Personalizing the Impersonal: Corporations and the Bill of Rights," *The Hastings Law Journal* vol. 41 (1990), p. 578.

cannot act as an effective counterweight to the large corporation because of its own bureaucratic tendencies. However, minimizing governmental responsibilities does not negate the existence of concentrated power; it merely leaves it in private, unaccountable hands.

To make corporate power accountable clearly requires the development of a notion of economic rights, something that a number of scholars have given considerable attention to and that need not be reviewed here.[32] Dwelling on the details of these proposals here would, in fact, direct attention away from the primary prerequisite of any such successful effort: the need for a broad-based political movement that places corporate accountability at the heart of its program. However, one modest step that can be mentioned here would be to require that all corporate boards of directors include representatives from their workforce and from the communities where the company's activities are located. Failure to extend democratic arrangements to the prerogatives of corporate power will leave untouched control over the internal operations of corporations, which includes how and where society's resources will be used. Harnessing corporate power by making it politically responsible is necessary; otherwise, the democratic possibilities of American society will be increasingly diminished.

The scope of corporate power extends, of course, well beyond the realm of economic activity. With often unparalleled political influence, the large corporation occupies a preeminent position in America today; its power is so pervasive that it is typically taken for granted. Therefore, returning to Walter Weyl, a Progressive Era reformer and a founding editor of *The New Republic,* is useful because, writing from the vantage point of the early twentieth century, when the large corporation was relatively new, Weyl was able to see the impact of corporate power on democracy that more recent observers tend to ignore. For Weyl, America had, in fact, become a *plutocracy,* not simply because men of wealth ruled but because the "new system of industrial organization," through its "wealth and prestige" and "the allegiance of like minded but poorer men, exert[s] an enormous, if not preponderating, influence over industry, politics and public opinion."[33]

---

[32] See, for example, Gar Alperovitz and Jeff Faux, *Rebuilding America* (New York: Pantheon Books, 1984); Samuel Bowles, David Gordon, and Thomas Weisskopf, *Beyond the Wasteland* (Garden City: Anchor Books, 1983); Martin Carnoy, Derek Shearer, and Russell Rumberger, *A New Social Contract* (New York: Harper and Row, 1983; Martin Carnoy and Derek Shearer, *Economic Democracy* (New York: M. E. Sharpe, 1980).

[33] Walter Weyl, *The New Democracy: An Essay on Certain Political and Economic Tendencies in the United States* (New York: Harper & Row, 1964 [1912]), pp. 78, 84. For a concise summary of Weyl's thinking, see Scott Bowman, *The Modern Corporation and American Political Thought: Law, Power, and Ideology* (University Park: Pennsylvania University Press, 1996), pp. 92–6.

It is difficult to be optimistic about the prospects for confronting such an entrenched system of power. Business interests so thoroughly dominate campaign giving, lobbying, the media, and think tanks that few dissenting voices challenging the corporation can be heard. It appears that the new civic religion demands bowing down at the altar of big business. Indeed, to suggest that the public interest may be separate from, or even opposed to, the interests of private profit making and corporate prerogatives may be the most politically incorrect form of speech today. Yet, the growing economic polarization in America would seem to provide fruitful ground on which to raise these issues. The economic arrangements of the past generation, often known as the post–World War II "social contract" (stable employment, steady wage increases, pension and health benefits), are in tatters. Fewer and fewer Americans are covered by private pensions or health insurance, and daily come attacks on the welfare state. A winner-take-all mentality is on the rise that, if unchecked, will surely weaken the bonds that are necessary for reasonable democratic relationships. Given the class-based patterns of nonvoting and the large group of disaffected voters, there may exist the potential to forge a movement to challenge the direction of public policy and current economic arrangements. If nothing else, Patrick Buchanan's 1996 bid for the Republican presidential nomination, as well as Jesse Jackson's 1988 bid for the Democratic nomination, indicates the strong undercurrent that exists in this direction. The time has long been ripe, and with the Cold War over now may be ready, for a reexamination of corporate power and its relationship to American society.

To do this, one must confront the forces of global capitalism, which appear to be not only unchecked but ideologically unchallenged. Much is now heard about how global economic forces rule the day. Nations must submit to these forces or risk losing out in the competition for investment and jobs. However, if on the global scale market forces have been unleashed, on closer inspection what may be taking shape is a form of competition among different national varieties of capitalism. Despite all the talk of the equalizing influence of global capital on wages and government policies, multinational corporations continue to meet a wide array of different mandates set by nation-states on such issues as wages, working conditions, domestic content requirements, and local partnership arrangements, just to mention a few.[34] The rhetoric of globalization is often used simply to stifle domestic political initiatives. It is for this reason that Piven and Cloward stress that "globalization is as much a political strategy as economic imperative."[35]

---

[34] For an elaboration of this point, see William Greider, *One World, Ready or Not: The Manic Logic of Global Capitalism* (New York: Simon and Schuster, 1997).

[35] Frances Fox Piven and Richard Cloward, *The Breaking of the American Social Compact* (New York: New Press, 1997), p. 5.

Challenging the prerogatives of corporate power raises questions that go to the very heart of how our society functions. Robert Lynd, in a metaphor appropriate for this work, realized that this kind of questioning leads to an examination of the social structure itself: "To attempt fundamental change in institutions, of a kind that affects the basic character of organized power in a given society, without changing the social structure of that society is like trying to drive a car forward with the gears set in reverse."[36] Thus, the task at hand requires nothing less than a fundamental reexamination of how American society is structured.

In the current political climate, raising these issues may seem quixotic. As the corporate community strengthens its hold over much of public policy, the citizenry appears quiescent; it is easy to despair. Thus, it is worthwhile to recall the words of Max Weber on the personal challenges confronting those who strive for political change. "Politics," he wrote, "is a strong and slow boring of hard boards." Change, he added, has been made only by those who have "reached out for the impossible," and to do this requires the "steadfastness of heart which can brave even the crumbling of all hopes."[37]

[36] Robert Lynd, "Power in American Society as Resource and Problem," in Arthur Kornhauser, ed., *Problems of Power in American Democracy* (Detroit: Wayne State University Press, 1957), p. 26.

[37] Max Weber, *From Max Weber: Essays in Sociology,* (New York: Oxford University Press, 1958), p. 128.

Index

Ackard, Patrick, 91n54
Adams, Walter, 2n5, 3n6, 9n35, 35n2, 44n26, 45, 100n5
air bags
  debate over regulation related to, 121–6
  provision in Intermodal Surface Transportation Efficiency Act (1991), 172
  Reagan administration rollback of regulation, 113–14
Air Force, 63
air pollution
  auto industry concerns and actions related to, 84–5
  Californian policies to control, 83–6, 158
  issues covered, 118–19, 157
  motor vehicle emissions as source of, 10–11, 83, 84n31, 157
  toxic inventory (1987), 159
  See also Clean Air Act; emissions standards
Alberger, Bill, 136–8
Allen, Alexandra, 160n11
Allen, Frederick Lewis, 8n29
Allen, Merrill, 62
Alperovitz, Gar, 194n32
AMA. *See* Automobile Manufacturers Association (AMA)
Amalgamated Clothing and Textile Workers, 148
Amberg, Stephen, 7n26
American Association of Port Authorities, 152
American Automobile Manufacturers Association, 155

See also Motor Vehicle Manufacturers Association
American College of Surgeons, 63
American Federation of Labor and Congress of Industrial Organization (AFL–CIO), 149
American International Automobile Dealers Association (AIADA), 115, 140–1, 145
American Medical Association, 63
American Motors, 40, 100
antitrust
  annual style change, 40
  post–World War II investigations of U.S. auto industry, 41–2
  GM–Toyota joint venture, 46–50
  movement, 193
  smog consent decree, 85–6
ASF. *See* Automobile Safety Foundation (ASF)
Aston Martin, 36
Audubon Society, 78, 87, 120
auto emissions. *See* Clean Air Act; emissions standards; air pollution
auto fuel economy. *See* fuel economy standards
auto industry, Germany, 45
auto industry, international, 36, 38f, 53
auto industry, Japanese, 36
  assembly plants in North America, 45
  Big Five, 180
  GM–Toyota joint venture, 46–9
  origin of lean production in, 37, 39
  trade with United States, 148, 174, 179–80
  See also import quotas
auto industry, Korea, 36

197

auto industry, United States
  acquisitions of Big Three (1980s), 50
  annual style change, 40
  Clinton nominee for NHTSA, 176
  competition from foreign automakers,
      43–4
  concentration trend (1920s–1950s), 40
  current consumption of materials and
      goods, 9
  economic history, 34–9
  downsizing, 35
  financial crisis (1980s), 135, 139
  fuel economy (CAFE), 169
  government financial assistance
      (1980s), 97, 104–8
  profits and losses, 34–5, 113, 139,
      170–1
  increased political influence (1970s),
      91–3
  influence on societal institutions, 7–
      12
  international aspects of, 35–6
  literature related to, 5–7
  relations with labor unions, 50–2
  lobbying, 89–93, 160, 167–70, 183–6
  Mexico, 44
  operations outside United States, 44
  pervasive power of, 183–5
  political impact of economic losses,
      98–100, 113–14, 170–1, 174–5
  pollution control under Clean Air Act
      (1970), 87–8
  plant shutdown threats, 81, 91, 93,
      127–31
  recalls, 71–2, 81–2
  safety committee (1916), 56
  safety legislation (1965–66), 67–74
  small cars, 43–4
  trade associations, 56–8, 70, 84, 115,
      119, 155–6, 167, 183
  transformation of worldwide, 53
  See also Chrysler, Ford, General
      Motors
Auto Pact, U.S. and Canada, 149n43
auto safety. *See* air bags; National Traffic
    and Motor Vehicle Safety Act;
    safety standards; traffic fatalities
Automobile. *See* auto
Automobile Manufacturers Association
    (AMA), 56–8, 60, 70
Automobile Safety Foundation (ASF),
    57–8
Automotive Importers of America, 115
Automotive Materials Industry Council of
    the United States (AMICUS), 115,
    140

Babson, Steve, 37n7
Bailey, Patricia, 48
Ballard, Hoyt, 21n13
Ballard, J. G., 7n23
Baran, Paul, 7
Barnard, John, 5n14
Barnet, Richard, 192n29
Barnett, Phillip, 157n7
Barrow, Clyde, 26n38
battery technology, 162
Bauer, Raymond, 19
Bendixson, Terrence, 5n10
Bentley, Arthur, 19
Bentsten, Lloyd, 140
Bergmoser, J. Paul, 104
Bieber, Owen, 49
Big Three. *See* auto industry, United
    States
Bilirakis, Michael, 160–1
Blumenauer, Earl, 187
Block, Fred, 31n62
BMW, 45
Boggs, Tommy, 101
Bollier, David, 81n21, 122n22
Bowles, Samuel, 194n32
Bowman, Scott, 2n4, 194n32
Boxer, Barbara, 167
Bradley, Stephen, 96n71
brain injury, 172, 178
Braverman, Harry, 191n24
Breglio, Vince, 159
Brilleck, Thomas, 150n45
Brock, James, 2n5, 3n6, 9n35, 35n2,
    44n26, 45, 100n5
Brock, William, 149
Brown, Gary, 101
Bruce-Briggs, B., 5n10
Bryan, Richard, 164, 166, 167–71
Bryner, Gary, 157n6
Buchanan, Patrick, 195
Buell, Ronald, 5n10
Bugas, John, 70
Burford, Ann Gorsuch, 120
Bush, George
  campaign for President (1988), 156,
      158–9
  fuel economy standards, 162, 166,
      169
  CAA (1989), 120
  Task Force on Regulatory Relief,
      Chair (as Vice-President), 116
  trip to Japan, 173
Bush administration
  auto industry–government relations
      during, 154–5, 177
  battery technology research project, 162

Clean Air Act (1990), 156–62
congressional effort to raise fuel economy standards, 163–71
fuel economy standard raise (1989), 167
trade policy, 173–5
vehicle safety standards, 171–2
business
  blaming government regulation for recession (1970s), 90–1
  in neomarxist theory of state dependence, 23, 25–6
  opposition to Chrysler bailout, 100
  political mobilization (1970s), 27, 90–1
  political power, 22–3, 31
  dominance over regulatory process, 79
  state dependence on, 23–5, 28
Business Council, 71
Business Roundtable, 100, 119, 152, 183
Byrd, Robert, 159

CAA. *See* Clean Air Act (CAA)
CAFE. *See* fuel economy standards
Caldwell, Philip, 104
Califano, Joseph, 69
Calvani, Terry, 47
Card, Andrew, 183–4
Carnoy, Martin, 26n38, 194n32
Carter, Jimmy, 97, 102, 104, 105–6, 108, 112
Carter administration plan to help auto industry, 104–8, 116, 118
Cavanagh, John, 192n29
Center for Auto Safety, 76, 118, 127n51, 170, 184, 186
Center for Auto Safety v. Les Thomas, 127
Chamber of Commerce, 90, 119, 152, 177, 183
Chandler, Alfred, 6n15
Chayne, C. A., 65
Chen, Donald D. T., 14n48
Chesebrough, Harry, 71
Chrysler
  air bags, 125
  campaign contributions, 160
  Daimler-Benz merger, 36–7
  domestic content legislation, 147
  joint-venture between GM and Toyota, 48–50
  fuel economy (1975), 95
  fuel economy rollbacks (1985), 128–31
  government bailout (1979), 34, 97–104

import quotas, 139, 173
  Reagan administration stance toward bailout, 103n15
  vehicle safety, 62, 66
Chrysler v. Department of Transportation, 123n27
Clanton, David, 47
Clawson, Dan, 168n27
Claybrook, Joan, 108, 118, 121n20, 122n22, 126, 134, 177
Clean Air Act (CAA)
  amendments (1977), 92–3, 118
  amendments (1981), 118–21
  amendments (1990), 156–62
  original legislation (1970), 83, 87–8, 89–93
  Reagan administration revisions, 118–21
  targeting mobile-source pollution, 87
  See also air pollution; emissions standards
Clinton, Bill, 154, 175
Clinton administration
  auto industry–government relations during, 154–5, 175
  auto-related trade agreement, 179–80
  NHTSA, 175–6, 177–8
  Partnership for a New Generation of Vehicles (PNGV), 176–7
  vehicle safety initiatives, 177–8
Cloward, Richard, 23, 78n7, 188n14, 195
Coalition for Vehicle Choice (CVC), 167–8
Cohen, Richard, 157n6
Coleman, William, 123
competition
  among early auto companies, 39–40
  effect of auto style changes on, 40–1
  in international auto industry, 35–6
Connor, John, 69
Consumer Product Safety Commission, 77
consumer protection regulation, 77
corporate average fuel economy (CAFE).
  See fuel economy standards
corporate power
  accountability of, 194
  definition, function, and scope of, 2–3
  making it politically responsible, 194–6
  scope of, 194
  of U.S. automobile industry, 1–2
corporations, large
  concentrated economic power of, 193–4
  control of capital, 25

corporations, large (*cont.*)
  international control of, 192–3
  limited compatibility with democracy,
      190–1
  making accountable, 194
  political rights of, 193
  purpose in structural organization of,
      191–2
Council on Environmental Quality (CEQ),
      77
Covair, 69
Crandall, Robert, 79n11, 88, 144n21,
      145n29
Crenson, Matthew, 22n19
Cutler, Lloyd, 72
CVC. *See* Coalition for Vehicle Choice
      (CVC)

Dahl, Robert, 19–20, 24
Danforth, John, 114, 126, 139–40, 174
Daimler-Benz (Mercedes), 36–7, 45, 115
Daimler-Chrysler, 36–7, 156, 183
Darman, Richard, 167
Davis, Michael, 162
Defenders of Wildlife, 120
deKieffer, Donald, 142
Delorean, John, 43
Department of Justice antitrust investiga-
      tions of auto industry (Post–World
      War II), 41
design, vehicle
  industry reluctance to improve, 61–3
  Nader's criticism of (1965), 69
  organizations pressing for safety-
      related changes, 63–4
  with passage of vehicle safety legisla-
      tion, 74
deregulation during Reagan administra-
      tion, 132–3
DeSola Pool, Ithiel, 19
Detroit. *See* automobile industry, United
      States
Detroit, Michigan. *See* Poletown
Dexter, Anthony, 19
Dingell, Debbie, 170
Dingell, John
  CAA (1981), 119–20
  CAA (1990), 159–61
  domestic content legislation, pro-
      posed, 149–51
  fuel economy, 167, 170
  representing auto industry, 161n14
  safety standards, 171
Ditlow, Clarence, 118, 129, 132, 170,
      186n10
Dole, Elizabeth, 125

Dole, Robert, 114, 155
domestic content legislation, proposed,
      135, 146–52
Domhoff, G. William, 21, 22, 24, 28
Donahue, John, 98–103
Donner, Frederick, 68–9
Doud, Douglas, 1
Douglas, Paul, 65
Dower, Roger, 14n48
Dowie, Mark, 82, 188n14
Drew, Elizabeth, 55, 68, 70, 72n67,
      72n68, 74–5
driver education, 58
Drucker, Peter, 1–2, 6n15, 7
Dudley, Kathryn Marie, 6n20
Dukakis, Michael, 158
Dye, Thomas, 2n3
Dyer, Davis, 42n20

Eads, George, 104n17, 118
Earth Day (1970), 87
Eastman, Joel
  highway safety establishment, 55n5,
      56n11, 56n12, 57n13, 57n14,
      57n16
  PCTS, 60n28, 61n32, 61n33
  safety standards, 66n48
  unsafe vehicle design, 62n34, 62n35
economic conditions
  during assistance to auto industry
      (1980s), 104–18
  effect of industry losses on political
      outcomes, 32
  political advantages of downturns in,
      31
Edsall, Thomas, 90, 156n5
Edwards, Richard, 191n24
Ehrlichman, John, 122
electric cars, 162
Electrical, Radio and Machine Workers,
      149
elitism, 17, 20
emissions standards
  automaker actions to limit regulation,
      94
  debate over Clean Air Act (1970),
      83–8
  regulation (1970), 76
  regulation of, 14
  relaxed standards under rescue of in-
      dustry, 106
  weakening of standards (1977 CAA
      amendments), 92–3
  zero-emission vehicles (ZEV) under
      California clean-air mandate, 158,
      162

See also air pollution; Clean Air Act
(CAA)
employment in U.S. auto industry, 35
energy crisis, 91, 97
Energy Policy and Conservation Act,
1975 (EPCA), 94–6, 127–32
Energy Supply and Environmental Coordination Act (1974), 91
Engler, Robert, 190n21
environmental effect of automobiles, 10–
12
See also Clean Air Act (CAA); vehicle emissions
environmental movement
development of (1960s–1970s), 77–8
reactivation during Reagan administration, 120
revival of, 188
targeting vehicle emissions control, 83
weakening influence of business on
public policy, 87–8
Environmental Protection Agency (EPA)
creation of (1970), 77
Clean Air Act (1970), 88, 91–2
pollution control and fuel economy
mandate of, 79
Reagan administration, 119, 120
EPA. *See* Environmental Protection
Agency (EPA)
EPCA. *See* Energy Policy and Conservation Act, 1970 (EPCA)
Epstein, Edward, 20n11
Equal Employment Opportunity Commis-
sion (EEOC), 77
Esposito, John, 85n32, 86
Estes, E. M., 93
Estes, Ralph, 192n28
Exxon *Valdez,* 11, 159

Fair Practices in Automotive Products
Act, proposed (1982), 147–52
Faux, Jeff, 194n32
Federal Trade Commission (FTC)
annual style change (1939), 40–1
antitrust investigations of auto indus-
try (post–World War II), 41
automobile warranties report, 80
GM-Toyota joint venture (NUMMI)
(1984), 46–9
GM-Toyota joint venture, congressio-
nal hearings, 47–9
Fenwick, Millicent, 150
Ferguson, Thomas, 27n44, 30–1
Fine, Sidney, 51n48
Fisher, Edward, 5n11
Fisher, Franklin, 41n13

Fitzgerald, John, 110
Fix, Michael, 104n17
Flatlow, Samuel, 85
Flink, James, 5n10
Flint, Michigan, 189
Ford, Gerald R., 95
Ford, Henry II, 91, 122
Ford Motor Company
air bags, 125
campaign contributions, 160
Carter administration plan to aid in-
dustry, 104, 106
Chrysler bailout, 100
domestic content legislation, pro-
posed, 146
fuel economy standards, 95, 127–31
import quotas, 136–9, 173
lobbying tactics, 89
Mexico, 44
ownership of other auto companies, 6,
36
Pinto, 82–3
safety equipment, optional, 63, 66
Fraser, Douglas, 102, 104–5
Friends of the Earth, 120
Freund, Peter, 5n10
fuel economy standards
Bush's opposition, 162
Clinton administration, 175, 177
Energy Policy and Conservation Act
(1975), 94–6
EPA mandate, 79
establishment of, 94–6
global warming, 163–4
legislation proposed to increase, 163–
71
NHTSA prohibition on increasing,
177
NHTSA responsibility for, 163
regulation of, 14, 76
rollback of, 127–32
savings and potential savings, 131–2,
171
setting of, 94, 127

Gandelot, Howard, 62
Garson, G. David, 19n6
Gaventa, John, 21n16
gasoline consumption. *See* fuel economy
standards
Gelsanliter, David, 6n22
General Agreement on Tariffs and Trade
(GATT), 141–43, 151
General Motors Corporation
air bags, 125–6
campaign contributions, 160

General Motors Corporation (*cont.*)
   Carter plans to aid industry, 104,
     106
   Chrysler bailout, 100–1
   conspiracy to dismantle public trans-
     portation systems, 13
   corporate structure and culture, 6, 43,
     50
   domestic content legislation, proposal,
     146
   downsizing, 173, 189
   fuel economy standards, 94, 127–31
   harassment of Ralph Nader, 69–70
   import quotas, 139
   joint venture with Toyota, 46–7
   lobbying, 160
   Mexico, 44
   occupant safety, 62, 63, 66
   Poletown, 109–11
   Saturn, 126
   size, share of economic output, 35, 42
   strikes against, 51
General Services Administration (GSA),
   66–7
Gibbons, Sam, 149–50
globalization, effect on auto industry, 53
global warming, 163–4, 171
Goldschmidt, Neil, 105, 106, 107, 123
Goldstein, Bennett, 86n36
Goldstein, Lawrence, 8n31
Gordon, Colin, 185n7
Gordon, David, 194n32
Gore, Al, 175
Gorz, Andre, 25
Graham, John, 122n23, 124n35
Gramm, Phil, 150
Green, Mark, 122n25
Greenpeace, 11n44
Greenspan, Alan, 169
Greenwald, Carol, 89n50
Greider, William, 53n51, 179n54, 180,
   195n34
Griemel, Karl, 111n49
Grilliches, Zvi, 14n13
Griswold, S. Smith, 85
GSA. *See* General Services Administra-
   tion (GSA)
Guerry, Dupont, 62
Gulf War, 166, 167, 168, 171

Haagen-Smit, A. J., 84
Haddon, William, 58n20
Haeusler, Roy, 62
Halberstam, David, 6n16
Hall, Elliott, 155, 169, 175
Halpern, Martin, 5n15

Hamper, Ben, 5n13
Hansen, Kirk, 89n48
Harfst, David, 187n11, 187n12
Hartke, Vance, 71, 73
head injury standard, 178, 187
Hearst, W. R., Jr., 60
Heaton, George, Jr., 41n15
Highway Safety Research Institute, 70
Hill, Frank, 6n16
Hillis, Elwood, 101
Hoffman, Paul, 56–7, 58n19
Hofstad, Lawrence, 66
Honda, 148, 155
Hoover, Herbert, 56
Howard, Howell, 86n36
Howes, Candace, 50

Iacocca, Lee, 48–9, 61, 98, 100, 122,
   125, 173
IHS. *See* Interstate Highway System
   (IHS)
imports, 43, 44, 127, 136–8, 173–4, 179
import quotas
   attempt to obtain (1991), 173
   for autos (1980s), 135–6
   Carter administration, 105
   congressional consideration of, 139–
     41
   considered by ITC, 136–9
   economic effects, 144–5
   lapse of, 145
   legal status, 142–3
   Reagan administration action related
     to, 116, 127, 141–4
   supporters and opponents, 144–6
   See also trade policy
Ingrassia, Paul, 6n17
institutions
   new institutionalism, 29–30
   in power elite theory, 20–21
Insurance Institute for Highway Safety,
   71, 189
Institute for Injury Reduction, 170
interest groups
   in Coalition for Vehicle Choice, 167
   expansion of, in 1960s and 1970s, 78
   political behavior of, 19–20
   as privileged business activity, 28
   support for assistance to auto industry
     (1980s), 115
   See also business; environmental
     movement; public interest groups
Intermodal Surface Transportation efficiency Act (1991), 154, 171–2
International Trade Commission (ITC),
   106, 136–8

Interstate Highway System (IHS), 12–13
  See also transportation policy
Isaac, Jeffrey, 25
ITC. *See* International Trade Commission
  (ITC)

Jackson, Henry, 87
Jackson, Jesse, 195
Jaguar, 36
Jeffreys, Steve, 51n49
Jerome, John, 5n10
Jessop, Bob, 26n38, 30
John, Richard, 95n70
Jones, Bryan, 6n19, 109n36
Jones, Daniel, 37n6
Johnson, Chalmers, 108n33
Johnson, Lyndon B., 69
Johnston, Jim, 31
Johnson administration, 85

Kaiser, 41
Kantor, Mickey, 179, 180
Kapp, K. William, 192
Kay, Jane Holtz, 5n10
Kaysen, Carl, 14n13
Keats, John, 5n8
Kefauver, Estes, 41
Keller, Maryann, 6n17
Kennedy, John F., 60
Kennedy, Robert F., 68–9
Kerourac, Jack, 7n23
Klein, David, 58n20
Krier, James, 83n30, 88n42
Kroll, Stephen, 86n35
Kunstler, James Howard, 183n2
Kuttner, Robert, 79n12
Kwoka, John, Jr., 49

labor unions, auto, 50–2
Lacey, Robert, 6n16
Lachman, David, 88n43
Lamrorghini, 36
Lasswell, Harold, 16
Lavelle, Rita, 120
Ledbetter, Marc, 164–5
lean production, 37, 39
legislation
  Clean Air Act (1970), 87–8
  Clean Air Act (1977), 92–3
  Clean Air Act (1981), 118–21
  Clean Air Act (1990), 156–62
  Energy Policy and Conservation Act
    (1975), 94–6
  Energy Supply and Environmental
    Coordination Act (1974), 91

Motor Vehicle and Schoolbus Safety
  Amendments (1974), 81
Motor Vehicle Information and Cost
  Savings Act (1972), 81
Motor Vehicle Pollution Control Act
  (1965), 87
National Traffic and Motor Vehicle
  Safety Act (1966), 67–75
related to social change in United
  States (1960s–1970s), 77–9
state seat belt legislation, 66, 125–6
tire safety (1966), 71
  See also public policy
legislation, proposed
  Bryan bill to raise CAFE standards
    (1990), 166
  domestic content law, 135, 146–52
  vehicle safety standards during Rea-
    gan and Bush administrations, 171
Lent, Norman, 151
Leone, Robert, 95n71, 115n7, 133
Leuchtenburg, William, 8
Levin, Doron, 50n46
Levine, Rhonda, 31n59
Lewis, David, 8n31
Lewis, Drew, 123
Lewis, Emily, 111n49
Lichtenstein, Nelson, 5n13, 5n14
Lindblom, Charles, 24–5, 190
Lochman, Michael, 139n6, 141n11,
  141n12, 143n16, 143n17, 143n19
Lovins, Amory, 11n42
Lovins, L. Hunter, 11n42
Lowi, Theodore, 77
Luger, Stan, 39n8, 118n10, 159n8
Lukes, Steven, 22n18, 26n39
Lynd, Helen, 8, 20
Lynd, Robert, 8, 20, 21n13, 23, 191, 196

Mackenzie, James, 5n10, 14n48
Magnuson, Warren, 55, 68–70, 73
Manley, John, 24n30
Marcuse, Herbert, 18n3
Martin, George, 5n10
Martinez, Ricardo, 177–8, 187
marxism. *See* neomarxism
Mashaw, Jeffrey, 187n11, 187n12
McCarry, Charles, 70n59, 72n66
McCarthy, Tim, 166
McDermott, John, 192n25
McNamara, Robert, 63
McQuaid, Kim, 56n10
Mehling, Harold, 62
Metzenbaum, Howard, 104–5
Meyer, Carl, 193n31
Meyer, Stephen, 5n13

Meyers, Arthur, 61n30, 69n57, 69n58
Meyers, Gerald, 104
Miliband, Ralph, 26, 28
Miller, Arjay, 66–7
Miller, G. William, 102, 103
Miller, George, 167
Miller, James III, 46, 47
Miller, Peter, 14n49
Mills, C. Wright, 20
Mining Enforcement and Safety Admin-
    istration, 77
Ministry of International Trade and Industry
    (MITI), Japan, 142, 143, 151, 155
Mitchell, George, 159
Mitchell, Robert Cameron, 120n18
Mitsubishi, 36, 49, 50
Moffet, John, 14n49
Mogensen, Vernon, 3n6
Mokhiber, Russell, 82n26, 88n47
Morgenstern, Richard, 164
Moritz, Michael, 99n4
Most Favored Nation (MFN) trading sta-
    tus, 142–3
Motor Vehicle Manufacturers Association
    (MVMA), 115, 119, 155–6, 167
    See also American Automobile Man-
        ufacturers Association; Auto-
        mobile Manufacturers Association
        (AMA)
Motor Vehicle and Schoolbus Safety
    Amendments (1974), 81
Motor Vehicle Information and Cost Sav-
    ings Act (1972), 81
Motor Vehicle Pollution Control Act
    (1965), 87
Moynihan, Daniel Patrick, 59, 60, 63n40,
    64n44
Murphy, Thomas, 100, 104
Muskie, Edmund, 87–8, 93
MVMA v. State Farm, 124–5

Nader, Ralph
    Chrysler bailout, 101
    Clinton administration, 177–8
    Covair, 69
    Ford safety options (1955), 63
    GSA safety standards, 66–7
    harassment by GM, 69–70
    industry disregard for occupant safety,
        62
    initial safety standards, 81
    NHTSA, 186
    joint venture between GM and
        Toyota, 47–8
    PCTS, 60n27, 60n29
    political power of business, 31
    role in passage of 1966 safety act, 54,
        67–8, 72
    traffic safety establishment, 55, 57,
        59n22, 59n26
    Reagan plan to aid industry, 115n6
    Unsafe at Any Speed, 69, 186
Nadis, 5n10
NAM. *See* National Association of Man-
    ufacturers (NAM)
Nash, Carl, 123n31
National Association of Manufacturers
    (NAM), 100, 119, 152, 177, 183
National Automobile Dealer's Associa-
    tion, 95
National Commission on Air Quality,
    118–19
National Farmer's Union, 152
National Grange, 152
National Highway Traffic Safety Admin-
    istration (NHTSA)
    air bag standard, 123–6, 172
    brain injury standard, 172
    Clinton administration, 177–8
    expanded authority of, 81–2
    final airbag ruling (1987), 126
    lowering fuel economy measures
        (1985), 114
    opposition to CAFE standards during
        Reagan administration, 129
    passive restraint standard, 123–6, 172
    Reagan administration, 134
    regulations promulgated by, 80–1
    responsibility of, 73, 79
    rollback of CAFE standards, 127–32
    seat belt ruling, 123–4
    social regulation, as part of, 77
National Highway Users Conference, 12
National Safety Council (NSC), 56, 58–9,
    71
National Traffic and Motor Vehicle Safety
    Act (1966), 14, 54–5, 67–76, 80
National Transportation Safety Board
    (NTSB), 77
Nelson, Gaylord, 87
neomarxism, 17, 25–7, 29, 31
Neumann, Franz, 17, 182
Nevadans (or West Virginians) for Fair
    Fuel Economy, 168
Nevins, Allan, 6n16
New United Motor Manufacturing, Inc.
    (NUMMI), 46–50
Nissan, 148
Nixon, Richard M., 87, 122
Nixon administration, 85
NHTSA. *See* National Highway Traffic
    Safety Administration (NHTSA)

NSC. *See* National Safety Council (NSC)
NUMMI. *See* New United Motor Manufacturing, Inc. (NUMMI)

occupant safety standards. *See* air bag; National Traffic and Motor Vehicle Safety Act; safety standards
Occupational Safety and Health Administration (OSHA), 77
O'Connell, Jeffrey, 61n30, 69n57, 69n58
O'Connell, W. H., 5n10
Offe, Claus, 25, 28
Office of Strip Mining Regulation and Enforcement, 77
O'Hara, James, 101
oil
 domestic production, 132
 embargo, 91, 94, 97
 global warming, 163–5, 171
 imports, 11, 132, 159, 163, 171
 legislative response to 1973 embargo, 91–2, 94–5
 price shocks and demand for small cars, 43–4
 spills, 11
 See also fuel economy standards
O'Neil, Thomas (Tip), 74
Organization for Petroleum Exporting Countries (OPEC), 132, 163
Orren, Karen, 30
Ottinger, Richard, 149, 152

Partnership for a New Generation of Vehicles (PNGV), 176–7
passive restraints. *See* air bags; seat belts
Pastore, John, 74
Peck, Raymond, 123–4
Peña, Federico, 177–8
Perot, Ross, 50
Perrow, Charles, 11n41, 192
Perrucci, Robert, 6n22
Pertschuk, Michael, 48, 70n61, 77n2
Peterson, Esther, 106
Peterson, Wallace, 91n55
Pinto, 82–3
Piven, Frances Fox, 23, 27, 28, 78n7, 188n14, 195
Plotkin, Sidney, 3n6, 18n3
pluralism, 17, 18–19, 21–2, 27, 29, 31
PNGV. *See* Partnership for a New Generation of Vehicles (PNGV)
Poletown, 108–12
political action committees (PACs), auto industry, 160
political behavior
 elite view of power, 20

pluralist view of power, 18–23
 related to social change (1960s–1970s), 77–8
 See also interest groups
political organizations, business-sponsored (1970s), 90
political science, 16, 17, 21, 29, 190n22
pollution control devices, 88
Polsby, Nelson, 18–19, 21
Poulantzas, Nicos, 26–7
power
 auto industry, sources of, 183–5
 factors shaping, 29
 pluralist account of, 18–19
 power elite theory, 20–1
President's Committee on Traffic Safety (PCTS), 59–60
Price, C. W., 56
Proxmire, William, 99
Public Citizen, 76, 126, 170
Public Health Service, 59
public interest groups, 77–9, 87, 90, 112, 120, 185, 188
public policy
 agencies related to auto industry, 4–5
 Bush administration, 154
 Carter administration, 112–13
 Chrysler bailout, 97–104
 highway development and subsidies, 12–14, 189
 financial rescue of auto industry (1980s), 104–8
 influence of auto industry on, 2–3, 76, 183–6
 neomarxist interpretation of, 25–6
 Reagan administration, 112–21, 135, 171
 recommendations for future, 187–96
 state dependence as, 28
 in traffic safety, 59–60
 See also legislation; trade policy
Pyle, Howard, 71

Rae, John, 5n9
Reagan, Michael, 24
Reagan, Ronald, 112, 113, 120, 148
Reagan administration
 air bags, 121–6
 assistance to auto industry (1980s), 112–18
 auto import quota policy, 135
 CAA, 118–20
 Chrysler bailout, 103n15
 fuel economy rollback, 127–32
 regulatory rollbacks, 113, 116–18
 smog consent decree, 86
 vehicle safety standards during, 171

recalls, 71–2, 81–2
Reeder, Robert, 5n11
regulation
  accompanying government rescue of
    auto industry (1980s), 104–8
  advent of auto safety standards, 54
  debate related to passive restraint
    standards, 121–6
  of fuel economy under EPCA (1975),
    94–6
  improvements instituted by, 186–7
  process, 116, 118
  provisions of National Traffic and
    Motor Vehicle Safety Act, 14
  rollbacks during Reagan
    administration, 113–14
  social regulation, 77–80, 91, 118, 121
  See also Bush administration; Clinton
    administration; Reagan administra-
    tion
Reich, Robert, 49–50, 98n1, 99n3,
  101n10, 103
Reilly, William, 167
Renner, Michael, 165
Reuss, Henry, 102
Reuther, Victor, 5n14, 52n50
Reuther, Walter, 52
Rhodes, James, 125
Ribicoff, Abraham, 68–70, 72
Riegle, Donald, 104, 161, 166
Roberts, Kenneth, 64, 66
Robertson, David Brian, 30n52
Robertson, Leon, 186
Roche, James, 69–70
Rockefeller, John, 167
Rogers, Joel, 27n44
Roos, Daniel, 37n6
Ruckelshaus, William, 88, 91
Rumberger, Russell, 194n32
Ryan, James, 110–11

Saab, 36
St. Clair, David, 5n12
Salter, Malcolm, 42n20
safety standards
  congressional response to concerns
    about (1956), 64–7
  during Reagan and Bush
    administrations, 171, 178
  fight over, 80–3
  GSA, 66–7
  industry recall campaigns, 71–2
  industry reluctance to recognize issue,
    61
  initial standards, 81

Intermodal Surface Transportation
  Efficiency Act (1991), 171–2
lives saved, 186
passage of National Traffic and Motor
  Vehicle Safety Act (1966), 67–74
pre-1966 absence of, 54
public concern (1930s), 56–7
rules of National Highway Traffic
  Safety Administration, 79, 81n18
SUVs, 188–9
See also air bags; head injury
  standard; National Traffic and
  Motor Vehicle Safety Act; seat
  belts; traffic fatalities
Saturn, 126
Schattschneider, E. E., 22, 76n1
Scheuerman, William, 3n6, 136n1
Schneider, Kenneth, 5n10
Schultze, Charles, 69
Schumpeter, Joseph, 23
Schwartz, Gary, 5n12
Seaman, Barett, 99n4
seat belts, 66, 125–6, 172
Senate hearings on auto industry
  concentration (1955, 1957), 41
Serrin, William, 5n14, 51
Sharp, Philip, 167
Shearer, Derek, 194n32
Sherman, Joe, 6n21
Shnayerson, Michael, 162n15
Sierra Club, 78, 87, 120
Simon, William, 92
Sinclair, Upton, 6n16
Skowroneck, Stephen, 29–30
Slater, Rodney, 178
Sloan, Alfred, 6n15
Smith, Roger, 109
smog. *See* air pollution
smog consent decree, 85–6
Snell, Bradford, 13n47, 40, 41
social regulation, 77, 79, 91, 118, 121
Sonosky, Jerome, 70–2
Sorenson, Ted, 70
Sousa, Barbara Ann, 143n19
sport utility vehicles (SUVs), 188–9
Starr, Kenneth, 184
state-centered theory, 17, 29–31
state dependence on large corporations,
  23–6, 28, 31, 184
*State Farm Mutual v. Department of
  Transportation,* 124
Steed, Diane, 125, 131, 168
steel industry, 136
Stepp, Marc, 103
Stern, Philip, 168n28

Stewart, Jackie, 170
Stieglitz, William, 81
Strobel, Lee Patrick, 83n28
structuralism, 23–8, 29
Studebaker, 56
Studies in American Political Development, 30
Sununu, John, 167
SUVs. *See* sport utility vehicles (SUVs)
super car project, 176–7
Suzuki, 36, 49
Sward, Keith, 6n16, 51n47
Sweezy, Paul, 7

Taylor, William, 31n61, 109n37, 115n6
Teamsters Union, 67
technology
    battery technology research, 162
    post–World War II automobile innovations, 42–3
Tierney, Susan, 177
Timmons, William, 101
Tobin, Richard, 82n25, 118n14
Toyota
    domestic content legislation, proposal, 148
    joint venture with GM (1983), 46–7
    lean production system, 39
    trade agreements, U.S.-Japanese (1989–1996), 155
    trade associations, increased political influence (1970s), 90
    See also auto industry, United States
trade policy, U.S.
    auto industry support (1989–1996), 155
    for autos (1980s), 135
    under Bush administration, 173–5
    to protect auto industry (1913–1934), 39–40
    See also import quotas; Voluntary Restraint Agreement (VRA)
trade protection. *See* import quotas
traffic fatalities, U.S., 10, 54, 56, 57, 65, 68, 186
traffic safety. *See also* safety standards
    congressional studies related to, 65–7
    establishment of uniform rules (1924), 56
    industry-sponsored Automobile Safety Foundation, 57–8
Traffic Safety Now, Inc., 125
transportation policy, U.S., 5, 12–14, 55, 189
Truman, David, 19, 23

Truman, Harry S., 51
Turner, Donald, 85

U.S. Public Interest Research Group, 160
United Auto Workers (UAW)
    assistance to auto industry (1980s), 115
    Carter plan to aid industry, 104, 106
    Chrysler bailout, 100
    domestic content legislation, proposal, 146–8, 152
    emissions regulation, 87
    fuel economy regulation, 95, 167
    GM-Toyota joint venture, 47, 49
    history, 50–53
    import quotas, 139, 173
    postwar demands in auto industry, 51
    rollback of government regulation, 76–7, 93
    safety legislation, 67
    trade relief, 136–8
Unsafe at Any Speed (Nader), 69, 186
Ursin, Edmund, 83n30, 88n42

Vogel, David, 22–3, 77, 78n6, 78n8, 93n64
Volkswagen, 115
Voluntary Restraint Agreement (VRA). *See* import quotas; trade policy
Volvo, 155
VRA. *See* import quotas; trade policy

Waddell, Brian, 30n57
Waitzman, Norman, 122n25
warranties, 80
Watt, James, 120
Waxman, Henry, 157n6, 157n7, 160–1
Webber, Alan, 42n20
Weber, Max, 196
Weidenbaum, Murray, 119, 120n19
Weinberger, Caspar, 80
Weisskopf, Thomas, 194n32
Wetstone, Gregory, 157n7
Weyl, Walter, 194
White, Joseph, 6n17
White, Lawrence, 41n14
Whiteside, Thomas, 70n60
Whitney, Simon, 41n15
Wilderness Society, 120
Wilson, Charles, 192–3
Wilson, Graham, 177n49
Wilson, James Q., 190n22
Wilson, Woodrow, 8
Womack, James, 37n6

Worldwatch Institute, 165
Wright, J. Patrick, 42n21
Wylie, Jeannie, 6n20, 110n38

Yago, Glenn, 5n12

Yao, Richard, 143n18, 143n20
Yates, Brock, 43

ZEV, zero emissions vehicles. *See* emissions